THE GOSPEL OF THE COMFORTER

by
Daniel Steele, S.T.D.
Recent Professor of Systematic Theology in Boston University

Author of
Binney's Theological Compend Improved (co-author)
Commentaries on Leviticus, Numbers and Joshua
Defense of Christian Perfection
Half Hours with St. John
Half Hours with St. Paul
Love Enthroned
Milestone Papers
A Substitute for Holiness: Antinomianism Revived

COMPLETE AND UNABRIDGED

SCHMUL PUBLISHING COMPANY
NICHOLASVILLE, KENTUCKY

COPYRIGHT © 2018 BY SCHMUL PUBLISHING CO.
All rights reserved. No part of this publication may be reproduced or used in any form or by any means—graphic, electronic, or mechanical, including photocopying, recording, taping, or information storage or retrieval systems—without prior written permission of the publishers.

Churches and other noncommercial interests may reproduce portions of this book without prior written permission of the publisher, provided such quotations are not offered for sale—or other compensation in any form—whether alone or as part of another publication, and provided that the text does not exceed 500 words or five percent of the entire book, whichever is less, and does not include material quoted from another publisher. When reproducing text from this book, the following credit line must be included: "From *The Gospel of the Comforter* by Daniel Steele, © 2018 by Schmul Publishing Co., Nicholasville, Kentucky. Used by permission."

Published by Schmul Publishing Co.
PO Box 776
Nicholasville, KY 40340
USA

Printed in the United States of America

ISBN 10: 0-88019-617-3
ISBN 13: 978-0-88019-617-8

Visit us on the Internet at www.wesleyanbooks.com, or order direct from the publisher by calling 800-772-6657, or by writing to the above address.

Contents

	Preface 7
I	Names of the Holy Spirit 12
II	The Holy Spirit and the Trinity 24
III	The Personality of the Holy Spirit 29
IV	The Executive of the Godhead 34
V	The Work of the Spirit Before the Day of Pentecost 40
VI	The Paraclete's Conviction of Sin 46
VII	The Paraclete's Conviction of Righteousness 54
VIII	The Paraclete's Conviction of Judgment 58
IX	The Pentecostal Attestation 65
X	The Gain of the Paraclete 74
XI	Praying to the Holy Spirit 84
XII	The Law of the Spirit 89
XIII	Miracles of the Holy Ghost 99
XIV	The Spirit's Work in Regeneration 104
XV	Christ Our Sanctification 116
XVI	The Witness of the Spirit 129
XVII	Christ's Two Receptions and Two Bestowals of the Holy Spirit 142
XVIII	The Paraclete's "Ecce Homo" in The Believer 154

XIX	The Holy Spirit and Conscience	158
XX	The Unity of the Spirit	167
XXI	Enlargement of Heart by the Holy Spirit	176
XXII	Knowing the Holy Spirit	182
XXIII	The Freedom of the Spirit	192
XXIV	Testings of the Holy Spirit	200
XXV	The Holy Ghost and Singing	205
XXVI	Preaching in Demonstration of the Spirit	212
XXVII	Walking in the Comfort of the Holy Ghost	238
XXVIII	Spiritual Babes and Spiritual Men	247
XXIX	The Spirit Presiding Over the Church	251
XXX	Dishonoring the Holy Spirit	256
XXXI	The Fulness of the Spirit	271
XXXII	The Unclaimed Deposit	276
XXXIII	Rivers of Living Water	280
XXXIV	The Extraordinary Gifts of the Spirit	284
XXXV	Blasphemy Against the Holy Spirit	294
XXXVI	The Holy Spirit the Conservator of Orthodoxy	300
	Appendix	320

Dedicatory

TO MY TWO DUTIFUL CHRISTIAN DAUGHTERS,

CAROLINE BINNEY STEELE
AND
MARY GRACE STEELE,

AND

TO ALL OTHER BELIEVERS IN CHRIST WHO ASPIRE TO A
KNOWLEDGE OF THE MOST VITAL CHRISTIAN DOCTRINE, AND
TO A REALIZATION OF THE DEEPEST SPIRITUAL EXPERIENCE,
THROUGH THE ABIDING COMFORTER,

THIS VOLUME

IS PRAYERFULLY AND HOPEFULLY INSCRIBED

Preface

THIS BOOK IS EXPERIMENTAL and practical rather than theological. But since every scriptural experience must be based on the truth apprehended by the intellect, there should be a clear and scientific statement of this truth. Hence the first few chapters of this volume on the various offices of the Holy Spirit are filled with arguments in proof of His personality and divinity, after the style of the systematic theologians. The scriptural proof texts will be found in the notes.

One of the favorable signs of the times is the increasing number of books on the Holy Spirit. Quite an extended examination of these recent volumes reveals in nearly all of them one obvious defect, the omission of the direct witness of the Spirit to the believer's adoption into the family of God, and His agency in entire sanctification in this life. In guarding against these omissions, we ourselves may have omitted some important topics in a theme so vast as that which is the subject of this volume. If we have done so, we ask the forbearance of the Christian public for our inadequate treatment of a theme which has occupied our thoughts during more than a quarter of a century. As we advanced the subject enlarged in our thought until we had transcended the limits of a single volume. For this reason a long chapter in eight sections on "Assurance Through the Spirit" has been reluctantly omitted. It may be the Lord's will that my life be so prolonged as to enable me to expand it into a future volume. If this be so, in the words of St. Peter, "I will endeavor that you may be able after my decease to have these things always in remembrance."

—D. S.

Milton, Mass., Nov. 8, 1897

THE FATHER'S PROMISE OF THE SPIRIT

I will pour out my *Spirit* unto you. Proverbs i.23

I will pour out my *Spirit* upon thy seed. Isaiah xliv.3

I will put my *Spirit* within you. Ezekiel xxxvi.27

I will pour out my *Spirit* upon all flesh. Joel ii.28

THE SON'S PROMISE OF THE SPIRIT

How much more shall your heavenly *Father* give the *Holy Spirit* to them that ask him. Luke xi.13. (This has been called the dawn of Pentecost.)

I will pray the *Father*, and he shall give you another *Comforter*, that he may abide with you forever; even the Spirit of truth. John xiv.16.

The *Comforter*, which is the *Holy Ghost*, whom the *Father* will send in my name. John xiv.26.

When the *Comforter* is come, whom I will send unto you from the *Father*, even the *Spirit* of truth, which proceedeth from the *Father*, he shall testify of me. John xv.26.

It is expedient for you that I go away: for if I go not away, the *Comforter* will not come unto you; but if I depart, I will send him unto you. John xvi.7.

When he, the *Spirit* of truth, is come, he will guide you into all truth: whatsoever he shall hear, that shall he speak. He shall glorify me: for he shall receive of mine, and shall show it unto you. John xvi.13, 14.

Behold, I send the promise of my *Father* upon you. Luke xxiv.49.

Wait for the promise of the *Father*, which ye have heard of me. Acts i.4.

But ye shall receive power after that the *Holy Ghost* is come upon you. Acts i.8.

Theology without the Holy Spirit is not only a cold stone, it is a deadly poison. —Prof. Beck of Tübingen

The place given to the Holy Spirit in the heart of the most decided Christians is altogether out of proportion to that which it occupies in the Word of God. —Bishop Ryle

The Father and His unmerited grace, the Son and His expiatory sacrifice, have been much more studied in our day than the Holy Spirit, His person, His work, and all that new world which He creates in the heart. —Adolph Monod

Man is a vessel destined to receive God, a vessel which must be enlarged in proportion as it is filled, and filled in proportion as it is enlarged. —Godet

The Holy Ghost on the day of Pentecost descended into the temple of His apostles, which He had prepared for Himself, as a shower of sanctification and a perpetual Comforter. —Augustine

Chapter I
NAMES OF THE HOLY SPIRIT

THE FIRST NAME that is found in the Bible is *Ruach Elohim*, the Spirit of God. He moved upon the face of the waters. The word *spirit* literally signifies *breath*. All nations express things immaterial by the use of the most subtile material representatives. The best symbol for the invisible, immaterial thinking agent in man is the wind or breath, that kind of matter which is the thinnest and has least of the grosser elements. Says Martin Luther: "They who desire to speak of God without these material envelopes strive to scale heaven without ladders. For it is necessary, when God reveals Himself to us that He should do this through some veil or kind of wrapper, and say, 'Lo, under this *involucrum*, or cover, you certainly grasp me.'" The Old Testament form of statement is not that God is spirit, but rather that he has the Spirit and sends Him forth out of Himself.

This may have suggested to the thoughtful Hebrew that the Spirit is God and is a personality distinct from Him from whom He proceeds.

The only other Old Testament designation is the *Holy Spirit*. This occurs only in Ps. li.11 and Isa. lxiii.10, 11. In the New it is very common. The adjective *holy* cannot be distinctive of the quality of purity which is not found in equal degree in the Father and the Son. Both are holy. Hence, as it is not descriptive of an attribute peculiar to the Spirit, we infer that it points to the peculiar office of the Spirit, in the redemptive scheme, *to make men holy*. The *Holy* Spirit, then, is the scriptural term for *the Sanctifier*, a term not found in the Scriptures as a designation of the Spirit. Holy Spirit is a name in English preferable to Holy Ghost, for the reason that words like men flourish and decay. Ghost and ghostly were once dignified words, as "ghostly adviser" for spiritual adviser. But these words have become degraded so that it would sound strange to us and repulsive to hear the words "the Ghost of God." Hence we commend the American revisers for substituting uniformly Holy Spirit for Holy Ghost.

When the time came for Christ to depart He introduced a new name to designate the Spirit whom He would send to continue His work— the *Paraclete*, a term used only four times in the four Gospels, and all of them in the consolatory address in John xiv.-xvi. and translated "Comforter," strengthener, from the Latin *confortare*, to strengthen. In I John ii.1 it is translated "advocate" and is descriptive of Christ, our intercessor in heaven. *Paraclete* is a Greek word signifying either, passively, the near called, as an assistant, monitor, teacher and guide; or, actively, the near caller, calling the believer near to God, or giving access to Him by inspiring confidence and strength. He is also called the Spirit of truth or reality, because He is the inspirer of revealed truth, which He makes blessedly real to the believer in Christ.

Twice He is styled the *Spirit of grace*, since He is the dispenser of the divine favor to all men, either by conviction of sin in order to bless them by turning them away from their iniquities, or by imparting to believers spiritual life, witnessing to their adoption and perfecting their holiness.

He is called also the *Spirit of supplication* because He teaches us how to pray and for what to pray; the *Spirit of revelation* because He reveals Christ to the eye of faith; the *Spirit of wisdom* because He imparts wisdom; the *Spirit of adoption* because He certifies the believer's sonship; and the *Spirit of Christ* because He was sent by the Father through the mediation of the Son. He is called the *Spirit of God* because He is one with God in His nature. This leads us to the scriptural proofs that the Holy Spirit is consubstantial with God and is a person. The two doctrines of the personality and the divinity of the Spirit go together. The identity of God and the Spirit of God runs through the Holy Scriptures. Whoever the Spirit is, there is no distinction between Him and God, just as there is no distinction between the man and the spirit of the man (I Cor. ii.11).

In the description of the guilt incurred by an apostate from Christ to Judaism is found another phrase descriptive of the Holy Spirit as the Spirit of grace (Heb. x.29). If this is not the irremissible sin, it is sin at its climax. The Son of God is trampled down with ruthless scorn and hatred, His "precious blood" is counted as that of either an ordinary man or that of a guilty criminal. Then the description reaches the summit of wickedness, the sin of all sins, the irremissible sin— "and insulted the Spirit of grace." Most modern exegetes say that the Spirit is thus called because He is the gift of grace. But by referring to Zechariah xii.10 we find the expression "Spirit of grace and supplication," evidently implying that the Spirit is "the source of grace" and the inspirer of all true prayer (Delitzsch). He is the source of grace not only in His own person, but He is the channel through which the love of the Father and the grace of His Son are poured upon penitent believers. The importance of the Spirit's office in human salvation cannot be overestimated. The Father's love and the Son's self-sacrifice in the scheme of redemption are ineffectual without the Spirit's personal agency in applying the provisions of salvation. He is the appointed and indispensable almoner of the divine bounty and messenger of the King's pardon. If a city has a bureau of charities, its poor who proudly refuse its help and rely on the general benevolence of the city government, and starve because of their folly, are no more unreasonable than are those who admit that they are sinners, but are trusting in the fatherhood of God for forgiveness, ignoring His bureau of pardon, through the mediation of His Son, as administered by His accredited commissioner, the Spirit of grace. Many Christians who are almost destitute of spiritual strength might become strong through the more abundant life which Christ came to bestow, if they would honor with an intelligent faith that personality whom He has appointed as the Lord and giver of life.

He is also styled the Spirit of truth. "What is truth?" Jesus Christ declined to answer Pilate's question, not because the truth is a simple term too difficult to define but because the truth most needed by the selfish Roman procurator had a moral element which he had no capacity to receive. Christ could make blind eyes see, but He could not make a blind soul perceive while persisting in a course of sin. Moral truth can be apprehended only by an active moral sense in sympathy with it. To awaken this sense in dead souls was one part of the mission of Christ. The other part was to reveal the truth. "To this end was I born, that I should bear witness unto the truth." All saving truth is centred in His person. "I am the truth;" not abstract, but concrete, in the form of facts adapted, man's faculties, or truths cast in a human mould. Truth is conformity to fact or reality. Eternal happiness in building on the granite of reality and laying every hewn stone by the plumb line of truth. There can be no other destiny for a character thus constructed. But sin is a lie. The motive to the first human sin a lie. "Thou shalt not surely die." All the woes of the human generations and eternities are serpents oiled up in that delusion. Yet eternal wellbeing is in Christ for every one of the serpent-deceived race who will receive Him by faith. For spiritual realities do not address our physical senses, but our faith. The great danger lies in the pleasing delusions of sin and our proneness to embrace them in preference to sober truth. I do not compliment my race nor do I misrepresent them when I say in the words of the great American showman, "Men love humbug and sham." They delight in being beguiled and duped. This strange infatuation for what is false is what gives Satan his chief power for doing harm. For no truly wise man wants to foster illusions. They end in pain, and if persisted in they lead to eternal sorrow. No sane man ever chose naked evil or pain as an ultimate end. He always chooses what seems to him at the time a good, a means of happiness. The mind has the power to invest the chosen object with all the colors of the rainbow, though it be as black as midnight. The drunkard sees happiness in the cup where the serpent lies concealed. He could see the serpent if he wished. The worldling sees supreme good in millions of money, being wilfully blind to the day just ahead when he would give it all for "an inch of time" in which to prepare for eternity.

 To dispel these illusions and break their power to decoy men to eternal ruin the Son of God came into the world. He revealed the real good, which is His Father's approval. His love is heaven. He disclosed the infallible standard by which to estimate things. But Jesus Christ, who is the incarnation of truth, has withdrawn His visible presence from our world. How can He now help us to divest ourselves of delusions destructive to our eternal blessedness? He has left a successor whose office it is to testify of Christ and to reveal Him and His standard of values to us. He takes of the things of Christ and shows them unto us. Without His agency the absent Christ would be forgotten and His power to sway each successive generation keeping abreast of the ages would have been entirely lost. Even the memory of Him would have perished, as President Warren intimates in his hymn to the Holy Spirit:

> "I worship Thee, O Holy Ghost,
> I love to worship Thee;
> My risen Lord for aye were lost
> But for Thy company."

It is His office in respect to the truth revealed by Christ to make it real and vivid to men bewildered and seduced by falsehoods. Sinful pleasures sway them because they are near and present. The Holy Spirit brings eternal verities near and makes them outweigh the vanities of this life. He supplies a new measuring rod, a sense of eternity, and convicts the soul of folly in neglecting its happiness millions of ages hence. He lifts every man at some point in probation to a mount of vision above the mirage, where, as Longfellow says,

> "Uplifted the land floats vague in the ether;
> Ships and the shadows of ships hang in the motionless air."

In this golden hour the disenchanted soul freed from all illusions gets a view of realities unfolded by the Spirit of truth. Happy indeed is he if from that view his future life is conformed to those realities. Unspeakably wretched will he be if he comes down from this mount of vision unchanged in moral purpose, and sinks into the shadowy illusions of sin for the rest of his life to pursue phantom pleasures and to grasp bubbles till smitten by the arrow of death, a forgotten reality. The most precious hour in a sinner's life is this hour of correct spiritual vision commonly spoken of as conviction of sin. Then it is that the Spirit of truth becomes the reprover by holding up to the soul two pictures, the dark reality of what it is, and the bright possibility of what it still may be by being "not disobedient to the heavenly vision." But if the soul refuses to obey and persists in this refusal till disobedience hardens into fixedness of character, there will sooner or later be another vision which will awaken remorse; by the dark reality of what is and hereafter must forever be will ever hang the splendid ideal of what it *might have been*, the most doleful words in the English language. Again, the designation Spirit of truth might have been translated Spirit of reality. He is thus called by Jesus because He works in human souls only through the instrumentality of truth. He regenerates only through Christian truth. Men are begotten children of God through the word of God. They are sanctified through the truth. The truth is the instrument; the Spirit is the efficient worker. The stability of the new life consists in having the "loins girt about with truth." Victory in warfare is through a vigorous wielding of "the sword of the Spirit, the word of God." When the Spirit convicts of sin, He takes such religious truth as He finds in the mind and makes it vivid and real. Conviction is the distinct realization of the person's lack of conformity to the requirement of the truth. There is no proof that the Holy Spirit ever acts immediately upon the soul without the medium of some truth lodged in the intellect affording light for the activity of the will. Successful preaching is by manifestation of the truth accompanied by the demonstration of the Spirit. The failure of many preachers arises from their dependence solely on the saving efficacy of the truth without the Spirit's office to make it real. There is a legend that the eloquent head of a monastery died and that while his body was lying in state before burial one of Satan's imps took possession of the corpse, raised it to seeming life, and preached an orthodox sermon through the lips of the dead abbot. The evil spirit returned to pandemonium and boasted of his exploit. When asked by Satan whether he did not run the risk of converting some soul by his orthodox sermon, he replied: "Sire, do you not well know that orthodoxy without the unction of the Spirit never saves, but always damns?" John Wesley asserts that an impenitent man may be as orthodox as the devil, who believes and trembles, but is not improved in character by his faith and his fear.

Where the truth, the Spirit's instrument, is only partially presented, His work is defective, as in the case of souls moved to a religious life by singing joyful hymns, as "Sweet By and By," and by a suppression of the awakening truths of original depravity and the deserts of actual sin, the holiness of the law and the terrors of the Lord. Such fragmentary views of God's character as exhibit only His fatherhood, concealing His unbending justice in upholding the majesty of law in the punishment of sin, limit the Spirit to the production of a short-lived verdure on the stony ground. Nevertheless, the Spirit may find in some Pagans and Mohammedans truths of natural religion sufficient to inspire them with the fear of God and to make them His servants, but He cannot assure them of pardon and sonship to God till they have heard of Jesus Christ and have received Him by an obedient faith both as Saviour and Lord (John i.12). Such will be saved through Christ though they know Him not, but they can have no assurance of salvation till they have believed in Him. The Spirit gives reality to the Old Testament, the prophetic record, and to the New Testament, the historic record of Christ's life. He impresses upon us the fact that Jesus is living and present— that He is what

He was. His birth, His sermon on the mount, His parables, His miracles, His farewell discourse, His high-priestly prayer, His words on the cross, to Spirit-illumined souls do not belong to a distant antiquity, but are perpetually as fresh as the morning paper. The Spirit telegraphs the Gospels across the chasm of centuries and millenniums as recent news from heaven. "What are you so greedily reading, grandpa?" said a child to a Bible-studying saint of four score years intently reading the word of God. "News," was the reply. To the spiritual mind Christ is present giving life to His words spoken eighteen hundred years ago. Thus He verifies His own promise, "Lo, I am with you alway, even unto the end of the world." Thus He makes His words spirit and life. Statesmen are present in the governments which they have founded. Thus Washington is present in the American Constitution, and Bonaparte in the Code Napoleon. Authors are present in succeeding ages in their books. Thus Homer and Plato are marching down the generations. But the presence of Christ through the Comforter is entirely different. It is a real spiritual and personal presence, invisible to all, but felt by the truly regenerate. "The Paraclete takes of the things of Christ and shows them to us. He shall testify of me.* He shall glorify me." It is said that the personal presence of Napoleon on the field of battle was equal to a re-enforcement of ten thousand men. But he could not be present in every battle of the French down the ages, for the allied nations caged him up in St. Helena, and death soon imprisoned him in the tomb. But Jesus Christ is present to every tempted believer and in every Waterloo of His church, not as a hallowed and inspiring memory, but a veritable personality, manifesting Himself to the loving heart. This is true because the Comforter is emphatically the Spirit of Christ. To fail to realize this truth is not to have heard whether there be any

*See Appendix, Note A

Holy Ghost. We are to be on our guard against commingling the risen Son of God with the Spirit. They are distinct personalities while one in substance. The Spirit is the organ through which the Son now communicates with the believer and with the world. He is the revealer by whose activity in human hearts redemptive truth is transformed into knowledge in such a manner that faith becomes knowledge (Eph. iv.13). The Holy Spirit is the channel of reality. He gives eyesight to the spiritually blind. He gives visibility, substance, color and weight to truths which are as airy nothings to the sense-imprisoned soul. Vague, shadowy and unreal are spiritual truths to the carnal heart. The inward vision, the spirit of revelation (Eph. i.17) is wanting. "Whom the world receiveth not, because it seeth him not, neither knoweth him." Granite realities indeed are gospel truths to him who has received the Comforter. The sordid earth and the shining orbs are soap bubbles in comparison. The things that are seen are temporal and evanescent, and the things that are not seen are changeless and eternal. Thus the Holy Spirit leads us up to that mount of vision where we see things with God's eyes, where the world's reals become the believer's unreals, and the things unreal to blind unbelief become real to open-eyed faith. The feet which press this mount will not be lured by mammon from ministries to the Master.

> "As by the light of opening day
>   The stars are all concealed,
> So earthly glories fade away
>   When Jesus is revealed."

The truly spiritual man, actuated by a motive power incomprehensible to the natural man, must appear visionary and fanatical. He is like a train moving up a steep grade with no locomotive; a ship moving against wind and waves with neither sail nor oar nor engine;

or a magnet uniformly pointing to the pole swayed by a power too subtle for our coarse senses to grasp. Yet it is a very shallow philosophy which rejects the Paraclete and His work in the believing soul because the divine worker is invisible, and at the same time assents to the demonstration of Sir Isaac Newton that all the heavenly bodies are impelled by an invisible force called gravitation, and to the masterly argument of the great American mathematician, Prof. Benjamin Pierce of Harvard College, that all physical force originates in spirit. The last chapter of his "Mechanics" demonstrates the spiritual origin of force. How glaring the inconsistency of those who accept this conclusion of a spiritualistic philosophy in the realm of physics and of metaphysics, and in the realm of theology reject the revelation of a spiritual agent morally transforming believing souls because of His invisibility!

Such people to be consistent ought to abstain from riding in an electric car, reading by an incandescent light, and communicating by an electro-magnetic telegraph or telephone because the imponderable agent is invisible and mysterious.

In attempting to awaken and call forth from the tomb dead souls, the great purpose of gospel preaching, it is a fatal mistake to neglect the Spirit of reality. The truth, however clearly unfolded and eloquently applied, will be no substitute for this grand factor in human salvation. Here again is the failure of much Sunday-school teaching and preaching which is evangelical in doctrine. It is unevangelical in spirit because it does not depend on the Spirit of truth to give vividness and reality to the gospel. The picture is thrown upon the canvas, but in the absence of the eye-opener who purges the film from blind eyes there is no vision. The day of judgment, heaven and hell are fables to the natural man till made solid realities by the Holy

Ghost. Rhetoric is no substitute. Pyrotechnics are not power. They may fill the pews with admirers; they will never crowd the altar with penitents.

Chapter II
THE HOLY SPIRIT AND THE TRINITY

THE DOCTRINE OF the personality and divinity of the Holy Spirit is intimately connected with the most mysterious yet most practical fact of revelation— the fundamental doctrine of the Trinity of God. It is mysterious because it is above reason, not contrary to it, and lies wholly in the realm of faith. It is practical because it is inseparably involved in all true Christian worship and is the mainspring of all effective evangelism. It is fundamental because its removal from the Christian system subverts every distinctive doctrine. It protects all such truths, especially the exceeding sinfulness of sin and the efficacy of the atonement. Unitarians have been accustomed to say that philosophy sustains their denial of the Trinity. This is a great mistake. The latest utterance of philosophic theism is that the Unitarian conception of Deity is utterly inadequate to preserve His personality and moral attributes from degenerating into naturalism and pantheism, and that the Trinitarian conception is the only effectual safeguard against such an outcome and the only rock on which reason can securely rest. I will briefly show you the logic of this movement of modern philosophy towards Trinitarianism. The advance movement of thought in this century, far from expelling the Trinity from its place in the mind of Christendom, has caused it to strike deeper root and grow with fresh vigor. This is the argument in a nutshell: Love, the basis of all God's moral attributes, cannot exist in that simplicity, that abstract self identity of the divine nature which is the essence of the Unitarian conception. Why? If God existed from eternity before He created a person on whom His love could pour itself, He was from eternity having the active, diffusive principle of love in His bosom, the very substance and substratum of His being, with no object to love. This is unthinkable! Eternal love without a personal object! Hence philosophy must either deny the existence of love in God, together with all its manifestations in the forms of holiness, justice, wisdom and truth, or supply such an object from eternity. This first alternative divests God of all His moral attributes and takes us more than half way to atheism. The first verse of St. John's Gospel supplies an object of the Father's love before His first creative act: "In the beginning [from eternity] was [not was created] the Logos, and the Logos was with God [face to face is the idea in the Greek], and the Logos was God." This Logos became flesh, and while tabernacling in humanity had a memory which went back beyond the creation of the universe to "the glory which he had with the Father before the world was." In these words of unsurpassed majesty, which no creature ever dared to use, we have an enlargement and enrichment of the concept of Deity in striking contrast with what Phillips Brooks called "the meagre God of Unitarianism," a simple, abstract unity, a mere cause or primal force. Hence the necessity of at least a dualism of persons in the divine nature to sustain the completeness of the divine life and character. The New Testament reveals such a dualism and adds the Third Person as essential to the perfection of full-orbed divinity. Hence we see that the Trinity is not a doctrine which has been arbitrarily imposed upon faith by external authority overriding reason, but it is one which accords with reason, after it is revealed, and explains and supports Christian experience. Every evangelical believer who through faith in Christ by the illumination and impulse of the Holy Spirit has had conscious access to the Father resulting in forgiveness and communion, has tested the doctrine of the Trinity and found it true. Its deniers must reckon with the best philosophy representing the demands of the highest intelligence; when they must convince of their stupendous delusion the millions who have through faith in the divine Christ experienced the witness of the Spirit attesting their adoption and assuring them of forgiveness. But every growing Christian verifies the truth of the Trinity every day of his life. He comes to the Father through the mediation of the Son and receives the Holy Spirit as the comforter, helper, guide, light, life and wellspring of joy, just as every astronomer proves the truth of the Copernican theory of the solar system by using it and arriving at results experimentally verified by the use of his telescope. "Through him [Christ] we [Jews and Gentiles] both have our access in one Spirit unto the Father" (Eph. ii.18).

The best statement of the Scriptures about God is that He is one in nature with a threefoldness which we call personality, that He has a Son who is not a creature, whose existence is grounded not in the divine will, as our existence is, but His being is grounded in the divine nature so that He has all the attributes of God. His sonship dates not from His human birth but from eternity, being the I AM before Abraham was born (John viii.58, Revised Version, margin). The Spirit proceeds from the Father and the Son, having their nature; the Father is self-existent. The Son's being is grounded in the Father, and the Spirit's existence rests on the Father and the Son from whom He proceeds. The Trinity, dimly disclosed in the Old Testament, is clearly revealed in the New Testament after Pentecost, when the Third Person came with power as the successor of the Son in the administration of the kingdom of God on the earth. The succession, which is indicated by the words Father, Son and Holy Ghost, is a philosophical progress and culmination. God reveals Himself to all men in His Son; He communicates Himself in the Holy Spirit to all who believe in the Son; He reveals Himself to man's intellect that through it He may transform the heart and make it a partaker of the divine nature, not divine as He is divine, but holy as He is holy. This succession also intimates the order of the dispensations unfolded on the earth. We have every reason to believe that dispensation of the Spirit is the last and most glorious era of Christianity on the earth, that the second coming of Christ will be to judge the world and wind up human history on this planet, and not to inaugurate the dispensation of Christ's bodily presence again with its limitations to one place at the same time. We do not believe that the order of progress is to be reversed after reaching its climax in the dispensation of the Paraclete, who is to abide with believers forever. It is certain that faith in an invisible personality is a higher exercise and more blessed than faith in a visible manifestation. This is hinted at by the risen Christ to Thomas, "Because thou hast seen me, thou hast believed: blessed are they that have not seen and yet have believed." We are living in the best era for spiritual development which this world will ever see — the era of Pentecost. Let us make the best possible use of it and profit by its wonderful privileges, the indwelling Comforter bringing the Father and the Son to abide in us forever. Just note the gradation of honor in respect to the dwelling of God among men: 1st. One nation was specially honored when Jehovah made His dwelling in the midst of the camp and the pillar of cloud and of fire betokened the presence of the King of kings and the Lord of lords. 2d. God selects one human body and soul for His abode; for in Jesus dwelt all the fulness of the Godhead bodily. And, lastly, we reach the climax, the whole Trinity dwelling in every true believer who evinces perfect love by unhesitating obedience. This eclipses all the millennial glories this side of the glassy sea, the new heaven and new earth. Hence the reasonableness of our conclusion that the descent of the Holy Ghost is the completion of Christian theology, and His indwelling in the believer is the crowning honor and blessedness. "In the person of Christ," says Joseph Parker, "truth was outward, visible and most beautiful; in the person of the Holy Spirit truth is inward, spiritual, all-transfiguring. By the very necessity of the case the bodily Christ could be but a passing figure, but by a gracious mystery He caused a Himself to be succeeded by an eternal Presence, 'even the Spirit of truth, which abideth forever.'"*

---

*See Appendix, Note B

Chapter III
THE PERSONALITY OF THE HOLY SPIRIT

IT MAY BE impossible to give an exhaustive and accurate definition of personality as applied to the distinctions in the Godhead. The term "person," borrowed from the stage as its Latin derivation shows, *per* and *sonare*, to sound through, or to speak through a mask, hence a character in a play, may not be the best word to denote these distinctions. Be that as it may, the Christian world has accepted it, and it is now impossible for any one man to displace it by a better word. As applied to a human being, it implies that the body is not the real man, but the spirit which acts through the material organism. Thus we infer that spirituality is one element of personality, which implies self-consciousness, intelligence, desire, moral discrimination, identity and freedom of will. To these attributes of personality we may add power, or causality, which cannot originate in matter. The free agent in a limited sphere is a first cause. He causes his own moral acts. He is the sole creator of character.

Now if we examine the Holy Scriptures we will find

that these marks of personality are all applied to the Holy Spirit. This is not clearly seen in the Old Testament, though when it is read in the light of the New it is manifestly there also. We know that there are personifications of qualities in Hebrew poetry, and that Wisdom is described figuratively as speaking and acting as a person dwelling with God from eternity, and giving counsel to Him in creation. But in the Gospels and Epistles we have no poetic flights of the imagination, but the most simple prose statement of facts and truths. There is no trace of poetry in the last discourse of Jesus in the solemn and tender hour between the Paschal supper and the agony in the garden, when He sought to prepare His disciples for the sadness, loneliness, despair and fear which they would experience in a few hours. Then He used no dark parables, no vague generalizations, no doleful elegies. He spoke plainly and definitely of another Comforter to take His place, do the same work that He had done in teaching and guiding, and that He would stay forever. He would be a presence, a person who though invisible would be really nearer to them than He had been, because He would be in them, more than compensating for the withdrawal of His bodily form. Note the personal pronoun relating to the Holy Spirit in the following brief promise, "I will pray the Father, and he shall give you another Paraclete, that he [*not it*] may abide with you forever; even the Spirit of truth; whom the Father will send I my name; whom the world cannot receive, because it knoweth him not: but ye know him; for he dwelleth with you. He shall teach you all things." Count the times the masculine personal pronoun is used, he and him. We are aware that *pneuma*, spirit, is grammatically neuter, but it has no more a neuter signification when applied to the Comforter than it has when applied to man (I Cor. ii.11) and to God the Father (John iv.24). Hence the pronoun relating to the Holy Spirit should never be *it* or *itself* as in Rom. viii.16, rightly changed to *himself* in the Revised Version. In the words "He shall glorify me," by no just law of interpretation can personality be denied of the first word while predicated of the last.

Says Dr. John Owen: "It is impossible to prove the Father to be a Person, or the Son to be a Person, in any other way than we may prove the Holy Ghost to be so. For He to whom all personal properties, attributes, adjuncts and operations are ascribed, and to whom nothing is ascribed but what properly belongs to a person, He is a Person; and so are we taught to believe Him to be. Thus we know the Father to be a Person, and the Son also... There is no personal property belonging to the divine nature that is not equally ascribed to the Holy Ghost." "The Holy Ghost *spake*" (Acts i.16); "it is not ye that speak, but the Holy Ghost" (Mark xiii.11). The Paraclete speaks of Himself as having authority in the Church. "The Holy Ghost said, Separate me Barnabas and Saul for the work whereunto I have called them." In their journey Paul and Silas "were *forbidden* by the Holy Ghost to preach the word in Asia." The Holy Ghost made elders at Ephesus, "bishops to feed the church of God " (Acts xx.28). Such verbs as these describe His personal acts. He teaches, comforts, guides, sanctifies, testifies, glorifies, distributes gifts as He wills, makes intercession and is grieved. "If a wise and honest man should come and tell you that in a certain country where he has been there is an excellent governor who wisely discharges the duties of his office, who hears causes, discerns right, distributes justice, relieves the poor and comforts the distressed, would you not believe that he intended by this description a righteous, wise, diligent, intelligent person? Could you imagine him to mean that the *sun* or the *wind*, by {heir benign influences, rendered the country fruitful and temperate, and disposed the inhabitants to mutual kindness and benignity; and that the governor is a mere figure of speech? It is exactly thus in the case before us. The Scriptures tell us that the Holy Spirit governs the Church, appoints overseers, discerns, comforts, strengthens and disposes all things according to the counsel of His own will. Can any man credit this testimony and conceive otherwise of the Spirit than as a holy, wise, intelligent Person? Can such expressions refer to quality, an effect or influence of the power of God, who doeth all these things *figuratively*; that He has a *will* and *understanding* figuratively, is *sinned against* figuratively, and so of all that is said of Him?

"It is true that some things peculiar to persons are sometimes ascribed to things; as charity is said to hope, to believe, to bear; the Scripture is said to see and foresee, to speak and to judge. The heavens and the earth are said to hear, and the fields to be joyful, and the trees to clap their hands. But these ascriptions are only *occasional*, and a plain description of the things themselves is given us in other places. But as to the Spirit of God, the constant uniform expressions concerning Him are such as declare Him to be a Person, endowed with all personal properties."*

Our final proof of the personality of the Spirit is derived from the requirement of faith, which is the only door through which God comes into the human soul. The stronger the faith the larger the capacity to receive the divine guest. Faith attains its highest vigor when it grasps a personal object and not an abstraction, the blesser and not the blessing. God in Christ awakens faith in a higher degree than the attempted conception of an infinite Being boundless and vague. Faith culminates in its strength where it addresses a personal Father revealed in a personal incarnate Son and claims the personal Paraclete. Grace then flows

---

*Dr. John Owen, "On the Spirit," Chapter III.

into the soul in largest streams, in Mississippi's and Amazons "of living water." Hear the testimony of a professor in Cambridge University, England:*
"If reference to personal experience may be permitted, I may indeed 'here set my seal.' Never shall I forget the gain to conscious faith and peace which came to my soul not long after a first decisive and appropriating view of the crucified Lord as the sinner's sacrifice of peace, from a more intelligent and conscious hold upon the living and most gracious personality of that Holy Spirit through whose mercy the soul had got that blessed view. It was a new development of insight into the love of God. It was a new contact as it were with the inner and eternal movements of redeeming goodness and power, a new discovery in divine resources. At a 'time of finding,' gratitude and love and adoration gain a new, a newly realized reason and motive power and rest. He who with His secret skill, and with a power not the less almighty because it violates nothing, has awakened and regenerated the man, now shines before his inner sight with the smile of a personal and eternal kindness and amity, and is seen standing side by side, in union unspeakable yet without confusion, with Him who has suffered and redeemed, and with Him who laid the mighty plan of grace and willed its all-merciful success." This testimony of Prof. Moule to a work of grace after regeneration hinges on the condition of his getting a "conscious hold upon the living and most gracious personality of the Holy Spirit," a "hold " possible only to him who has already been born of the Spirit.†

---

*H.C.G. Moule, principal of Ridley Hall and author of "Veni Creator."
†See Appendix, Note C

Chapter IV
THE EXECUTIVE OF THE GODHEAD

FOR SEVERAL YEARS our mind has been laboring to invent some concise expression for the sum of all the offices of the Third Person of the Trinity in the transformation, sanctification and habitation of souls who fully believe in Christ Jesus. At last Dr. Hodge has struck out with his die the very coin which our own mint has failed to stamp and contribute to the currency of Christian experience and theological discussion. "The Holy Ghost is the executive of the Godhead." This clear-cut conception and expression of the work of the Spirit is exceedingly beautiful because it is indisputably true. Law emanates from the Father, mercy and judgment are committed to the Son, while the executive of both Persons is the ever-blessed Spirit. Here we have the three departments of government—the legislative, the judicial and the executive. Through the Holy Spirit the Father and the Son operate on human souls, reproving, regenerating, witnessing and sanctifying. We now see how a person may honor the Father and in a measure the Son and yet fail of attaining the highest spiritual grace through a failure to honor the Holy Ghost, the blessed Comforter; just as a man may show all proper respect to the lawmaking and law-interpreting departments of our own government, and secure their action, and then miss his purpose at last by ignoring the last link necessary to its realization—the executive officer, without whose agency statutes and courts are ineffectual. We fear that there are many Christians who inadvertently fail in their tribute of respect, faith and worship to the Holy Ghost, regarding Him as an impersonal emanation or influence streaming from God, or as only another name for the Father, who can just as well without Him reach and transfigure their sin-stained souls through the blood of the Lamb that taketh away the sins of the world.

To human reason this looks very plausible. But Christian experience, especially in its advanced stages, has proved it to be fallacious. We must believe in the Holy Ghost as an indispensable agent in the production of spiritual life both in its incipiency and in its fulness. There is a sense in which He is now the most important active factor in the production of Christian character. The work of the Father in the gift of the Son and the work of the Son in pouring out His own blood as a sin offering are completed past acts. But the work of the Spirit in each individual believer is incomplete. They very greatly mistake who suppose that He fully accomplished His mission to our world on the day of Pentecost, or at the farthest when He had inspired the last word of the New Testament, and that He then withdrew, leaving the Church under the reign of fixed spiritual laws. Such a creed as this chills the soul and deadens all the fires of faith and love. Let the entire Church come to a full realization that the Comforter came to abide and that He is now descending in personal Pentecosts as certainly and as demonstrably in the consciousness of every perfect believer as He did in the upper room in Jerusalem, then will the glory of the dispensation of the Spirit begin to be generally seen and "the executive of the Godhead" receive fitting honor. "To have faith in Christ and not to have faith in the Spirit seems to be a great contradiction; yet we submit it for the judgment of candid inquirers whether this very contradiction is not strikingly exhibited in the case of almost all who profess to be followers of Christ. To know the Father, we must know the Son; to know Christ, we must know the Spirit."* This is our privilege: "Ye shall know him. He shall testify of me." We suspect that much of the repugnance among good Christian people to an instantaneous sanctification comes from a sort of a naturalistic view of the kingdom of grace left to the operation of fixed laws in the absence of the King. They forget that the King has left in His stead a personal successor and vicegerent clothed with omnipotent power. "The day of Pentecost was a pattern day; all the days of this dispensation should have been like it, or should have exceeded it. But alas! the Church has fallen down to the state in which it was before this blessing had been bestowed, and it is necessary for us to ask Christ to begin over again. We of course in respect to knowledge—intellectual knowledge of spiritual things—are far in advance of the point where the disciples were before the Pentecost. But it should be borne in mind that when truths have once been fully revealed and made a part of orthodoxy, the holding of them does

---

*"Love Revealed," George Bowen

not necessarily imply any operation of the Spirit of God. We deceive ourselves, doubtless, in this way, imagining that because we have the whole Scriptures and are conversant with all its great truths the Spirit of God is necessarily working in us. We need a baptism of the Spirit as much as the apostles did at the time of Christ's resurrection."* That was not a mere dash of rhetoric which fell from the pen of John Fletcher when he spoke of the Pentecost as the opening of "the kingdom of the Holy Ghost." He has the signet ring of our glorified King Jesus, and reigns over the family on earth as the Son of man reigns over the family above. He has not shut Himself up as an impersonal force in the tomb of uniform law, but He walks through the earth a glorious personality, with the keys of divine power attached to His girdle and with the rod of empire in His right hand. He works miracles in the realm of spirit as did Immanuel in the realm of matter. The new Creator of the soul performs a greater work than the original Creator of man, inasmuch as the former works upon material which is capable of an eternal resistance to His plastic touch, while in matter there was no such antagonism.

In that sublime formula of worship, the *Te Deum Laudamus*, which has dropped from the lips of dying sires to living sons for fifteen centuries, there is found this sentence referring to the work of Christ in opening the dispensation of the Spirit, "When Thou hadst overcome the sharpness of death, Thou didst open the Kingdom of Heaven to all believers." To make the Church realize the presence of "the executive of the Godhead," there must be more praying in the Holy Ghost, more preaching with the demonstration of the Spirit, more singing with the spirit and testifying as the Spirit giveth utterance, with

---

* "Love Revealed," George Bowen

the attesting fruits of the Spirit, love, joy and peace. There must be more faith in the Holy Spirit as the greatest gift that men can wish or that heaven can send. We belie His presence when in our fruitless lives we present Him as a barren tree with no golden fruit to attract and feed hungry souls. This poor, blind world, which apprehends only sensible things, physical causes and effects, must be lifted up by the lever of sanctified character from the low plane of naturalism to apprehend the presence of the supernatural on earth, the standing miracle of Christianity — the Holy Spirit dwelling in human hearts and transfiguring human lives. How glorious will be that era when the brief *credo*, "I believe in the Holy Ghost," has descended from the head into the heart of the Church, or has ascended from an intellectual assent into assured knowledge (John xiv.17). Then, and not till then, will Jesus, the glorified Bridegroom, have the entire heart of His bride, for then will the Spirit, the Bridegroom's looking-glass, fully reflect His loveliness to her eyes as the chief among ten thousand. "He shall glorify me; for he shall receive of mine, and shall show it unto you." How cheering the thought that this period of intense spiritual illumination and power is not fixed by the decree of God in the distant future, but that it may be inaugurated in our own day by a simple, all-surrendering faith in Christ's promise of the Comforter. There are indications of the dawn of that returning day of Pentecost when the Spirit shall be poured out in His fulness upon all who "know the exceeding greatness of Christ's power to usward who believe." The eastern sky has streaks of light betokening the sunrise of a day of power. Christians of every name, lone watchers on the mountain tops, now see the edge of the ascending disk, and are shouting to the inhabitants of the dark valleys below to awake and arise and behold the splendors of the King of day.

Reader, the perfect restoration of the reign of the Spirit

over the Church involves your personal co-operation, the entire consecration of your heart, your victory over the world, your crucifixion with Christ, the entire cleansing of your heart and the transformation of your body into "a temple of the Holy Ghost, the habitation of God through the Spirit." Are you ready to be nailed to the cross? By the "you " I mean the old self-life. You should be willing to enter into that state of conscious deadness to self in which the great German reformer was when he said, "If any one knocks at the door of my breast and says, Who lives here? I will answer, Not Martin Luther, but Jesus Christ."

Chapter V
THE WORK OF THE SPIRIT BEFORE THE DAY OF PENTECOST

THIS IS AN INQUIRY into an obscure subject, but necessary for the clear setting forth of His contrasted work as the Paraclete.

1. The conviction for sin does not seem to have been so pungent. Men were driven back from their apostasies by repentance, more through the scourge of divine judgments, wars, locusts, plagues, captivities, than by an inner sense of the exceeding turpitude of sin.

2. The Old Testament conversion was a moral change wrought by the will of the penitent, influenced by the Spirit of God, rather than a new creation or a new birth. The very surprise of Nicodemus indicates that the idea of regeneration as a radical spiritual transformation was unfamiliar to the Jewish mind. The predominant purpose may be changed from vice to virtue in reliance on divine help, as in the case of reformed drunkards, without regeneration. This is our idea of conversion during the period of Mosaism and under the preaching of John the Baptist. To assert that

John's converts were spiritually changed is to declare that John lost in a few months more regenerated probationers for Jesus than Methodism ever lost in her entire history of a hundred and fifty years. There are many Old Testament converts in our modern churches.

3. There was no assurance of acceptance with God certified to the penitent soul, no witness of the Spirit, in fact no pardon, but rather the pretermission of sins, as Paul teaches in Rom. iii.25, where he uses παρεσις, passing by, for αφεσις, forgiveness.

4. Old Testament piety was characterized by bondage, the New by freedom. Those who were as children under tutors and governors were made free by Christ, free indeed. For where the Spirit of the Lord is there is liberty, the dungeon doors swing open and the fetters fall.

5. It naturally follows that there was no permanent state of reconciliation, because there was no permanent basis for it in an atonement made once for all and all-sufficient during all time. (See the Epistle to the Hebrews, where the failure of the altar offerings to remove the consciousness of sin is emphatically announced.) There was, through the offerings, a temporary peace of mind attained, but no satisfaction concerning the whole standing of the sinner before God. Full pardon was in the future. O Israel, wait for the Lord. He *will* redeem Israel from all his sins. The legal sacrifices of the sincere and penitent Israelite availed to maintain his corporate membership in the Old Testament covenant, and to secure an operation of grace; but still the Holy of Holies remained closed to him, and he was destitute of that knowledge of personal salvation without which he was not "made perfect as pertaining to the conscience." He could not attain that inward consciousness of perfect reconciliation with God and perfectly satisfied longings after salvation and that undisturbed peace which is enjoyed by the genuine believer in Christ under the dispensation of the Comforter.

6. There was no conscious indwelling of the Spirit in Old Testament saints because there was no new or spiritual man in which He could abide. Hence their experiences, with a few extraordinary exceptions like David, were sombre, not sunny. Outside of the Psalms and Isaiah there is little gladness and less exultation. The fruit of the Spirit is joy. They had not the tree, the abiding Comforter, how could they have the fruit? The kingdom of God is righteousness, peace and joy in the Holy Ghost. They had in imperfection two thirds of the kingdom, ceremonial purity and legal righteousness, an intermittent peace, but to the joy of the Holy Ghost they were strangers because He did not dwell in their hearts. The notion of divine sonship as conferred upon Israel as a nation, and then upon the anointed king, is found in the Old Testament. But the sonship of individuals is a glorious gospel promise, the distinctive prerogative of believers in Christ. John i.12: "To as many as received him gave he power to become the sons of God." For this reason one such believer is greater than John, whose spiritual stature overtopped all the saints before him, even Abraham, the founder, and Moses, the lawgiver, of the Hebrew commonwealth.

7. Of course entire sanctification except in a ceremonial sense was not enjoyed by the Old Testament saints. This could not be in the absence of the indwelling sanctifier. This again is held up as an attainment in Messianic times. Ezek. xxxvi.25-29: "I will sprinkle clean water upon you." In enumerating these defects in Old Testament saints I have spoken of them generally. It will be easy to find an exception to each point which I have made, as Enoch, who had assurance; David, the joy of forgiveness; and Isaiah, who was sanctified by the symbolic coal of fire laid upon his lips. But the exception proves the rule.

To the objection that I have given the Holy Spirit no eminent place in Old Testament experiences, I answer that He has all the place that can be assigned to strong outward influence, but not a conscious indwelling in the individual. In fact, the gifts of the Spirit before Pentecost were largely external rather than internal, rather gifts than grace; such as skill to Bezaleel, prescience to the prophets, strength to Samson, valor and administrative ability to the Judges and the kingly instinct to Saul. After Pentecost there were outward gifts arbitrarily bestowed; as *charismata*, distributed by the Spirit severally to whomsoever He will; but the chief gift was the Spirit Himself permanently abiding in the soul as the sanctifier, the endowment of power, the wellspring of joy and the inspirer of all gracious dispositions. The graces of the Spirit, especially the grace that leads the choral procession, *Love*, are infinitely superior to all the outward gifts of tongues, interpretation, healing, etc.

The operations of the Spirit on the world at large and on impenitent Hebrews before Pentecost effected little more than to create a basis of responsibility. Few seem to have been savingly influenced. His striving with the sinners before the flood (Gen. vi.3) was a signal failure, only one family being saved. Nehemiah (ix.20) says of the vast host of disobedient Israelites in the wilderness, "Thou gavest also thy good Spirit to instruct them, and withheldest not thy manna from their mouth." They seem, like modern sinners, to have appropriated the manna, but to have rejected the instructions of the good Spirit, for only two or three adult men who left Egypt out of a million got into Canaan. We do not say that all except these failed to attain eternal life, for Moses is certainly in heaven. Nor is this failure a matter of surprise when we consider that the distinct mission of the Spirit had not begun, and that in pre-Pentecostal times He had very poor tools to work with— the light of natural religion in pagan minds and the types and shadows of Mosaism with which to move the Hebrew heart. But since the ascension He has had all the facts and wonderful realities of the gospel of Christ.

The distinctness of the Spirit's work since the ascension of Christ is apparent to all readers of the New Testament. Dean Alford is so impressed with this fact that he writes in capitals these words descriptive of the office of the Comforter, that it is TOTALLY DISTINCT from all His previous working. These are some of the characteristics of His mission:

1. *Distinct* promise; the Spirit of promise, *the* promise of the Father.
2. An *instantaneous* coming, an event as sharply defined in history as the birth of Christ.
3. Permanence; He came to stay, to *abide* forever.
4. He enters into the interior personality of the believer, and dwells within him, putting the law of God, the law of love, into his innermost heart, the source and nutriment of a new life interpenetrating his soul in a manner as mysterious as the coexistence of the Trinity of persons in one divine nature.
5. His whole work has a most intimate relation to the person of Christ, as if to hold up a mirror to reflect the form of the invisible and glorified Saviour into the consciousness of the believer, affording a spiritual manifestation of Christ.

"When I say that pious Jews and our Lord's disciples before the day of Pentecost were strangers to the great outpouring of the Spirit, I do not mean that they were strangers to His directing, sanctifying and enlivening influences according to their dispensation... Nevertheless they were not fully baptized. The Comforter who visited them did not properly dwell in them. Although they had wrought miracles by His power, 'the promise of the Father' was not yet fulfilled to them. They would have been puzzled with such questions as these: 'Have ye received the Holy Ghost since ye believed?' 'Is he fallen upon you?'

'Is the love of God shed abroad in your hearts by the Holy Ghost given unto you?' 'Is the fountain springing up into everlasting life opened in your breast?' ...If these and like questions would have perplexed the apostles before Christ had opened His spiritual baptism and set up His kingdom with power in their hearts, we ought not to be surprised that professors who knew only the baptism of John should ingenuously confess they 'never heard there was a Holy Ghost [to be received] since they believed.' Nor should we wonder if devout Jews and easy Laodiceans should even mock and say, 'You would have us filled with new wine;' but 'we are rich and increased in goods, and have need of nothing.' 'The water of our old cisterns is preferable to the new wine of your enthusiastic doctrine, and our baptismal ponds to your baptismal flames.'" (Fletcher.)

Chapter VI
THE PARACLETE'S CONVICTION OF SIN

"AND HE, WHEN he is come, will convict the world of sin." Of what form of sin? Not of those social offences called crimes, violations of the precepts and prohibitions of the decalogue, the basis of the criminal code in all civilized countries. Human courts are competent to convict of crime. Nor does the Spirit convict of those injuries to ourselves known as vices, moral delinquencies not named in the Ten Commandments. Conscience is sufficient to convict of these, aided by self-love and self-respect. But human law and conscience combined cannot eradicate evil from the heart. Philosophy has tried it and failed. Poetry, especially comedy and satire, have ineffectually attempted to convict the world of sin in all past ages. They have chastised cutaneous sins, denouncing the drunkard, the glutton, the opium user, the fornicator. All these were self-condemned before the shaft of ridicule was hurled at them. Each of them could say:

"I see the right, and I approve it too;
Condemn the wrong, and yet the wrong pursue."

But is not God's law thundering from Sinai a sufficient witness to convict of sin? No, it never did convince the world that sin is evil *per se*, a thing to be abominated, to be abhorred and shunned because of its inherent hatefulness and unspeakable vileness. The divine law is effectual only as it causes sin to be dreaded and avoided merely because of the punishment which will surely visit it. There is needed more than an accuser and punisher of sin, a power which can not only probe and search the heart and turn it inside out, exposing to the sunlight all its loathsome leprosies, but a power which can effect a radical cure. The sinful heart needs a surgeon so sharp-sighted as to detect this deadly disease under all its disguises of euphonious names, and a physician so skilful as to apply an effectual remedy. That healer of the sinful soul is the divine Comforter, mercifully sent, not to torment the world by forbidding its pleasures, but to bless the world by turning it away from its iniquities. Sins of every kind are the fruit of an invisible root to which they bear no outward resemblance. This root is too subtle for human laws and courts to see. It requires anointed eyes. No human philosophy had ever found the sum and substance, the poisonous essence of sin, in unbelief. How can this be the all-inclusive sin? Is not historic doubt respecting persons and events innocent and even commendable? To such questions of a shallow rationalism we answer that unbelief in respect to Christ is more than withholding intellectual assent to a historic record. It is ingratitude towards a Benefactor and Saviour, and rebellion against a rightful Ruler, a refusal to bow the knee to the personal revelation of God. The cause of this unbelief is not intellectual, arising from a lack of evidences, but moral, arising from a lack of willingness. Christ is rejected because He lays the axe at the root sin, plants a hedge of thorns across the path of sinful pleasure, and kindles a consuming flame in the house of the worldling's idols. The Holy Spirit convicts unbelievers of a lie when they pretend that their unbelief toward Christ is merely honest doubt. It is because faith in Him draws after it what is conceived to be the unpleasant obligation to obey Him, that they are unbelieving. In fact, the Greek Testament has but one word for unbelief and disobedience. In truth and verity, however boldly and persistently the world may deny it, the fact is that unbelief in respect to Christ lies in the will so corrupt that it hugs sin and will not let it be taken away by the Son of God, who came into the world and submitted to the shame and agony of the cross for this very purpose. Not all unbelievers are as honest as the African chief, Sekeletu, with whom David Livingstone met in his explorations. Says that great missionary: "Sekeletu pressed me to name anything I desired, and it should be given. I explained that my object was to elevate him and his people to be Christians. He replied, 'I do not wish to learn to read the Book, for I am afraid it might change my heart and make me content with one wife, like Sechele [a converted chief]. No, no, I want always to have five wives at least.'" Here is a frank admission that the difficulty in believing in Christ does not lie in defective evidence of His right to rule the heart and life, but in the purpose of the sinner to have his own way. Equally frank was that son of Abraham, a Pole, who, when asked by an American Christian whether the Jews' rejection of Jesus, the Messiah, was because they would not believe or because they could not, spitefully replied, "Ve vill not believe, ve vill not believe." But gospel-hardened sinners do not have such candor. Instead of acknowledging the real obstacle in their own will, they devise some pretext, some intellectual difficulty in the way of faith, with which they sophisticate conscience and excuse their godlessness. The Spirit of inspiration teaches that the sin of unbelief denies God's moral attribute of truth. "He that believeth not God's witness concerning his Son, that eternal life is in him [and in Him only], hath made him a liar" (I John v.9-12).

It is a favorite plea of those who reject Christ as their personal Saviour that faith is not in the province of the will, and that consequently we are not accountable for it as the pivot of destiny. But this falsehood is shown up by the Holy Ghost, who ever insists that the culpability of unbelief lies in the fact that it is a wilful, obstinate and persistent aversion to Christ's requirements. It is this activity of the Spirit in demonstrating the truth to every mind and conscience by showing *the things of Christ*, His divinity, His sinlessness, His condescending love evinced by His self-sacrificing life and atoning death, that renders every hearer of the gospel accountable to the Judge of the quick and the dead for his acceptance or his rejection of Jesus Christ as his rightful King. "He that believeth shall be saved; he that believeth not shall be damned." The convicting debate which the Spirit carries on with the world has this surprising peculiarity: The momentous question of eternal destiny does not turn upon man's treatment of God the Father, but rather his disposition towards His Son. This is the sin which towers above all and comprises all. "Because they believe not on ME." That is to say, the world did not believe in Him as God manifest in the flesh in the person of His only begotten Son, the appointed King and Redeemer of mankind. "For God, as He is in Himself, in the mystery of His own unapproachable being, as He dwells in the bright abyss of His own timeless eternity, before the glory of whose face the archangels veil their eyes, whom no one has known or can know except the only begotten Son and the Spirit who is one with the Father and the Son, can hardly become a distinct object even of faith to man." It is only when He vouchsafes to come forth out of His absolute Godhood, in the person of His Son and of His Spirit, that He is pleased to make Himself known to men by these two divine witnesses, the representatives of His glory, without whom no creature could know anything or believe anything about God.

Underlying the Spirit's argument in the inmost depths of the soul where character originates from free choice, is the doctrine of the supreme Godhood (corrupted into Godhead) of Jesus Christ. For if He were a creature, the highest in the universe next to the throne of God (Channing), it would be a sin to trust in Him rather than solely in the Creator. The Spirit recognizes the supreme divinity and not the creaturehood of the Son of man, the Son of God. For this reason orthodoxy in all the Christian ages has emphasized and exalted that primary truth which Luther, after the theological errors of the dark ages, so fully apprehended and so lucidly proclaimed, that evangelical, saving faith is the ground of all good in man, and the want of it is the source of all evil. This truth the Spirit's convincing agency always implies when He gives a clear perception of the deformity and damnableness of the absence of faith in Christ as the chosen state of heart. The Spirit demolishes all the subterfuges and excuses by which depravity endeavors to palliate unbelief and to whitewash the vileness of his ingratitude to Jesus Christ, his best friend and benefactor.

Another truth implied in the Spirit's conviction of the world is that present salvation and eternal life depend solely on faith in Christ for which there can be no substitute. By this declaration the pious, God-fearing pagan living up to his best light is not excluded from salvation.

He evinces that he has the spirit of faith and the purpose of righteousness which are accepted in the involuntary absence of a knowledge of the historic Christ. He has engraven on his own character, through co-operation with the universal activity of the Holy Spirit, the imperfect outlines of the image of Christ, styled by Joseph Cook "the essential Christ." When the apostles demonstrated to the conscience of the Jews that there was salvation in no other name, not even in Abraham their father nor in Moses their lawgiver, they were convicted of the most stupendous crime possible, but not beyond the forgiving grace of their disowned and crucified Messiah. Great as was their first crime of murdering their King, their second offence of rejecting His claims did not place them individually beyond His pardoning mercy, if they would repent and believe, although it sealed their national doom. Their unbelief vitiated all their fancied righteousness sought from the law and rendered it detestable and all their sacrifices abominable to the searcher of hearts. They were preeminently guilty of unbelief. The temporal consequences to their nation manifestly confirm the assertion that it was the most heinous of all sins. The Spirit not only convicts unbelievers of wilful sin, but He also convicts the regenerate of "sin improperly so called" (Wesley), a wrong state of the sensibilities lying back of the will. Even after the will has, through the new birth, been brought into the attitude of submission to Christ, there remain tendencies and propensities perilous to the spiritual life and antagonistic to the new principle of love to God which is now enthroned within. This rendered many of the Corinthians "carnal," so that Paul hesitated to call them "spiritual," though they were, "as babes in Christ," possessing a feeble spiritual life instead of that more abundant life which Christ came to impart. This lingering carnality, "the easily besetting" or closely clinging sin, styled by Delitzsch "the indwelling evil," was the force which was impelling many of the Galatians downward instead of upward; for, having begun in the Spirit, they were ending in the flesh. We must ascribe to the same cause that lack of perfect loyalty and perfect devotion to Christ in all of Paul's band of missionary helpers in Rome, Timothy excepted, of whom the sorrowful apostle says, "For they all seek their own, not the things of Jesus Christ." By such a remark as this the apostle to the Gentiles does not de-Christianize those members of Christ's body who are still actuated by selfishness. Rather he represents them as weak and defective believers who have not yet submitted to a total self-crucifixion as a prerequisite to perfect love to Christ. Paul does not include himself and Timothy in this class (Phil. ii.19-21).

A light estimate of sin is the bane of modern Christian thought.* It is attended by a depreciation of the moral law. Since the law underlies the atonement, whatever lessens the majesty of the law detracts from the necessity and value of the atonement. Thus these fundamentals all suffer loss when one of them, sin, law, atonement, is discounted. To these three vital doctrines we may add the pardon of sin and sanctification, together with eternal retribution. When one of these doctrines is undervalued, all are soon weakened. Says Principal Moule: "A full, strong current of opinion in the professing Church of Christ runs at the present day directly against a grave, thoroughgoing doctrine of sin and its correlative truths of eternal judgment and of the unspeakable need of the atoning blood and of a living personal faith in the crucified and risen One. One would think that some earnest teachers had learned, by some other path surely than that of the Word of God, to look with temperate eyes upon sin as a phenomenon sure at last to disappear under long processes of divine order." The final evanescence of moral

---

*See Appendix, Note D

evil is a pleasing delusion of liberalism which cannot endure the idea of sin as an eternal blot on the face of the universe. A careful, candid study of the parables of Christ shows the human family in the day of judgment separated and sentenced to the opposite destinies of punishment and reward with no hint of an ultimate reunion. Moral evil as a finality under the government of omnipotent goodness is a problem of less difficulty than the permission of sin by absolute holiness. The argument which justifies the arbitrary non-prevention of sin will justify its sovereign non-extinction. But we need no such argument. God has only one way for the extinction of sin, the blood of His Son presented by penitent faith. He will never crush sin with an almighty trip hammer, as Universalists desire; nor will He crush the sinner into nonentity to suit annihilationism. Hence final impenitence can have no other sequence than everlasting misery. Without any revelation Plato comes to this conclusion. His moral reason demanded it. Hence it is not unreasonable. What is the remedy for inadequate and superficial views of sin as a transient, cutaneous disease soon to be outgrown by the soul? Preach earnestly and persistently the office of the Paraclete as the convincer of the stupendous sin of unbelief toward Christ, of righteousness and of judgment to come. Liberalism can be cured only by the awakening truths of Christ's gospel. No office of the Comforter can be neglected without moral disaster, which always overtakes those who advance beyond the New Testament in their fancied progress. "Whosoever goeth onward and abideth not in the teaching of Christ hath not God" (II John 9, Revised Version).

Chapter VII
THE PARACLETE'S CONVICTION OF RIGHTEOUSNESS

THE SPIRIT'S CONVICTION of righteousness— His exhibition of a perfect model of righteous human character— was as necessary for the moral recovery of fallen men as the conviction of sin. By the dark picture of what the sinner is, must be suspended the bright ideal of what he ought to be. This ideal no fallen man is able, without the Spirit's aid, correctly to portray. He alone can photograph it upon the prepared tablet of the soul. Conviction of sin prepares the tablet. In the normal unfolding of the child there arises the ability to discover the distinction between right and wrong. But this moral sense is so drugged from childhood upward with the threefold opiates, selfishness, worldliness and fleshly-mindedness, that the soul has no conception of the high moral attainments for which it was created, and comes to look upon it as becoming and inevitable to desire sensual pleasures, to seek after them and indulge in them with only such limitation as self-love may suggest. The ordinary course of education in all pagan families, and in many homes nominally Christian, is such as tends more and more to inflame the worldly and fleshly stimulants of action, more and more to draw the youth out of quiet meditation into the race-course of intellectual emulation, athletic strife, business competition, or the whirlpool of sensual pleasure. The world is full of false notions of honor and false estimates of interest. Hence the natural man knows nothing of a perfect attainable righteousness. Study the moral character of the pagan gods of the most cultured nations; for here, if anywhere, we may find among the gods worshipped by these nations an expression of their highest ideals of righteousness. But we find on Mount Olympus among the gods of Grecian and Roman mythology only deified lust, deified hatred, deified theft, deified jealousy and deified bloodthirstiness.

Nor is there anything in the best human philosophies in heathenism that can be safely held up as the pattern of perfect righteousness. Ignoring the fact that man at his climax reflects the image of his Creator, philosophy denudes Him of all the human virtues, piles up a lot of abstractions and negations powerless to purify and elevate human society, and then wonders that it is steadily sinking into the depths of hopeless moral degeneracy.

Study the pagan poets, their epics and tragedies, their satires and comedies, and their lyrics also, and you will no longer express your surprise at Plato's exclusion of the poets from his ideal republic. Instead of delineating the portrait of spotless righteousness, they glorify human vices, and with all the splendors of genius they so adorn the contentions and debasing passions of men as to incite to their imitation.

Even in Christian lands some modern writers who reject Christ have gone back to paganism, and have raised from the dead the idea that *might is right*, a monstrous idea which was laid in its grave by Socrates more than twenty-two hundred years ago. But what is the Comforter's irrefutable proof of the perfect righteousness of Christ? He Himself answers, "Because I go to the Father, and ye see me no more." The world placed Him between two thieves; but God, who cannot err, has set Him between Himself and the Holy Spirit, far above all principality and power. Never was the righteousness of the world so contradicted as when He to whom Barabbas was preferred, was received by the Father amid the acclamations of all the holy orders of intelligences around His throne. The pure and perfect righteousness of Jesus is now forever vindicated. "Despised and rejected of men," yea, of all men, — for what the Jews, the best nation, did, all other nations would have done, — He has been received and adored by all the heavenly world. This is a sufficient proof of His righteousness.

But how do we know that He has been thus received? It is true that no human eye saw Him after the cloud received Him from the sight of His upward-gazing disciples. It is also true that no angelic witness of the reception and coronation has come down to this world and made oath to this glorious fact. But a greater witness has come down, and is now testifying to every human conscience that Jesus sits enthroned with His Father. This testimony is twofold: first, in the inspired gospel record where the fact stands undisputed; and, secondly, in the heart of every hearer of the gospel, where the duty of penitent faith in Him is urged upon the conscience as the first and greatest duty. It may be that "the fulness of time" for which God waited before He "sent forth his Son" (Gal. iv.4) was the period required for the demonstration of the world's utter inability to originate those moral ideals which could turn men from sin to righteousness. He waited till the

Greeks, the most aesthetic nation, had reached the perfection of art in painting, sculpture and architecture; till the greatest orators had uttered their matchless speeches; till the greatest poets had been laurel crowned; till the greatest philosophers had uttered their "divine peradventures," and till all the leading ethnic religions had set up moral monstrosities to be worshipped in their temples; till Greece amid the splendors of art was rotting in licentiousness, and till all-conquering Rome, on her seven hills burning the incense of her adoration to Might, was pouring contempt on all the passive virtues, meekness, patience, forgiveness and philanthropy. Then God permitted His well-beloved Son to unite Himself with humanity, to present to all men the perfect model of character, and to teach every man the duty of reproducing that sinless character in himself. Then, as a crowning gift, to render the gift of His Son available in the highest degree, He sent down the divine Paraclete to assist man's wandering eye to gaze steadfastly upon this divine and human model of holiness, and to steady his hand to copy the matchless beauties of that heavenly pattern. This was the second work of the Comforter, to convince the world of righteousness, because this too was a work which He alone could accomplish.

Chapter VIII
THE PARACLETE'S CONVICTION OF JUDGMENT

JUDGMENT IS THE SANCTION of law. Since Jesus came not to destroy the law but to fill it full of meaning, His commission to the Paraclete must effect the same purpose to honor the law by declaring its sentence against sin. Says Tholuck: "The meaning of our Lord's words is, When the divine principle of the Spirit shall spread among my disciples and produce its extraordinary effects in mankind, people will be forced to confess that the power of the evil spirit which opposes me in the ungodly feelings of men is broken. By the incarnation and coming of the Saviour an inward judgment was commenced in the hearts of men of which the last judgment is only the outward manifestation." The atoning death of Christ declaring God's abhorrence of sin and His mercy to sinners was the defeat of Satan, the usurping ruler called "the god of this world." Christ Jesus through death conditionally emancipated every human soul from Satanic bondage, and thus "destroyed him who hath the power of death, that is, the devil."

But how can the casting out of "the prince of this world" demonstrate that every one who refuses to trust in Christ with true obedience and to seek justification through reliance on the atonement for sin made by Him will be found on the left hand of the Judge and hear his own condemnation pronounced in the last day? Our answer is this: All who take on the Satanic character must expect the Satanic doom; all who bear the devil's image must share his destiny. So all who bear the likeness of Christ will share His glory. "After the whole dilemma between sin and righteousness is clearly set forth, the Spirit finally announces the judgment of Satan in such a way that He not only comforts believers with the perfect comfort declared in Rom. viii.33, 34, but also reproves unbelievers with that awful judgment, as a last sting, in their inmost hearts, *Will ye then absolutely be and continue the devils? Will ye bejudged with him?*" (Stier.) Satan is condemned now for our benefit if we yield to the Spirit's voice in our hearts and accept the righteousness which Christ provides and the Comforter inworks; or we abide with God's great adversary in the judgment if we continue in sin with the world. This third and last conviction of the Spirit clearly implies that in the estimation of the Spirit of truth the existence of the devil must needs belong to some fundamental article of saving truth without which we cannot correctly estimate the enormity of sin, the value of righteousness and the necessity of the atonement by which it was procured. In this third conviction the victory of righteousness over sin is completed. In this our salvation is infallibly secured if we but will it. The Spirit never coerces a free agent.

The discussion of the three convictions which the Paraclete effects in men, especially men who are enlightened by gospel truth, shows in what way He glorifies the

Son of God. The first question is, Why does He not glorify the Father? He does. If the Father and Son are one in nature, as the Son asserts (John xiv.9), it follows that honors ascribed to the Son glorify the Father. "He that acknowledgeth the Son hath the Father also" (I John ii.23). There can be no jealousy between them, because they are one in divinity, and in their distinct personalities they aim at one purpose in the scheme of redemption.

The personality of the Son is much more easily grasped by men's narrow minds, because it is divested of that vagueness and abstract infinitude which belong to our conception of God. Hence, the Son's personality having been exhibited in a concrete form, within the limits of humanity, has become far more affecting and influential, when contemplated with all its historic incidents, lowly birth, poverty, youthful toil, kindly deeds, beneficent miracles, wise sayings, transparent parables, rejection by the Jews, arrest by the midnight mob, unjust condemnation, tragic execution and glorious resurrection. It is this historic setting of the Son's personality which the Holy Spirit can use with the best effect in producing conviction of sin. The only element which we have failed to enumerate needful for this result is assent to distinctive Christian truth, especially to Christ's claim of supreme divinity. Truth separate from a sense of the authority of God does not convict of sin and spiritually vitalize man's moral nature. Says Dr. Walker, "Conscience will enforce no moral duty unless it sees God in it." It will respond to no other voice than that of the moral Ruler and final Judge of all free moral agents. So long as Jesus was regarded as a man only, His preaching had meagre results in the number of His disciples. But after His supreme divinity was demonstrated by His conquest of death, ascension to heaven and effusion of the Holy Spirit, men were converted by the thousands in a day. Like causes produce like effects in every age. Wherever in dependence on the

VIII: THE PARACLETE'S CONVICTION OF JUDGMENT   61

Spirit of truth the whole gospel is preached, including Christ's triumph over the grave in proof of His Godhead, unbelievers are convinced of sin, righteousness and judgment. But wherever Jesus Christ is presented as a model of moral excellence, but a mere man like ourselves, there is no conscience awakened to see the enormity of sin and to turn from it with a perfect loathing. Revivals can no more come from such preaching than orange groves can spring up and bear fruit among the glaciers of Alaska. Genuine conversions must be preceded by a painful sense of the enormity of sin, which comes only from the belief that Christ is the divine Saviour. This belief, though not saving, is the necessary stepping-stone to that all-surrendering reliance on Him as both Saviour and Lord which is the condition of salvation. It is not enough to know Him historically as the Son of man. He must be known as the Son of God. This knowledge flesh and blood cannot impart. "No man can say Jesus is Lord, but in the Holy Spirit" (I Cor. xii.3, Revised Version). This gracious ability to arrive at a belief in the supreme divinity of Christ is imparted to all candid readers of the entire New Testament who have a disposition to follow whither the truth may lead. It is not enough to read the first three Gospels. The sincere inquirer must proceed to the fourth if he would be convinced that the Son of man is also the Son of God, equal to the Father in power and glory. Then he will hear Him say, "All things [attributes] that the Father hath are mine: therefore said I, that he [the Comforter] taketh of mine and shall declare it unto you" (John xvi.15). Thus the Comforter glorified Christ by attesting His perfect power to save from the guilt of sin through faith in His blood shed as a conditional substitute for the punishment of sin.

Then the Comforter, as "the Spirit of adoption," glorifies Christ as the Saviour by crying in the believer's heart, "Abba, Father." This inspired feeling of sonship is the gift of Christ. "But as many as received him, to them gave he the right to become children of God, even to them that believe on his name." Thus the three divine Persons are glorified in the new birth of a soul.

> "With joy the Father doth approve
> The fruit of His eternal love;
> The Son looks down with joy and sees
> The purchase of His agonies;
> The Spirit takes delight to view
> The contrite soul He forms anew;
> And saints and angels join to sing
> The growing empire of their King."

Again, the Paraclete glorifies Christ by inwardly revealing Him as the chief among ten thousand and the one altogether lovely. In that wonderful address respecting the coming and offices of His successor, another Comforter, in John xiv.-xvi., aptly styled the Trinitarian Discourse, Jesus says respecting every disciple who evinces the genuineness of his love by his obedience, "I will love him, and will manifest myself unto him." That this is not a spiritual phenomenon attending regeneration is evident from the fact that those whom Christ thus addressed were already regenerated. This is implied in His prayer in John xvii., appropriately called His high-priestly prayer: "They are thine... They are not of the world, even as I am not of the world." Then He prays for a further work to be wrought in them: "Sanctify them through thy truth... I sanctify [consecrate to the one work of redemption] myself, that they themselves may be truly sanctified." With respect to these two future events, Christ's manifestation to the believer and His sanctification, the inference is natural that the former is intimately connected with the latter as a means to an end. The manifestation is by the Holy Spirit, the representative of Christ, who does not manifest Himself, but magnifies, glorifies, deifies the personality of the Son of God, for whom He is cleansing the heart as the temple of His everlasting abode.

In entire sanctification the Holy Spirit violates no law of mental philosophy, but strictly conforms His work to the nature and faculties of the mind. The stronger affection expels the weaker. Drop golden eagles plentifully in the path of beggars scrambling for cents, and the awakened thirst for gold will cure the mania for copper. The superior banishes the inferior. It was Dr. Chalmers who eloquently discoursed on "The Expulsive Power of a New Affection." To expel all proneness to sin, all that is required is to inspire an unconquerable love of holiness, not in the abstract, but as embodied in a person in the sphere of the human affections, a person who by his self-sacrifice has laid in our minds a foundation for eternal gratitude. Then will this new affection instantly expel all base loves and keep them out so long as this new affection is enthroned within. Now it is the office of the Paraclete to inspire this affection. This He does by pouring light upon the person of the divine Christ, making Him a bright reality, a sun above the king of day, infinitely superior in splendors. This manifestation of Christ in the heart was an experience of Paul in addition to His revelation of Himself to the eye and the ear of the chief persecutor as he drew near to Damascus. The outward manifestation arrested his career of hostility to Christ; the inward revelation awakened an undying love, the motive power of that heroic course of labors, privations, perils and sufferings which ended when Rome's imperial axe severed his head from his body. During all this period, as Chrysostom says, "Paul had Christ speaking within himself." Thus by deep inward revelations, as well as by outward manifestations, was the great apostle prepared, as every preacher should be, for the work of the ministry. Well does Bengel argue that the Son of God must first be revealed *in* the preacher before He can be revealed *by* him. This revelation of Christ in Paul's consciousness was the sum and substance of that "excellency of knowledge of Jesus Christ, for whom he suffered the loss of all things." The time of this inward revelation of Christ by the Holy Spirit is unknown. The exegetes agree that it is not identical with Saul's vision of the risen Christ, and that it must have occurred afterward, either in Damascus, in Arabia, or after his return from that country while sojourning in his native Tarsus.

Chapter IX
THE PENTECOSTAL ATTESTATION

WE REMARK THAT Pentecost is the final, indispensable and standing attestation of the Lordship of Jesus Christ and of the truth of all His declarations. In other words, the gift of the Paraclete, not merely as a solitary event, but as a perpetual dispensation of grace and power, is absolutely necessary to the perfection of the Christian evidences. The resurrection of Christ, according to Paul in I Cor. xv. and all Christian apologists, is the fundamental proof of His divine mission. It is my purpose to show that this greatest miracle, taken by itself as an isolated event, without the standing and perpetual attestation of the Pentecostal dispensation as a predicted sequence, would have been insufficient for the establishment of Christianity against the universal opposition of Jews and Gentiles, including ten imperial edicts of persecution and extermination beginning with Nero, A.D. 64, and ending with Diocletian, A.D. 313. Much less would it have been sufficient to perpetuate the gospel eighteen hundred years as a system dominating the world's best thought and keeping in advance of the progress of the ages. We mean to say that the empty tomb without the tongues of fire descending from generation to generation on Spirit-baptized believers would have been inadequate to the permanent enthronement of Christianity over mankind. If "another Comforter" had not succeeded Christ, His mission, with all His miracles, including His victory over the tomb, would have been a failure, and His sermons and parables would long since have been forgotten. This idea is beautifully expressed in the first verse and the last of President W. F. Warren's hymn.*

> "I worship Thee, O Holy Ghost,
>   I love to worship Thee;
> My risen Lord for aye were lost
>   But for Thy company.
>
> "I worship Thee, O Holy Ghost,
>   I love to worship Thee;
> With Thee each day is Pentecost,
>   Each night nativity."

If the Paraclete had come to testify of Himself and to do an independent work irrespective of Christ, His mission would not have conserved the memory of Christ, but would have eclipsed it. If He had come in the name of the Father to maintain the meagre unity of God in the bare and simple sense taught by so-called liberal Christianity, the outcome would have been the final oblivion of Jesus Christ following the denial of everything supernatural in His birth and ministry.

But He proceeded from the Father and the Son specially charged with the office of testifying of the Son, yea,

---

*No. 272, Hymnal of the Methodist Episcopal Church

of glorifying Him, not only in the gospel record, which He should inspire, and in the doctrines to be unfolded in apostolic sermons and epistles, but by His indwelling presence in the consciousness of believers, revealing Christ in them in a manner wholly indescribable but blessedly real and certain. We do not wonder at the tenacity with which western Christianity has insisted on the "*filioque*" (and from the Son) in the creed respecting the procession of the Holy Ghost. This enlargement of the creed not only conserves the dignity of the Son of God and harmonizes with His Trinitarian address in John xiv—xvi. and with other texts in which the Paraclete is called the "Spirit of Christ" (Rom. viii.9), the "Spirit of Jesus" (Acts xvi.7, Revised Version) and "Christ" (Eph. iii.17), but it is confirmed by the experience of all who testify that the Comforter "has taken up His lasting abode in their hearts." (Alford.) These rejoice in a wonderful magnifying of Christ and in an inexpressible increase of love to Him. If troubled before by doubts of His divinity, their doubts are forever dispelled, and "in the Holy Spirit" they gladly and spontaneously "say, Jesus is Lord" (I Cor. xii.3, Revised Version). They are as sure of his Godhead as was Thomas in the presence of his risen Master when he exclaimed, "My Lord and my God" (John xx.28). A notable instance of deliverance from doubt on this fundamental doctrine of orthodoxy by the baptism of the Spirit occurred in the experience of Dr. Wilbur Fisk at Wellfleet early in his ministry.*

This intimate identification of the Spirit's mission with the person of Christ and the success of His work was because in the wisdom of God it was seen to be necessary to the establishment and universal spread of His kingdom. There is truth in the argument that the existence of the Church as the visible exponent of Christ's kingdom is the

---

*See his Life by Dr. G. Prentice

great proof of the resurrection and divinity of its Founder. This is true. But our contention is that the Church, which was not organized when Jesus Christ, its living head, ascended, would not have had a beginning on the earth without the Pentecostal gift. This idea has found expression in that beautiful and inspiring formula of worship, the *Te Deum Laudamus,* called by Canon Liddon "at once a hymn, a prayer and a creed," in these sublime words, "When Thou hadst overcome the sharpness of death, Thou didst open the Kingdom of Heaven to all believers." This dates the founding of the Church on the day of Pentecost. It was then that Christ, in the person of the Paraclete, like the sunrise described by the poet Horace, *Altera dies, sol idem* (Another day, the same sun), gathered together the Church of the firstborn of the Spirit on the earth, the first to receive the Spirit of adoption and to head the procession of redeemed souls through all the Christian ages.

Without Pentecost the resurrection of Christ would soon have been confounded with the prodigies of the Greek and Roman mythologies. There would, after a few years or generations, have been no one interested in defending this historic fact, and after the death of the apostles there would have been no witnesses to the resurrection power as a transforming spiritual experience. The historical facts without a spiritual life built on them, preaching and defending them and dying for them a martyr's death, would have had no champion to advocate them and to perpetuate the remembrance of them.

We do not read that the company of disciples was at all increased by the story of the resurrection of Christ repeated again and again during nearly fifty days. This bare historic fact made no converts. Facts alone, though miraculous, and truth alone, though undoubted, have no regenerating power. Only life can beget life. For seven weeks the company of believers had all the facts of the gospel except the ascension complete, and for ten days they had the climax, the ascension of Christ, but there was no increase of their numbers. But on the fiftieth day three thousand believed on Jesus as the divine Saviour. Something must have happened. There is no effect without a cause. In this hidden cause lies the secret of the final triumph of Christ. Let me illustrate. In the late American Civil War, in the absence of Gen. Sheridan, the Federal commander in the valley of Shenandoah, his army was unexpectedly attacked in camp and routed. They threw down their arms and ran like frightened sheep. This scared herd of soldiers without arms suddenly turned about, met and conquered the over-confident foe, regained their lost artillery and camp and drove Gen. Early and his Confederate army in a disorderly flight and captured his artillery. What caused the change from a disgraceful rout to a glorious victory? It was the sudden arrival of their valiant commander riding bareheaded at breakneck speed. What caused the sudden great victory of the gospel? What produced the conversion of three thousand in a day? It was the sudden arrival on the field of the divine Commander in the mysterious, invisible, conquering personality of another. It is vain to attribute the initial force of Christianity to the conversion of Saul of Tarsus. You have first to account for his sudden transformation from a bloody persecutor. But he was not converted during the fifty days after the crucifixion. Even if he had been it would be as paradoxical to ascribe the first triumph of Christianity to the accession of a persecutor as it would be to attribute Sheridan's victory, plucked out of defeat, to the presence of the chief of Gen. Early's staff rallying the running Federal soldiers to fight the army he had just deserted in treason to the Confederacy.

In every generation there are needed living witnesses to corroborate the resurrection of Christ. For these on the witness stand of every age He has made provision in the gift of the Holy Ghost. "Believers started to life when He did, and their resurrection is a triumphant proof of His resurrection." On the day of Pentecost the astonished Jews saw a hundred and twenty duplicates of the resurrection of Jesus. A feeble, almost pulseless life they had before, but now they have a stalwart and abundant life. Every Christian who has had a personal Pentecost is a new attestation of the basal proof of Christianity, the resurrection of its Author. Every believer, if he lives at the summit of his privilege, is to an unbelieving world a risen Christ. O Spirit divine, multiply on the earth the number of such fac-similes [sic] of the resurrection of the God-Man as shall overwhelm the scepticism of the world and bring hosts of unbelievers to crown Jesus Lord of all!

"It is the vocation of every believer, in every generation, to afford in his own person the evidence that Christ has risen. Art thou a Christian? Thou art one whom Christ has chosen to convey to men the proof that He is risen. This is thy vocation. Wilt thou roll back the stone upon the sepulchre and make the world believe that Christ is still there? This thou art actually doing if thou walk not in the Spirit."*

Pentecost is not only a convincing and perpetual proof of the Messiahship of Jesus, but it is also an attestation to His righteousness. What was the world's judgment of His character is shown in their crucifying Him as a malefactor between two thieves. Why do I say the world did this when only a few individuals out of hundreds of millions had any part in this appalling wickedness? Because the few were exponents of the many. Jesus was rejected not only by the Jews; "He was rejected of men," as He is to-day rejected by every natural heart. Majorities everywhere, even in so-called Christian lands, choose Barabbas and condemn

---

*George Bowen

Jesus of Nazareth, shouting, "Crucify! crucify!" His reputation with men needed vindication, and Pentecost was that vindication. How? He declared that when He should go to the Father He would receive the promised Holy Ghost as the great gift which He would bestow upon men. John's words imply that this gift could not be imparted before Jesus was glorified. Hence the effusion of the Spirit is a proof to all men that the despised and crucified Son of man has been received at court, approved of his Father and crowned Lord of all. This is God's justification set over against man's condemnation. Have we any Scripture for this? Listen. "He will convict the world in respect of sin and of righteousness, because I go to the Father." My reception in heaven will reverse my rejection on earth. God's approval outweighs man's vilification.

The Pentecostal gift demonstrates Christ's omnipotence. Just before He stepped from God's footstool to His throne He said, "All power is given unto me in heaven and in earth." No person can give what he does not possess.* To bestow a personality all powerful is to possess all power. The Holy Spirit has all power. In creation He "moved upon the face of the waters" and "garnished the heavens." In Providence, by the Spirit, the successive generations are created and the face of the earth is renewed (Ps. civ.30). The Spirit distributes nine extraordinary gifts, and among them "the working of miracles" (I Cor. xii.10).

The gift of the Spirit by Jesus in the same way proves His omniscience, "for the Spirit searcheth all things, yea,

---

* Early in the nineteenth century there was an African pastor of a Methodist Episcopal church in Boston whose name was Snowden. It was in the days of Channing, when the Unitarians were more Biblical than they are in modern times in the advocacy of doctrines, or rather in the indication of their negations. To this negro preacher a Unitarian pastor one day in a bookstore propounded this question: "Father Snowden, what was the Son before the Father gave to Him all power?" Instantly this self-educated, or rather Spirit-educated Ethiopian replied, "What was the Father after He gave the Son all power?"

the deep things of God" (I Cor. ii.10). This text also proves the omnipresence of the Son of God, as does the fact that the Spirit in convicting the world is present with every soul as a reprover, and in uttering in the heart of every child of God, "Abba, Father," He is with every believing soul present as a Comforter. The personal giver must have all the attributes of the personal gift.

In the conclusion of this argument we infer from the identity of attributes of the giver and the gift that our opinion of the one must determine our opinion of the other. "Tell me," says George Bowen, "what think ye of Christ, and I will tell you what you ought to think of the Spirit. Or tell me what ye think of the Spirit and I will tell you what ye think of Christ." Unworthy, narrow and vague opinions about the Spirit imply the same in your conception of Christ. Because the Spirit is practically nearer to us, being the finger of Christ's power, belittling views of the Spirit are more disastrous. "The Spirit in the believer testifies of Jesus, that He has ascended on high and that He is the Mediator between God and man. The Spirit is powerful just according to the degree in which the believer yields himself to His influences and makes way for Him in his affection, in his intellect and in his life." Are not heaven and earth waiting, groaning, travailing for such a testimony to the crucified and risen Saviour as has not yet been given in the Church on earth? To reveal Christ the believer is in the world and the Spirit is in the believer. Am I thus revealing Christ, His condescension, purity, love, unworldliness, meekness, all-suffering and unchangeableness, in every part and parcel of my life? Are my talents, tastes and opportunities made over to Christ to witness for Him? Only when the witnessing Spirit came down were the apostles, though brimful of ten thousand facts in the life of Jesus, able to testify to Him effectively. "Modern Christians have enough materials stored in their minds to make thousands of discourses about Christ, but our lips are sealed and our lives ineloquent until the Spirit of Pentecost come upon us and make Christ's truth live in us and shine through our transfigured lives." (George Bowen.)

Chapter X
THE GAIN OF THE PARACLETE

THE WITHDRAWAL OF THE visible Christ and the substitution of His invisible presence in the Paraclete whom He sent was the introduction of His disciples into a higher school of faith. Hitherto they had walked chiefly by sight. The miracles of their Master had appealed to their reason through the senses. They were not entirely destitute of faith, else they would not have forsaken their fish-nets and followed the Man of Nazareth. But their faith was weak; it needed to be exercised and developed by struggles in a far different arena. They must be taught the spiritual nature of Messiah's kingdom. The visible presence of Christ as a veritable man had been a help to the primary lesson they had already learned; it would be a hindrance to the advanced lesson now to be learned. They must learn that deliverance from sin and restoration to true holiness consist not in outward ceremonials and prescribed rituals, nor in abstract truths grasped by the intellect, but in a vital union with a personal Saviour effected by the Spirit. While Jesus sat there before them in the body the mystery of this spiritual union was altogether beyond their comprehension. The enigma could be explained only by His removal. "It is expedient for you that I go away." This expediency is strongly stated by Draseke as quoted by Stier: "The old Messiah in the flesh is with them; *therefore* the new Comforter, the Spirit, is far from them. What hindered their being comforted? Jesus Himself, who, comforting, stood before them, was the hindrance. As long as He, this Messiah, bearing all the prophetic marks upon Him, stood before them in person, this, His person, continued to be a foundation and prop to that system of vanities which bewitched their heads and hearts. The form must pass away from their eyes before the Spirit could enter their souls. It was good for them that Jesus should go away. Before He, the Christ after the flesh, went away, the Christ after the Spirit could not come. When the former vanished the latter appeared."

The visible, tangible Messiah was the false foundation of all their erroneous notions about a splendid worldly kingdom. The ascension of Christ, the removal of His human form from the eyes of His disciples, was necessary to initiate a purely spiritual kingdom, the basis of which is faith in a risen and invisible Messiah enthroned in heaven. For the same reason the bodily absence of Christ will continue till He descends to judge the quick and the dead and terminate the probationary history of mankind on the earth. His reign as a visible king for a thousand years would be a long step backward. It would destroy the conditions of the development of that stalwart faith which Christ has pronounced specially blessed: "Blessed are they that have not seen and yet have believed."

Again, it was expedient for Jesus to substitute for His

visible presence the invisible Comforter for the emancipation of the Jews from "the letter that killeth" — a complex ritual which they had for more than fourteen centuries obeyed with a mechanical precision. This altar ritual, chiefly of bloody sacrifices typifying the atonement in Christ's death, had accomplished its purpose and should now be laid on the shelf as one of "the beggarly elements" — a rudimentary and preparatory dispensation. Also the burdensome law of ceremonial purity, designed to lead a sinful nation up to the idea of spiritual purity, must now be abrogated because it had become a yoke upon the neck of an unspiritual people.

How can this ingrained hereditary worship of "the letter that killeth" all joyful freedom of service be done away without destroying the religious spirit? Christ herein exhibits divine wisdom. He enforced no ceremonial law, nor did He formally abrogate any. But He inculcated the true spirit in which that law should be administered while the Mosaic dispensation should continue. He did not command fasting, but corrected its disgusting ostentation, while intimating that it was not in harmony with His joyful gospel, but, rather, as incongruous as a new patch on an old garment (Matt, ix: 15-17, Revised Version). He did not abolish bloody sacrifices, but prescribed the spirit of reconciliation in which they should be laid upon the altar. He knew that faith in His atonement would supersede the altar ritual without its formal repeal. He did not re-enact the law of tithes, but He insisted that while it continued it should be accompanied by justice, mercy, faith and love. He sought to enthrone in all hearts supreme love to God as the sum of all duties toward God. Then He sends down the Spirit of love, who sheds abroad the love of God in the heart. This inspiration of the evangelical Spirit gradually overcomes the spirit of bondage to the letter, the legal spirit, first in Stephen, then in Saul of Tarsus, and then in the whole Gentile section of the

Church, and finally in Peter and the believing Jews. Thus the whole Levitical law is quietly laid aside without a convulsion destructive of faith in revelation. To accomplish this amazing change it was necessary that the God-Man should retire and the God-Spirit should be His successor.

It is quite obvious that Christ's efficiency in His saving contact with human souls is indefinitely increased by His representative, the Comforter. While on the earth in the limits of the body His range of beneficent effort must be restricted to a few of the many millions of mankind. His method was to individualize. In healing He laid His hands on every one. There was no healing in the mass. If men's diseased bodies required individualization, much more do their depraved souls. Through the Paraclete the Great Physician can simultaneously medicate millions of sin-sick souls on all the islands of the sea and in both hemispheres wherever His gospel is preached. "After the ascension, wherever there was a believer there was an omnipotent Christ. A thousand cities might simultaneously behold the displays of His power. On the day of Pentecost a thousand of the fiercest enemies of Christ laid down their weapons and proclaimed Him Lord to the glory of God the Father. The hearts of His own immediate disciples, so imperfectly subdued during His ministry, having been brought into complete subjection by the outpouring of the Spirit from the throne of their risen Lord, He went forth conquering and to conquer. It was sufficiently manifest then that Christ had all power in heaven and in earth." (George Bowen.)

But not only is the quantity of His work multiplied infinitely, but the quality is vastly improved through the mission of the Spirit. While in the body on the earth the work of reconstructing fallen human nature must be done from the outside, at a distance from the centre of personality within. But the Spirit can interpenetrate the soul, impart spiritual life, and lodge the transforming principle in the very core of our being. Yea, He Himself, with my free consent makes my heart His domicile, His earthly holy of holies, thus imparting and conserving holiness at the fountain of action and character. This He can more effectually do than did Jesus in the flesh. For the Comforter does not take up His abode in my body merely, nor in my intellect, nor in any one of my mental powers; but in my spirit, which He found as a mere unused capacity and filled with His subtle energies which stream forth, quickening intellect, sensibilities and will, chastening every bodily appetite, and in this way sanctifying the material organism through which my spirit acts. Not in what *we know*, but in what *we are*, does the Spirit take up His abode. Taking possession of the unexplored recesses of my spirit, the Holy Spirit, after my voluntary surrender and self-effacement, is in a position to inspire and safely guide me individually through all the perils and turning points of my probation. Thus I am, through the Paraclete, on more intimate terms with the Lord Jesus than ever was "that disciple whom Jesus loved" and who leaned on His bosom. It is this spiritual privilege, this closer intimacy with God in His Son, that makes the least in the kingdom of God, the spiritual kingdom established on the day of Pentecost, greater than John the Baptist, even though he was greater than Abraham, the founder, and Moses, the lawgiver, of the greatest nation on earth in God's eyes. Hence we emphatically indorse the strong declaration of Alford, especially his capitalized words: "This 'the Comforter will not come if I go not,' is a convincing proof that the gift of the Spirit at and since the day of Pentecost is something TOTALLY DISTINCT from anything before that time; a new and loftier dispensation."

The declaration that it was expedient, or "good," as Luther translates it, for Christ to go away in order that the Comforter might come, proves the fact that the work of the Holy Spirit is so indispensable a complement to

His own work that His bodily withdrawal, which is the condition of the Spirit's advent, should awaken great joy in the hearts of His disciples. A few disciples, comparatively, had seen Him in His humiliation, rejected of men; now One was to come who should be a mirror in which all disciples in all lands and in all generations should see Him glorified, and, seeing, "should be transformed into the same image from glory to glory." Without Jesus radiant with divinity, the Comforter would have nothing to reproduce in the heart of the believer. "It would be like removing from the photographer's studio the person whose features the sun is about to fix on the plate prepared to receive them."

The radical dissimilarity between the old and the new dispensation is seen in the following particulars: In the old dispensation the Spirit externally wrought upon men, but He did not in His person dwell in believers; His working was occasional and for a short time; He did not permanently abide in them. He was external; He did not incarnate Himself in believers. His action was intermittent, irregular, and apparently without any law. He came and went like Noah's dove, finding no abiding place. But in the new dispensation there is a "law of the Spirit" by which all believers may receive Him as a permanent dweller in the heart, as another dove seen by John the Baptist descending upon Jesus and abiding on Him as a part of His person. In the Old Testament the Spirit bestowed gifts of an intellectual and physical nature—prophecy to the seventy elders, skill to Bezaleel, the kingly feeling to Saul, and strength to Samson. But the Comforter dispenses the various graces, such as saintly inward virtues, love, gentleness, goodness, etc. "Affianced of the soul, the Spirit went oft to see His betrothed, but was not yet one with her; the marriage was not consummated until the Pentecost, after the glorification of Jesus Christ."

Another great gain to the disciples in the exchange of

the bodily presence of Christ on the earth for His spiritual presence in their hearts, by the Comforter's coming and indwelling, was in the clearer evidence of his Messiahship and divinity. Doubtless the disciples at the first intimation of Christ's intended departure asked of one another, "What proofs can we hereafter point to that we have not followed a pretender if the great miracle worker removes? His amazing miracles have been our chief argument with our enemies hitherto. Nothing can supply their place in even keeping ourselves from serious doubts. What shall we do?" Little could they possibly comprehend that an invisible divine Person could descend from heaven, enter into their very being, pouring a light more resplendent than the sun upon the person of Christ, giving an intuitive perception of His supreme Godhood as indisputable as any self-evident truth of the human reason. They knew nothing of the self-evidencing power of the Spirit to glorify the Son of God in their consciousness and to plant their feet for evermore on the sunlit summit of full assurance and certain knowledge so frequently spoken of by Paul under the strengthened word *epignosis*.

The death of Christ was deemed by His disciples as the greatest possible disaster, but it redeemed a world of sinners lost. So the departure of their Master was deemed a privation for which they could imagine no compensation, but it removed the barrier which kept Him from access to their inmost selves. Hitherto He had been imprisoned within walls of flesh obstructing the full communication of Himself to their hearts, just as the unbroken alabaster flask kept the delicious perfumes from filling all the house, every crack and crevice, with its pervasive odors.

When the God-Man was on the earth He was farther from His disciples, even when He washed their feet, than the sun is from the earth, 93,000,000 miles away. But when He came in the form of the Comforter this distance was annihilated. The disciples now have an eternal sunrise within their hearts. They are ensphered in the Spirit, who reveals Christ. They are enveloped in His personality; they are "in Christ."

"To have the Holy Spirit of God coming through the human nature of our Lord, entering into our spirits, identifying Himself with us, and becoming our very own just as He was the Spirit of Christ Jesus on earth, — surely this is a blessedness worth any sacrifice, for it is the beginning of the indwelling of God Himself."

I am quite sure that many of my Christian readers will think that I have too highly colored the pre-eminent superiority of the conscious abiding of the Spirit within to the visible presence of Christ instructing, assuring and cheering His disciples. They may assert that they have no such experience, and yet that they love Christ. I do not doubt their testimony. The difficulty is easily explained. Their experience of the presence of the Holy Spirit is meagre and unsatisfactory, because they so little know and honor Him as a person. A person is sensitive when he is spoken of as *it* and treated as a thing. There may be a faith in Jesus that attains forgiveness, while a faith that claims the abiding Comforter as the Christian's heritage is lacking. He that believes in Christ for all that He has promised, "out of him shall flow rivers of living water." This promise has not become obsolete. There are many modern witnesses to its fulfilment, though the of the visible Church. Yet by a candid and patient study of God's Word, the ground of faith, and by a self-surrender and self-effacement which put the soul wholly in the hands of the Great Physician with unwavering trust, the utmost stain of evil may be removed, and the presence of Christ be as real as it was to Mary Magdalene.

There are many evangelical Christians who are resting in a head-knowledge of Christ to the exclusion of that heart-knowledge which comes from the presence of the Paraclete. It is in a sense true of them that "the letter killeth," while they might have the Spirit that giveth the more abundant life. The external knowledge of Christ is valuable but it may be used as a bar to that intimate internal knowledge of Him who dwells only where He is welcomed and enthroned. He comes to reign. Orthodoxy is commendable; but a trust in it and a reliance on the sufficiency of religious knowledge may obstruct the fulness of the Spirit. A pauper may be told that he may take from the open treasury of Dives as much silver coin as he can carry in his hands. After filling his hands a bag of gold coin is poured out, and he is permitted to appropriate all that his hands can hold. If he has ordinary wisdom he will drop the silver and grasp the gold. Thus Paul dropped Judaism, not because it was untrue, but because it was an obstruction to his appropriation of "the excellency of knowledge of Christ Jesus." He afterwards did what every Christian must do if he would realize the true, spiritual Christ within. When it pleased God "to reveal his Son" in Paul, some time after his conversion, probably in Arabia while in his three years' theological course under the tuition of the Holy Ghost, he ceased "to know Christ after the flesh," in contrast with knowing Him as a bright reality "after the Spirit," the source of ineffable bliss and transcendent life.

Resting in the external knowledge of Christ attained on the plane of nature is a life akin to legalism, a life of effort and failure which must be abandoned to open the door for the incoming and indwelling of the Holy Spirit. Even the apostles trained by Christ "had to let go, to lose, to die to their old way of knowing Christ, and to receive as a gift an entirely new life of intercourse with Him." This may account for the fact that there is so little reminiscence of the incidents in the earthly life of Jesus and even of His miracles in the Epistles of James, Peter, John and Jude, and scarcely any at all in Paul's. What power would come to the Church if its members would imitate the apostles in acquiring this new, efficacious and transforming knowledge of Christ imparted by the indwelling Spirit! Doubt would then find no dwelling place. Worldly pleasures would lose their seductive power.

"As by the light of opening day
The stars are all concealed,
So earthly pleasures fade away
When Jesus is revealed."

What a gain Christ intended the outpouring of the Spirit and His indwelling in the consciousness of His disciples would be in substantiating the truth of Christ's resurrection as an undeniable fact to the onlooking world! Says George Bowen, "Is not the great thing wanted this, that the Spirit of God should be so poured out on Christ's people that men should be made aware of His presence with them and of His presence at the right hand of God?" The work of the Holy Spirit in my heart is God's credential to me individually. All that Christ did for me profits me nothing if the Holy Spirit does not come into my heart and bring it all home to me. As Christ fulfilled and ended the ceremonial law, so the Paraclete is the complement of the gospel and the end of the "law of sin."

Chapter XI
PRAYING TO THE HOLY SPIRIT

THE FACT THAT there are only a few instances of prayer to the Holy Spirit, and these are only when He is named with the other Persons of the Trinity, has led some persons to refrain from praying to the Paraclete. But there are good reasons for the infrequency of prayer to the Third Person of the adorable Trinity.

When we take into consideration the disposition of the Spirit to conceal Himself in magnifying the Son and the Father revealed in the Son, and when we note the fact that the Holy Spirit is the inspirer of the Bible, it is natural that there should be a comparative silence respecting honors ascribed to Himself. He may purposely have omitted from the Acts of the Apostles, the Epistles and the Revelation, the record of the adoration of Himself by men and angels. This would have been in harmony with His mission to glorify Christ and not Himself.

Again, to give prominence to His claim to be worshipped might interfere with our dependence on Him to suggest what we should pray for and to make intercession within us. "If it is His special function not only to speak to and deal with, but also to speak and work through, the man whom He renews and sanctifies, we can just so far understand that He the less frequently presents Himself for our articulate adoration." Yet there can be no question of its rightfulness and propriety, inasmuch as His equality with the Father and the Son is assumed in the prescribed formula of baptism: "In the name of the Father, and of the Son, and of the Holy Ghost." The form of benediction also implies prayer to the Third Person of the Trinity. "The grace of our Lord Jesus Christ, and the love of God, and the communion [communication] of the Holy Ghost, be with you all" (II Cor. xiii.14), is an act of adoration to the three alike. The same may be said of the blessing pronounced upon the seven churches in Rev. i.4, where the perfection of the offices of the Holy Spirit is spoken of in the Hebrew idiom of sevenfoldness. It is to be noted also that in this text the Spirit is not mentioned after the Son, but after Him whose name signifies "he who is, and was, and is to come," *i.e.*, Jehovah. Says Prof. Moule, "The believer's relation to the Spirit is *not so much* that of direct adoration as of a reliance which wholly implies it."

The Scriptures ascribe divine titles and attributes to the Holy Spirit equally with the Father and the Son (Acts v.3, 4; Acts xxviii.25 with Isa. vi.9; Heb. iii.7-9 with Ex. xvii.7).

The equality of the three divine Persons in unity is formulated in the Christian covenant and commission: "All power is given unto me in heaven and in earth. Go ye therefore, and make disciples of all nations, baptizing them into the name of the Father, and of the Son, and of the Holy Ghost" (Matt, xxviii.18, 19).

Richard Watson, the standard theologian of Methodism for one hundred years, says on this text: "The form exhibits three persons without any note of superiority or inferiority, except the mere order in which they are placed.

It conveys authority in the united name, and the authority is therefore equal. It supposes... faith, that is, not merely belief, but, as the object of religious profession and adherence, trust in each, or collectively in the one name which unites the three in one. It implies devotion to the service of each, the yielding of obedience, the consecration of every power of mind and body to each, and therefore each must have equal right to this surrender and to the authority which it implies." (Institutes, Vol. I, page 635.)

It should be borne in mind that all orthodox believers must pray to the Holy Spirit when they pray to God. For the Christian concept of God is that in the one divine substance there are three subsistences, the Father, the Son and the Holy Spirit, or three Persons in the one divine nature. This may not be distinctly before the minds of some Christians when they pray. Nevertheless, prayer reaches its full evangelical development and efficiency in the consciousness that through the divine Son we have access by the one divine Spirit unto the Father (Eph. ii.18). The treasures of devotion of the whole Church, the products of holy men who have composed petitions and hymns, contain invocations to the Holy Spirit, such as *"Veni, Creator Spiritus,"*

> "Come, Holy Ghost, our souls inspire
> And lighten with celestial fire,"

and the *"Veni, Sancte Spiritus,"* thus in part translated by Ray Palmer:

> "Come, Holy Ghost, in love
> Shed on us from above
>   Thine own bright ray!
> Divinely good Thou art;
> Thy sacred gift impart

To gladden each sad heart:
O come to-day!"

Since the Spirit, equal in power and majesty to the Father and the Son, is the agent by whom both touch believing souls and impart the wealth of their love, it is natural that He should also be the object of devotion and that His ministration of grace should be invoked, at least in impassioned ejaculatory prayer.

Here we note an error in the Plymouth Brethren, who discourage prayer for the Holy Ghost because He was given once for all on the day of Pentecost. This error arises from overlooking two facts: 1. That the spiritual capacity of the normal believer is ever increasing and needs an ever-enlarging fulness of the Spirit. It will not do to confound mechanical fulness with vital fulness. Dr. William Arthur's illustration of the difference between these is worth repeating. At evening fill two vessels with milk, an earthen pitcher and a healthy baby. In the morning you will find the pitcher full and the baby empty and crying to be filled again. The Christian is not an earthen pitcher which can be kept mechanically full, but a "newborn babe desiring the sincere milk of the word, that he may grow thereby." Hence the propriety of constant prayer for the Spirit to be more and more fully realized. 2. Another fact not noted by the Brethren is the example of repeated asking and receiving of the Spirit even in Pentecostal days. On the first day after Christ arose the apostles received the Holy Ghost from the mouth of Jesus (John xx.22), and after forty days they were in a ten days' prayer meeting with one accord in prayer for the Holy Spirit in larger realization of His presence within them, as we infer from Peter's sermon and its glorious sequel, the tongues of fire.

The law of spiritual growth is by successive uplifts or baptisms of the Spirit. By a study of the Acts of the Apostles we find that the same persons who "were all filled with the Holy Ghost " (Acts ii.4) were a few days or weeks afterwards, again in answer to prayer, "all filled with the Holy Ghost" (iii.31).

"Prayer is the Christian's vital breath;
We enter heaven by prayer."

What is the object for which the believer prays except it be for an ever-increasing fulness of the Spirit?

But did not Christ refer to the Holy Spirit when He said to the woman at the well, "Whosoever drinketh of the water that I shall give him shall never thirst"? Yes, but the tense of the verb "drinketh" denotes continued appropriation. If the Christian thirsts for any other water, it is because he has ceased to drink of Christ's "living water." Says Bengel, "Truly that water, as far as it depends on itself, has in it an everlasting virtue, and when thirst returns, the defect is on the part of the man, not of the water." The life emanating from Christ must be constantly made our own anew. "He that cometh [continually] unto me shall never hunger; and he that believeth [uninterruptedly] on me shall never thirst" (John vi.35). Says Tholuck: "The figure means, this water will once for all be received into the inner nature, will be immanent in man, and will attend him through every stage of his being, even to eternity. The need of an increase of this water is not thereby excluded."

The Holy Spirit, of which water is a symbol (John viii.39), is as a river of life flowing from the Father and the Son (Rev. xxii.1) into all hearts open skyward, and incessant prayer for the Spirit keeps our hearts thus open. "How much more shall your heavenly Father be continually giving the Holy Spirit to them that constantly ask him."

Chapter XII
THE LAW OF THE SPIRIT

IN THE EPISTLE TO the Romans Paul speaks of the two laws or uniform and controlling forces— the law of sin producing spiritual death, and the law of the Spirit inspiring spiritual life which becomes eternal on the condition of persevering faith. In the thought of many people the Spirit is capricious in His action, and sovereign in the sense that He is a law unto Himself, observing no conditions and establishing no regular order of sequences by which His aid may be secured. Perhaps this error may be truthfully ascribed to that religious teaching which magnifies the sovereignty of God as exercised unconditionally. In some instances it may be traced to a misunderstanding of Christ's comparison of the mystery of the new birth to "the wind blowing as it listeth." He did not intimate that the winds are not under physical laws, but rather that science had not then, as it has not now, a knowledge of pneumatics sufficient to predict with infallible certainty what will be the direction and intensity of the wind an hour hence. Some infer that the Holy

Spirit acts on men in promoting revivals of religion with the same uncertainty and apparent lawlessness. Hence revivals come to a church like thunderstorms, without regard to any human conditions. This idea is confirmed by a faulty translation of a sentence in Peter's sermon in Solomon's porch, Acts iii.19, "Repent ye therefore, and be converted, that your sins may be blotted out, when the times of refreshing shall come from the presence of the Lord." This rendering of the text commands sinners to be ready for the blotting out of their sins whenever it may please God to send the times of refreshing. The correct rendering makes the times of refreshing or revival depend on the commanded human condition of repentance, "Repent… that so there may come seasons," etc. (Revised Version). In fact the Spirit is endeavoring to produce in every sinner penitence for sin and faith in Christ, in order that He may impart spiritual life and be God's messenger of adoption, inspiring the joyful cry, "Abba, Father." This is the purpose for which He is reproving the world. He yearns to inspire in every human soul the gladness of the filial feeling in place of the dread and foreboding of punishment which haunt conscious guilt. He delights to take up His abode in the believer. His personality interpenetrates ours just in proportion to the perfectness of our self-surrender. It is a wise remark of Dr. A. J. Gordon that the Spirit, like the wind, always moves toward a vacuum. By entire consecration make your heart vacant of all love of the world, and the Holy Spirit will come in Pentecostal power and fill the vacuum.

The reasons why so few are thus filled are various.

1. Many do not know that this fulness of the Spirit is

the privilege of all Christians. They think it is an exceptional experience of a favored few, "the elect of the elect." They think it is not modest to assume that they belong to this small company. This narrow view of the gift of the abiding Paraclete weakens faith. They dare not appropriate the gift which may not belong to them, and so they fail to realize their full heritage in Christ.

2. Others imagine that they must always have a propensity to sin, and that they must sin a little to keep them humble. As the fulness of the Spirit would not be consistent with depravity and occasional sins, they deem it not a normal experience, and abstain from effort to receive it.

3. Many fail because they do not know the law of the Spirit, the conditions by which He works His wonders in human hearts. Till within a very few years the whole race of men failed to utilize a mighty force in nature, the power of electricity, to light, heat and transport men, move the world's machinery and convey intelligence with the speed of lightning under the seas and over the continents. As we look back upon it what a slow and sleepy world it was, simply because it did not know the law of electricity or the conditions of all these utilities. But men began to study and to experiment, conforming to the ascertained qualities of this mysterious agent and gaining more and more power to harness this tremendous force to the chariot of human progress. What new electrical discoveries and inventions are in the future we cannot tell because we have not reached the end of the chapter of electrical knowledge. John Wesley used to tell his people that as believers they were weak because they were not more knowing. This is the cause of much of the weakness of modern Christians. They do not by day and by night study the law of the Spirit as Edison studied the law of electricity in the production of light and the reproduction of articulate sounds. Many nominal Christians "have

not so much as heard whether there be any Holy Ghost" consciously receivable by the individual believer in Jesus Christ. When by the diligent study of the Word of God they believe that the Spirit has a personal existence and that He stands at the door of their hearts and knocks, then they will be able to fulfil the conditions of His full incoming and permanent abiding. What hinders such a universal experience? Ignorance, unbelief, worldly pleasures, neglect of Bible study and prayer, satisfaction with mere formalism, unwillingness to be identified with the so-called spiritual extremists and cranks, and dislike to stand alone with Christ or to be crucified with Him. It is the law of the Spirit to enter in where the door is opened and He is cordially welcomed with His scourge of small cords to drive out everything which profanes the temple of the human soul and body. "For the temple of God is holy, which temple ye are."

4. But some are not consciously filled with the Holy Spirit because He comes as a refiner and purifier. They are unwilling to submit themselves to this painful purgation. They shrink from the crucible by which the divine Refiner sits till He can see His own perfect image in the mirror of molten gold purified of all dross. They admire the Son of God and desire to be conformed to His image, but they dislike the process of total and irreversible self-surrender and self-crucifixion. They cannot truthfully sing:

> "O that in me the sacred fire
> Might now begin to glow,
> Burn up the dross of base desire,
> And make the mountains flow!"

God can do His perfect work in a soul only when the will is in the attitude of complete, trustful submission. Only when the will thus bows to God's will does faith in His promises mount up to its climax. For this Paul prayed, "that ye may know what is the exceeding greatness of his power to usward who believe." Then he adds the measure of that power which stands ready to transfigure believers, "according to the working of his mighty power, which he wrought in Christ when he raised him from the dead." The greatest miracle in the universe, the miracle attested by men, by angels and by God, is the resurrection of His Son. Even the creation of the world was not so striking an exhibition of omnipotence. Yet Paul assures us that the same resurrection power in "its exceeding greatness" stands ready to work its wonders in "us who believe " with that faith which appropriates the largest promises of God. This highest upreaching of faith is possible only to the deepest submission of the human will. To this point of entire self-surrender every believer has the gracious ability to descend without the incentive of outward adversities, losses, bereavements. disappointments, persecutions and bodily afflictions. These, as in the case of Job, are necessary to the revelation to the world of our perfect trust, loyalty and submission to God, but not to the production of these virtues. Many have had the spirit of the martyrs who were never led to the stake. The axe and block were once deemed necessary to Christian perfection. But this is a mistake. God takes the will for the deed. We can climb to as high spiritual altitudes in the sunshine as in the storm; yes, to higher. There is such a thing as an equation of spiritual advantages. Those who are on the verge of the twentieth century may achieve as lofty Christian excellences as the believers who listened to the preaching of Peter at Pentecost. The gift of the Holy Spirit has suffered no diminution because of the intervening centuries. Like Christ, the giver of the Paraclete, He is the same yesterday, to-day and forever. Fulfil the conditions, and the humblest modern believer may receive Him in the perfect performance of His offices as graciously and as effectively as did the company in the upper room. The externals of sound and tongues of fire were no part of the essential and inward grace bestowed in the Comforter.

When any local church, any company of believers associated for spiritual ends, fulfils the social conditions,— all of one accord in one place making the reception of the Holy Spirit their only business for at least ten days,— Pentecost will be repeated in every essential particular. Their hearts will be purified by faith, and they will be endowed with a marvellous spiritual insight and courage and utterance.

It is not the law of the Spirit that His transfiguring power should decrease with the lapse of ages, nor with the spread of education and the growth of intelligence and culture. It is true that there is an intellectual pride with a pretence to culture which boasts that it has outgrown such so-called crudities as disfigured Christianity on the day of Pentecost. These over-wise philosophers insist that the doctrine that one personality, even though divine, can interpenetrate a human personality and consciously abide therein, violates all the known principles of mental philosophy and lays the foundation of various forms of fanaticism, in the end destructive of all morality and sound piety. Our reply to this is that the greater the value of a coin the greater its liability to be counterfeited. The highest possible experience for men dwelling in houses of clay is to be inhabited by God in the person of His Spirit. This is a mystery next to the incarnation of the Son of God in human form.

It is natural that the proclamation that both the body and soul of every believer may through simple faith become the habitation of God through the Spirit, should awaken the hostility of the great adversary of all goodness, and that he should endeavor to discredit this glorious privilege of the indwelling Paraclete by inspiring counterfeits grossly defective in moral character or greatly unbalanced in mental equipoise. This he has done in every revival of genuine spirituality since the first effusion of the Spirit of promise, as in the days of Luther and also in Wesley's times. But as men of common sense still continue to put gold in their purses despite the spurious coin occasionally uttered, so wise men and women will by the prayer of faith receive, as the greatest boon possible to mortals, the Holy Spirit as a distinct and permanently abiding blessing. Such wise people, if asked how can the divine thus dwell in the human, the infinite in the finite, and both personalities be preserved, will no more attempt to explain this mystery than they will the enigma of electricity filling a mass of iron while both remain unchanged, and that of the immaterial spirit inhabiting the material body while both retain their identity. The rays of the sun after passing through a double convex lens of ice will kindle a fire. So the Holy Spirit has kindled an inextinguishable fire in many an icy heart. The facts in both the natural and the spiritual realm must stand, though our poor philosophy is baffled in accounting for the manner of the facts. It is enough for us to know the conditions by which the facts are produced, where the fact itself is of transcendent value, as that man may be indwelt by God. This honor and blessedness, unknown to the patriarchs, to the Israelites, the chosen people of God, and even to the twelve apostles before Pentecost, is now offered to the most illiterate and obscure believer in Jesus Christ who will comply with the conditions by which a personal Pentecost may be experienced.

In answer to our exposition of "the law of the Spirit" as invariably cleansing and filling all who exercise an all-surrending faith, it may be alleged that Paul teaches that the Spirit performs the work of His offices in "every man severally as he will." This is said, not of the graces of the Spirit, but of the distribution of His nine extraordinary gifts enumerated in I Cor. xii.8-II. The Spirit Himself is Christ's gift to every one "who loves him and keeps his commandments." He is to be in us, and we are to "know him;" *i.e.* to be conscious of His abiding in us "forever." Not only the Spirit but also the Father and the Son "make their abode" with us. All this is promised in John xiv.15-23; not sovereignly to whomsoever the Spirit wills, but universally without exception wherever there is evangelical love to Christ evidenced by obedience. This it is which makes the least in the Pentecostal kingdom greater than Christ's forerunner, who was ranked by Him as superior to Abraham, the founder of God's earthly church, and to Moses, the lawgiver of the world.

Many people are so dazzled by the splendor of the outward and extraordinary gifts of the Spirit that they undervalue the infinitely superior boon of the indwelling of the giver Himself, imparting life and adorning with all the Christian graces. To put gifts above grace is an old mistake. Simon Magus is not the last instance of this kind. Many are now eager to possess the gift of healing who would not cross the street to receive the grace of perfected holiness. It is a very serious error to regard anything as superior to the fruit of the Spirit. Churches fall into it when, seeking after a pastor, they first ask, "Is he brilliant in the pulpit?" "Is he rhetorical, poetical, oratorical?" "If he is we must have him." The question respecting his piety, his fulness of the Spirit, his grip of faith, his knowledge of the Holy Scriptures, the basis of faith, and the indispensable qualification for such preaching as saves and sanctifies, is not emphasized, and frequently is not asked at all. Occasionally we find a church inquiring for a Barnabas. "For he was a good man, and full of the Holy Ghost and of faith: and much people was added unto the Lord." Yet his name, "son of exhortation," as in the Revision, is not suggestive of pulpit oratory of the classical sort.

The doctrine of the law of the Spirit is very beautifully

stated by Christ in His dialogue with the Samaritan woman at Jacob's well. "If thou knewest the gift of God, and who it is that saith to thee, Give me to drink, thou wouldst have asked of him, and he would have given thee living water." The gift which He would have bestowed was the Holy Spirit, according to John vii.38, 39, "This he spake of the Spirit, which they who believe on Him should receive: for the Holy Ghost was not yet given, because Jesus was not glorified." Note the invariable law of certain receiving following confident asking: If thou hadst asked, He would have given. There is the same invariable order of effect following cause in the spiritual realm as there is in the material realm. Turn the faucet, and you get a stream of water so long as the faucet is connected with the reservoir on a higher level. Try this a thousand times, and the same effect follows. Turn the spigot of true prayer, and the living water, the personal Holy Spirit, is poured out upon the thirsty soul. It has been well said that God answers all true prayer and wishes to receive more. In the bosom of the Infinite Father there is a shoreless and fathomless Lake Superior of living waters ready to fill millions and billions of human spirits when they supply the aqueducts. In fact, the main aqueduct was laid by God Himself on the day of Pentecost, and the water of life is brought to every door. To appropriate it we must lay the individual service-pipe.

> "Angelic spirits, countless souls,
>   Of Thee have drunk their fill;
> And to eternity will drink
>   Thy joy and glory still.
>
> "O little heart of mine! shall pain
>   Or sorrow make thee moan,
> When all this God is all for thee,
>   A Father all thine own?"

Before leaving this charming scene of Jacob's well, we call attention to another spiritual law. Not only does receiving depend on asking, but asking depends on knowing. "If thou knewest, thou wouldst have asked." Many souls wander for years in painful thirst because no one tells them of the supply of water within their reach. Hence the need of ceaseless testimony by those who have found the unfailing fountain. Hence the pressure of the missionary motive upon all who "have been made partakers of the Holy Ghost." Interest in Christian missions in pagan lands and city slums is a fair gauge of the spirituality of an individual and of a church.

If knowing depends on testimony, the inquiry arises, How many witnesses have we among our readers who can attest the fulness of the Spirit?

Chapter XIII
MIRACLES OF THE HOLY GHOST

THE QUESTION IS often asked, What are "the greater works" which believers in Christ shall do? This marvellous promise is found in His consolatory address a few days before His death. The chief topic of encouragement, comfort and hope is the Paraclete whom the risen Lord will bestow. His works will be more wonderful than the physical miracles of Jesus Christ. This is declared in John xiv.12-17. I quote Dr. Campbell's version, which is remarkable chiefly for its punctuation. It must be borne in mind that there is no punctuation in the original. "Verily, verily, I say unto you" — a formula "in which the Son of God speaks out of His coequality with the Father" (Stier)— "He who believeth on me, shall himself do such works as I do; nay, even greater than these shall he do; because I go to my Father, and will do whatsoever ye shall ask in my name. That the Father may be glorified in the Son, whatsoever ye shall ask in my name, I will do." It is worthy of note that this doing greater works, this survival of the supernatural from age to age, is not the exclusive prerogative of the apostles, but it belongs, to every one, however humble, who believes on Christ. Again, our greater works are done by the glorified Jesus on the throne above in response to our faith. In the same breath He declares that He will do the greater works which we shall do. This paradox He explains in His next utterance: "If ye love me, keep my commandments; and I will entreat the Father, and he will give you another Monitor to continue with you forever, even the Spirit of truth." This "Helper, Advocate; Greek, Paraclete" (Revised Version, margin) will be the divine agent sent down from heaven to do these greater miracles through believers in Christ. This brings us to "the miracles of the Holy Ghost" which in the Old Testament are physical, as when Ezekiel says, "The Spirit lifted me up and took me away." The same manifestation of supernatural physical power by the Holy Ghost was experienced by Philip: "The Spirit of the Lord caught away Philip, that the eunuch saw him no more." But the promise under discussion does not relate to miracles in the realm of matter, but rather to those in the province of mind, in the re-creation of the human soul, called figuratively birth from above, or the new birth, the resurrection of a dead soul, the new creation. This spiritual miracle is greater than any physical miracle wrought by Christ before He burst asunder the gates of death by His inherent power to take again the life which He had laid down, for the following reasons:

1. Physical miracles were temporal in their effects. Those raised from sickness died of disease in a few years. The multitudes fed by miracle hungered again in a few hours. The eyes into which Jesus by a word let in the light were soon darkened again by the shadows of the tomb. The tongue of the dumb loosened by the Son of man was

soon silenced by the touch of death. But miracles wrought in the transfiguration of the soul are enduring unto eternal life. "He that believeth on the Son hath eternal life" within the grasp of his free agency. Jesus healed the body for time, the Spirit heals the soul for eternity. "A healed leper may appear to be a greater miracle than a renewed soul, but in reality, in comparison, he is hardly a miracle at all!" (Joseph Parker.)

2. The results of spiritual miracles are far more valuable. Mind is far superior to matter. Hence "to minister to a mind diseased and pluck from the memory a rooted sorrow " is an achievement in a higher realm and of immensely greater value. For this reason Christ Himself did not place a primary emphasis on physical wonders as His credentials, and they are scarcely so much as referred to in the apostolic writings. Peter, who had seen them all, mentions them only once, and then only to Christ's murderers in Jerusalem, who were incapable of appreciating any higher proof of His Messiahship: "Jesus of Nazareth, a man approved of God among you by miracles and wonders and signs." St. Paul magnifies those spiritual marvels which God wrought by the Holy Spirit in the regeneration and sanctification of souls. In his estimation "the shining in our hearts to give the light of the knowledge of the glory of God in the face of Jesus Christ " was a greater act than the *Fiat lux* which illumined the first day of creation (II Cor. iv.6).

3. To transform a spirit from death to life, from sin to holiness, requires a higher power than any change wrought in matter. Spirit is a self-determining personality which may successfully withstand omnipotence, or rather, physical omnipotence is inapplicable to the production of spiritual effects. Sin cannot be crushed out of a soul with an almighty trip hammer. God can transform inert matter as He may will, but He is powerless to regenerate a stubborn human will; but in the presence of a

consenting will He displays to the astonished universe "the exceeding greatness of his power to usward who believe." Hence the age of the most notable miracles is now in the very zenith of its glory. They are visible in every land where the gospel is preached in faith. Boston has just witnessed the transformation of a burglar and drunkard into a missionary on the Congo. Recovered from the slums and converted in the Kneeland Street Rescue Mission, he immediately wrote to the governor of Maryland, the scene of his crimes, offering at his request to appear in court, testify against himself, and be sentenced to the penitentiary. In the absence of such a request he volunteered to go to a deadly clime to preach Christ mighty to save. "When the proud Brahman has received the truth as it is in Jesus, and extended the right hand of Christian fellowship to the meanest member of the lowest caste whom he has met at the Lord's Supper, a greater miracle has been wrought than in the healing of the lame or the raising of the dead." To put God's law "in the inward parts" of a tribe of thieves in India, as the Holy Spirit has done through Bishop J. M. Thoburn, transforming them into sons of God, "is more than to fill the firmament with stars." "Instead of the thorn shall come up the fir tree,... and it shall be unto Jehovah for an everlasting miracle that shall not be cut off." Spiritual miracles, in the regeneration of depraved and wicked men, are the standing proof of the divinity of the Holy Spirit. Regeneration, crowned with the entire sanctification of a soul once dead in sin, loving what God hates and hating what God loves, is the supreme miracle of the Holy Ghost vividly portrayed by Paul: "Fornicators, idolaters, adulterers, effeminate [catamites], nor abusers of themselves with mankind [sodomites], nor thieves [robbers, Conybeare and Howson], nor covetous [wantons, Conybeare and Howson], nor drunkards, nor revilers, shall inherit the kingdom of God " (I Cor. vi.9, 10). What a rogues' gallery is this! as vile a gang of criminals as ever broke jail. What can the Holy Spirit do with these but to abandon them forever? But, hold! let us read further: "And such were some of you; but ye washed yourselves [Revised Version, margin], but ye were sanctified, but ye were justified in the name of the Lord Jesus Christ, and by THE Spirit of our God." The Paraclete has transformed them all into a company of saints bearing the image of Christ and candidates for promotion to thrones beside the archangels. Bad men have been transformed into good men standing in the same shoes.

Chapter XIV
THE SPIRIT'S WORK IN REGENERATION

REGENERATION IS THE lodgement by the Holy Spirit of the new principle of life. This is love to God, which is the ruling motive of every genuine Christian. There is a radical and an essential difference between those who are born again and the best of those who lay claim to only natural goodness, a beautiful moral character revolving around self as a centre. But the great transition from spiritual death to spiritual life does not make the child of God at once complete in holiness. The Holy Spirit in sanctification does not work magically, nor mechanically like a washing machine, "but by the influence of grace, in accordance with the essential constitution of man, and in the way of a vital process, only by degrees completely renewing the soul." While the Spirit in the new birth touches the whole nature, the thoughts, the feelings and the will, so that the man is a new creature, his renewal is not complete in any part. At first he is in spiritual knowledge only a babe. His faith is unsteady and often mingled with distrust, while his love is not usually strong enough to secure uninterrupted victory over temptation. The enthronement of love does not immediately render the pleasures of sin unattractive, nor destroy the painfulness of self-denial, nor instantaneously change sinful habits. Such is the state of immature converts to Christ, "the flesh lusting against the Spirit." The Corinthians were characterized as "carnal, walking as men." We know that John says that "he that has been born of God sinneth not" when he is describing those whom he styles "fathers" or adult believers, just as Paul describes the same class as having "crucified the flesh with the passions and lusts.* Neither of these apostles is describing an ideal Christian, as some teach who deny the possibility of complete deliverance from depravity in this life. They are describing regeneration at its climax, the glorious possibilities of the birth from above, when it has culminated in perfected holiness.

Bishop Foster sums up the defects of the experience of regeneration in a "more comprehensive manner than we remember seeing in any theological treatise. He does not minify the experience of regeneration, but declares it to be a glorious experience. He, however, shows its defects in this manner: "I note, third, that dissatisfiedness of the soul with itself is a common experience of all regenerate souls, varying from intense distress at times to mild regret. Its experiences are not satisfactory. It has a prevailing consciousness of inexcusable defects. It does not reach its ideal. It feels the chiding of the Holy Spirit. It lashes itself with reprovings. It often carries an unhealed wound because of its unfaithfulness or failure to be what it feels it ought to be. There is the abiding consciousness that there is something better for it. When it is upheld and

---

*See Appendix, Note E

sustained in an average experience, and others think well of it, and there is no external failure visible to other eyes, it discerns inward poverties which grieve and distress it. It would love more, be more patient, more brave, more trusting, more cheerful, stronger, more robust; it would work more and do more and be more. There are holy yearnings in it after something higher and nobler. There is often a distressing sense of remaining evil in it. I think I am safe in saying this is universal experience, subsequent to the experience of regeneration. This has been called in our theologizing and in the theologizing of all the Christian schools, 'the remains of the carnal mind,' 'unextracted roots of inbred sin,' 'the spirit of the flesh,' 'natural corruption,' 'seeds of depravity,' 'the old man,' and by various other semi-scriptural names. These phrases all point to a fact, but not unfrequently a sensuous meaning is attached to them which leads wide apart from the truth which they aim to represent. They are supposed to represent some sediment or infusion in the soul or in the body, or in both, which must be washed out. What is meant and what is true is this: when the soul is forgiven and its affections are turned to righteousness, so that it passes from under the dominion of evil, impulses and inclination to evil are not completely eradicated. They still arise and assert themselves. They assail and disturb the peace of the soul. They have a constant tendency to prevail with it. They find support in its old habits and in its native lusts— that is, desires and cravings."* In the above truthful condensation of experience it will be noticed that the bishop teaches that we are not entirely sanctified at conversion— a doctrine often denied in the Church today. He teaches as John Wesley did, that there remains yet that which needs a farther work of the Spirit, which is called, in the language of theology, entire sanctifica-

---

*Merrick Lectures on "The Philosophy of Christian Experience."

tion, which supplements the defects of the soul still remaining after regeneration. The adverse influences and tendencies which continue after the new birth imperil the very existence of the new principle of love to God by overcoming and choking it, unless it is continually nourished and strengthened by divine grace. Strength is supplied to the believer by the inner presence of the Holy Spirit. His indwelling is by faith. If faith declines, the Spirit's sphere in the soul is narrowed. If confidence in God is "cast away" — a possible act against which we are warned in the Scriptures (Heb. x.35)— then the Spirit withdraws, or rather, is excluded by unbelief, and love, the vital spark of the spiritual life, expires. Hence the question whether the Spirit shall be a merely transient impulse toward purity, or a lasting power, depends on the free will of the regenerate soul. The parable of the sower is exemplified to-day in the case of those who have no depth of earth. Their love to Christ soon degenerates into a mere sentiment with little or no influence on practical life, and in a short time the sentiment itself entirely evaporates, and the soul becomes "twice dead, plucked up by the roots" (Jude 12). What is the safeguard against such a disaster? It is such an indwelling of the fulness of the Spirit as excludes everything contrary to the divine nature by filling and flooding the soul with a love that is ever enlarging the vessel and ever filling it to the brim. Then love is perfect in the sense that it is no longer mixed in kind and so weak in degree as to be unable to encounter the temptation successfully. Says Prof. Candlish: "The new life of Christianity is a unity, and though, on account of the imperfect and abnormal condition of most Christians, it does not show itself with perfect symmetry, yet it tends toward moral excellence and perfection in every direction, and the more vigorous the central principle of religious life is, the more will particular virtues be developed and increased." This is progress toward entire sanctification by the Holy Spirit, and is a necessary condition of that crowning work. The question is often asked, "Why does not the Spirit entirely sanctify when He regenerates?" We answer, it is because that neither the consecration nor the faith of the penitent sinner is adequate to this complete work. The person then surrenders his bad things, he lays down his arms, quits his rebellion and sues for pardon. This is all that his faith grasps. But he soon learns that a deeper consecration is requisite, that all his good things, his possessions, his bodily powers, his intellectual faculties must be fully consecrated to Christ. To pour all his money into the treasury of his imperilled country and to give his life by enlisting in her military service is far different from the act of surrender as a prisoner of war. In the next place, faith for entire sanctification is a far higher act, involving a deeper knowledge of one's spiritual needs and a larger comprehension of the vastness of the supply found in Jesus Christ. This deeper knowledge is not found in the spiritual babe.

Moreover, at the risk of being suspected of predestinarianism, I insist on another reason why the Spirit does not entirely purge the soul at the new birth. The impartation of spiritual life to a dead soul is wrought by the Spirit alone without the soul's co-operation, though it is active in repentance, faith and turning to the Lord. It is active in conversion, but passive in regeneration. Theologians would call the first a case of synergism and the second an instance of monergism. If our distinction between these works of the Spirit is correct, it affords a sufficient reason why entire sanctification could not be wrought by the Spirit at the time of the new birth. The old man cannot be crucified without the co-operation of the new man. He must sign the death warrant of that sin in the flesh which the Son of God by His sacrifice for sin has condemned, in order to make that condemnation effectual for the destruction of "the body of sin" (Rom. vi.6). "In implanting the new life at first, the Holy Spirit has to deal with a soul that is indeed essentially active, but in regard to spirituality insensible or opposed to the call of God. Hence this work is entirely due to divine power; we are His workmanship, created in Christ unto good works. But in the preservation and development of the new life the Spirit has to deal with a soul that is now spiritually alive and able and inclined to work in the same direction as His work."* In sanctification "we are God's fellow-workers" (I Cor. iii.9, Revised Version). Hence the momentous import of the exhortation of Paul, "Carry out with fear and trembling your own salvation. For it is God which worketh in you both to will and to work for his good pleasure."† The occasion for fear and trembling arises from the fact that God's work in me may fail to reach perfection because of my failure to work perfectly with Him. It is indeed a solemn and awful thing to be fellow-workers with the holy God in the production of the most valuable thing in the universe, a holy character. In the work of purifying ourselves while God is refining us how careful should we be lest through lack of faith in His exceedingly great and precious promises we should mar the work of His Spirit in perfectly conforming us to the image of His Son. As a slight motion may spoil the image which the king of day is imprinting on the prepared plate, so a little self-indulgence or heedlessness or wavering of faith may blur the image of Christ

---

*Prof. Candlish
†Dean Alford's version of Phil. ii.12, 13

which the Spirit is creating in me. I am responsible not only for all that I can do towards completed holiness, which is perfect consecration, but I am also responsible for all that the Holy Ghost can do with my co-operation.

The work of the Holy Spirit in the progressive sanctification of the newborn soul is indirect: in opening the heart to receive the truth,* the instrument of purification; in giving vigor to the spiritual life; in strengthening the will to resist temptation, and in diminishing the power of evil habits. It is repressive of depravity rather than totally destructive.

The entire eradication of the propensity to sin is by the direct and instantaneous act of the Holy Spirit responsive to a special act of faith in Christ claiming the full heritage of the believer. "When we learn that God claims us for His own, and when, after fruitless personal efforts to render Him the devotion He requires, we learn for the first time that God will work in us by the agency of His Spirit and by actual spiritual contact with Christ the devotion He requires, and when we venture to believe,... we find by happy experience that according to our faith it is done to us. The experience thus gained becomes an era in our spiritual life. We feel that we are then holy in a sense unknown to us before."† It is in reference to this distinctive act of the Sanctifier that it is noted by an emi-

---

*"In II Thess. ii.13, sanctification of the Spirit is placed in close connection with belief of the truth. And from Acts xxvi.18 we learn that not only forgiveness of sins, but a lot among the sanctified, is obtained by faith in Christ. This accords with the broad principles asserted in Mark ix.23, 'All things are possible to him who believes;' in Gal. iii.14, 'That we may receive the promise of the Spirit through faith,' and in Acts xv.9, 'By faith having purified their hearts,' and with a great mass of Bible teaching which I have not space to quote and expound. In Rom. vi.11, St. Paul bids us 'Reckon ourselves to be dead to sin, but living for God in Christ Jesus.' This reckoning is the mental process of faith, for it results in assurance resting upon the promise of God."— J. A. Beet's "Holiness as Understood by the Writers of the Bible," page 55.

†J. A. Beet's "Holiness as Understood by the Writers of the Bible," page 60.

nent expositor "that in the New Testament we never read expressly and unmistakably of sanctification as a gradual process." This is said in view of the almost universal use of the aorist tense of the verbs *to sanctify* and To this distinct and decisive action of the Holy Spirit in the extinction of proneness to sin, bringing the believer into the land of rest, in marvellous contrast with His previous wilderness experience, after His regeneration, there are too many intelligent and trustworthy witnesses to be lightly passed by as of no account. They assure us that they were truly converted and received the direct witness of the Spirit to their adoption; that they did not backslide, but grew in grace; that they were not conscious of living in wilful violation of any known law of God, and that they could testify that there is no condemnation to them who are in Christ Jesus. But they solemnly aver that through all their regenerate life, before receiving Christ for their entire sanctification, they were conscious of a strong inward enemy whom they were striving to bind and cast out but always failed; that by the study of the Scriptures they found that this rebel within was called "the old man," whom theologians style "original sin;" that after reading or hearing the testimony of those entirely consecrated souls who had through specific faith and importunate prayer found complete deliverance, they definitely sought for this distinctive work of the Holy Ghost, and at an ever-memorable date they emerged into a blissful consciousness of inward purity and profound peace far beyond all former experiences. This victory many have attested decades and scores of years. Dr. Asa Mahan, whose temper in his youth was so ungovernable that his father predicted that in a fit of anger he would kill some one and expiate his crime on the scaffold, and whose irascibility in the early years of his Christian ministry was the cause of untold grief, testifies to a change wrought by the Holy Spirit so great as to make the last forty years of his life years undisturbed by one gust of irritability, though he often met with insults and other occasions to call it forth if it had been slumbering within. The Sanctifier had cast out this demon and so adorned the place of his former abode with the fruits of the Spirit and so filled it with His own permanent fulness that he could not return though he may have "taken with himself seven other spirits more wicked than himself." The Lord be praised! There is a power which not only cleanses but also keeps. It is to be noted that the witnesses to whom we refer agree in testifying that this entire sanctification was subsequent to regeneration, and that it was accomplished by the Spirit in an instant, and not by the processes of growth.

This negative work of the Spirit in the eradication of inherited proneness to sin is followed by an illimitable development of all the Christian graces. One may reach the point where sin is all destroyed and love become perfect, *i.e.*, pure and unmixed, and yet his power of moral discernment and his mental enlargement be capable of increase through time and through eternity. His spiritual development will be commensurate.

Perfection in degree of love is never to be attained.

Perfection in kind is the gift of the Holy Ghost to the believer now.

There prevails in certain religious circles the doctrine that in the new birth a new nature is created, while the old nature, or old man, continues till physical death extinguishes his life. It is said that the old nature is nailed to the cross, but he does not die so long as the human spirit acts through a material organism. Denial of the possibility of entire sanctification in the present life is an obvious inference. Another outcome of this error is that depravity is necessary, and that it is beyond the reach of the Holy Spirit in the application of the blood of Christ which cleanses from all sin. Hence the notion of two natures existing in every Christian, however consecrated, so long as he is in the body, the one a new creation and therefore sinless, and the other sinful and beyond all hope of change for the better, is exceedingly mischievous, palliating and excusing evil propensities. When we speak of the Holy Spirit as the indwelling Sanctifier we will examine the alleged scriptural proofs of this doctrine. We insist that the work of the Spirit in the new creation of the penitent believer in Christ is not the creation of new faculties, but the rectification of those already existing, weakened and marred by sin. He has no need of a new reason, for even after the fall, reason in man grasps the same self-evident truths that exist in God. In fact, the modern teaching of philosophy is that truths of intuition are the activity of God immanent in the soul of man. His sensibilities, both natural and moral, have been damaged by the fall of Adam, and his will has become enslaved to his perverted affections and depraved desires. It is the office of the Holy Spirit to lift this yoke of bondage and to bring the newborn soul into the glorious liberty of the sons of God. He whom Christ Jesus makes free is free indeed. It is the slave that is emancipated and not a new being just created. Such a being would need no act of emancipation. It is the office of the Spirit to give the will the gracious ability to make holy choices, and to clarify the moral sense or conscience so that its decisions will all harmonize with ethical axioms or immutable morality. The "new creature" spoken of by Paul is a figure of speech for the vivid presentation of the transforming power of the Holy Spirit in the renewal of a soul badly shattered by sin. Conscience is restored to full activity both in its power to discern and its power to approve or to condemn. The human spirit may well be compared to a skylight in the dome of his being through which he was designed to have a vision of spiritual realities. But sin has darkened the windows and intercepted the heavenly vision. The remedy is not in the demolition of the old skylight and the setting of a new one, but in the thorough cleansing of the original window by One who by taking up His abode in that dome can always keep it transparent by His purifying presence. The process seems to be first to cause the law of God to shine into conscience, the light of forgiveness, then the light of purity, "having no more conscience of sin."

Another error obstructive of the spiritual life of all the so-called sacramentarian churches— more than half of Christendom— consists in a perversion of the meaning of Christ's words to Nicodemus, "born of water and the Spirit." Those who magnify the sacraments as saving ordinances, and some who do not teach baptismal regeneration, like the Methodist Episcopal Church, which uses the Anglican ritual abridged, teach that the words "born of water" refer to water baptism.* But others, including the writer, insist that these words have no reference to that ordinance, which was not made obligatory upon believers till after Christ's resurrection, years after his dialogue with Nicodemus. The identification of water baptism with the new birth has wrought untold harm to myriads of souls, deluding them with a shadow of the requisite for salvation instead of the substance, the impartation of spiritual life and initial sanctification symbolized by water. We sympathize with Weisse, though we cannot use his strong language, that to make regeneration depend upon baptism by water "is little better than blasphemy." We believe with Neander, Calvin, Grotius and other scholars, that Christ here intends the symbolic import of water, and not water itself, as an agent of cleansing, according to an ancient figure which expressed one idea by two nouns connected by *and* instead of a noun and an adjective, as, "we drink from *cups and gold*" for *golden cups*. Thus, "ye must be born of water

---

*See the first Scripture quoted in the "Order for the Administration of Baptism to such as are of Riper Years" in the ritual of said church.

and the Spirit" for the purifying Spirit. Desiring to give his distinguished hearer a clear idea of the change which the Spirit must work in the natural heart, he adds the idea of initial cleansing by using the word water. In like manner a more thorough purification is expressed by the words of John the Baptist descriptive of Christ, "He shall baptize you with the Holy Ghost and with fire," an agent of cleansing far more effectual than water in the purification of earthen and metallic utensils. We cannot here, as some do, read *and* as meaning *or*, "with the Holy Ghost or fire," meaning all who do not receive the Holy Spirit's baptism must be baptized with hell fire. We prefer the exegesis of Bishop Hopkins, "those who are baptized with the Holy Spirit are, as it were, plunged into the heavenly flame, whose searching energy devours all their dross, tin and base alloy." Here is a promise of a richer blessing, a more thorough sanctification and a far larger equipment for effective service than that which is enjoyed by the average Christian of to-day. "The purification at conversion, comparatively superficial, is only that which may be fitly symbolized by water baptism. But fire searches the inmost springs of life. The baptism of fire must be such a close and intimate contact of the holy God with the inner man, as to light up its dark secrets and burn out its uncleanness."*

---

*"The Baptism in Fire " Rev. Charles Edward Smith

Chapter XV
CHRIST OUR SANCTIFICATION

THE WORK OF EACH of the three Persons of the Trinity in the scheme of salvation is quite definitely stated in the Holy Scriptures. The Father originated the plan, the Son by His atoning death provided the means, the blood of sprinkling, and the Holy Spirit conditionally applies it for the soul's purification. But sometimes the work of the Spirit is ascribed to the Son. This seeming confusion perplexes the student of the Bible, till he learns that when the Son is spoken of as sanctifying it is always in a different sense from the Spirit's work of purification. In the interest of clearness of thought and of saving truth set forth as the cloudless noonday sun, let us note in what sense the sanctification ascribed to Christ in several texts differs from that internal work wrought by the Comforter. When Christ is spoken of as our sanctification, it is meant, not that He enters into the hearts of believers and cleanses them, but that He provides the purifying medium, His own shed blood, and the sanctifying agent, the Holy Spirit. The Son's work is external, the Spirit's is internal; or in philosophic terms, the work of the one is objective, that of the other is subjective; the one sanctifies provisionally and the other effectually. Now let us carry this distinction into Paul's letters to the Corinthians. In I Cor. i.2 they are addressed as "sanctified in Christ Jesus," and in iii.1 Paul "cannot speak unto them as spiritual, but as carnal, even as unto babes in Christ." How are these apparent contradictions harmonized? It will not do to say that Paul, to say nothing of the Spirit who inspired him, flatly contradicts himself. In the light of the distinction between provisional sanctification in Christ and actual sanctification by the Holy Spirit, a very beautiful harmony emerges. Through faith the Corinthians had been born from above, and had become "babes in Christ," and were now entitled to all the privileges which He had purchased for believers, among which was conditional sanctification. But since they had failed to appropriate their heritage by the exercise of faith, they were still strongly carnal in their leanings, as evidenced by their "envying, strife and divisions." They were provisionally sanctified in Christ; they were not actually sanctified by the Holy Spirit. The contradiction disappears. In the same way the contradiction between the statement that "Jesus Christ is the Saviour of all men" and His sentence of a part of them in the last day to eternal punishment disappears in the consideration that Christ is the conditional Saviour of all the human race, but the real Saviour of believers only.

In I Cor. i.30 Christ "is made unto us wisdom and righteousness, sanctification and redemption." This He is to every one who does by faith appropriate Him and become wise by believing divine revelation personified in Christ, the truth, and justified through faith in Him, and sanctified through the reception of the Spirit in His office as Sanctifier, and redeemed, soul and body reunited and glorified, through persevering faith in Him who shall change the body of our "humiliation," that it may be fashioned like unto His glorious body. This distinction between provisional sanctification in Christ and sanctification inwrought by the Holy Spirit secured by faith utterly excludes the doctrine of holiness imputed to persons whose hearts are still filled with depravity. One may die for another, but one cannot be holy for another. Sin and holiness are personal, and not transferable. Alford calls attention to the double conjunction in I Cor. i.30, between "righteousness, the source of our justification before God, and sanctification by His Spirit, implying that the Christian life is complete, the negative side and positive side are so joined as to form one whole." The piety of the Corinthians lacked the positive side. They were forgiven, but not cleansed. They had appropriated part of their heritage in Christ, justification, but they had not by an appropriating faith claimed sanctification. The Corinthian type of Christians has not become obsolete. In every age, with here and there an exception, it has been the prevailing type. This accounts for its failure to conquer the world. When the possible in Christian character shall have become the actual in the whole Church the world's evangelization will be speedily accomplished. That generation will see the glorious consummation.

In Heb. ii.11 "he that sanctifieth" is Christ, regarded as the author of the provision of salvation and of the agency of the purifying Spirit, who applies to "those who are being sanctified" the cleansing efficacy of the atonement on the condition of their faith in Christ.

In Heb. x.10 is another instance of sanctification by Christ provisionally, "through the oblation of the body of Jesus Christ once for all." That inward holiness which the altar ritual of the Hebrews with their interminable repetitions was unable to produce, has been rendered possible to every believer through the offering of the body of the adorable God-Man once for all. While the atonement sanctified no one, it renders possible the entire sanctification of every offspring of Adam who will trust in Christ for this purchased blessing.

Verse 14 has often been misunderstood as teaching that Christ brought to perfection the work of our inward sanctification eighteen hundred years before we were born: "For by one oblation hath he perfected forever them that are being sanctified." (Alford.) The sanctification which Christ thus perfected is provisional. As such it is eternally efficacious and incapable of improvement. It stands ready from age to age to be applied by the Holy Spirit to the inward cleansing of every believer. Nothing is lacking but the outstretching of an empty hand to grasp this pearl of great price. Under the atonement "all things are possible to him that believeth."

Verse 15 does not teach the witness of the Holy Spirit to the actual, inward work of entire sanctification, as some erroneously teach, but His testimony in the Old Testament to the coming of the days when the provisions for the inner purification will be complete, when the law will no longer be a galling yoke on the neck, but a joyful song in the heart. It is true that this inner change will be through the agency of the Holy Spirit, who, by shining on His own work, is a witness to its genuineness. But this is not a proof text of such a witness. Well says Delitzsch: "The Holy Ghost is the Spirit of prophecy, and from Him comes the whole God-inspired written Word. He also in that Word is the witness that with Christ's return to the Father all is accomplished, and nothing remains to be done to procure for us inward perfecting and a complete restoration to communion with God." Man's relation to God is no longer merely legal, but inward, evangelical and spiritual. He ceases from outward, compensative works, but concentrates his view upon the sanctifying and endowing grace already procured, and seeks to enter in and lay hold of it. This once-for-all provisional grace for justification and entire sanctification, according to Jeremiah, is the basis of the new covenant (Jer. xxiii.6).*

Many good Christians find it difficult to accept the doctrine of a definite and instantaneous work of the Holy Spirit subsequent to regeneration, because they cannot draw a sharply defined line between the incoming of the Spirit, the Lord of life, to impart life, and His second incoming to impart the more abundant life by the removal of all antagonisms thereto. When told that there is a difference between being free and being "free indeed," between the work of the Spirit in inspiring love and in perfecting love, they are still unable to construe to themselves satisfactorily this distinction. Hence they are inclined to reject the doctrine as an untenable theory.

But in the face of so much Scripture exhorting to holiness and commanding perfection and the fulness of the Spirit, and of so many promises and prayers relating to the same blessing as immediately attainable, is it not the wiser course to bind up this difficulty with two others pertaining to the Holy Spirit, which every evangelical mind believes, but none understands? The first mystery is involved in the question how the Holy Spirit was always in the world as the inspirer of all true piety in human hearts, from Abel to John the Baptist, and yet at a definite moment, on the day of Pentecost, the same Spirit came down from heaven into the world. Here is an enigma which orthodoxy universally fails to explain, and yet universally believes. For orthodoxy receives the doctrine of the Trinity, which implies the eternity and the omnipresence of the Holy Spirit, while the Bible asserts His agency in creation and His activity in human hearts

---

*See Appendix, Note F

in all the pre-Christian ages. Faith accepts this mystery which is too high for the grasp of reason. In a similar manner faith answers another question, how the Holy Spirit was in the heart of the man Jesus Christ, inspiring, illumining and guiding Him all His life up to the hour of His baptism, when the Holy Ghost descended upon Him and abode in Him. How could He be in Him thirty years, and then enter into Him at a definite moment?

Here is a question which reason cannot answer. Yet every believer in the New Testament assents to these unharmonized facts in the relation of the Holy Spirit to the humanity of Jesus Christ. If the Bible teaches that entire sanctification through the Holy Spirit is a crisis in Christian experience, subsequent to the new birth by the same divine agent, and if reason cannot draw an accurate boundary line between these two works of the Spirit, why should we not bind up this mystery in the same bundle with the two which we have just described, and relegate this difficulty to the domain of faith? The first immediate effect would be the cessation of the debate which exists even in Wesleyan circles; there being no more occasion for a theological controversy on this third question than there is in the case of either of the other two. The second effect would be that multitudes of earnest believers, having now emerged from the foggy metaphysics environing the subject of entire sanctification into the clear atmosphere of faith, would aspire with all the energy of their being to enter into the full spiritual heritage of the children of God, now clearly set before the eye of faith. A third effect would be: "He that is feeble among them at that day shall be as David; and the house of David shall be as God, as the angel of the Lord," in efficiency to resist sin and to sway unbelievers to bow to Christ. There would be a spiritual revolution in the Church, and vigor would supersede supineness, spiritual hunger would take the place of satisfied worldliness, harmony would succeed discord, and unity displace all tendencies to schism.

It is certainly logical to treat all the mysteries involved in the offices of the Paraclete alike; and it certainly is unreasonable to receive two of these mysteries by faith and to reject the third, not because of its lack of scriptural proofs as the ground of faith, but because of its lack of transparency to the eye of reason. Candid persons should be consistent, treating like difficulties in a like manner when they all stand upon the basis of the same supernatural revelation. But truth when it collides with men's pleasures, passions and wills never has a fair chance. President Mark Hopkins suggests that, if the proof that the three angles of a triangle equal two right angles abridged men's sinful indulgence, there would be many who would stoutly insist that they could not see the point of proof. This shows that unbelief originates in a moral rather than an intellectual cause. May it not be that much of the difficulty with the doctrine of entire sanctification arises from the heart and not from the head; not in a lack of evidence, but in a disposition to neglect the proofs of a work of the Holy Ghost which builds a hedge across the path of sinful desire, and kindles an unquenchable fire in the house of the heart's idols? Hence entire self-surrender to one's best light is absolutely necessary to perfect candor in his attitude towards God's truth. The least particle of self-will can obscure a great spiritual truth, as a hair, or platinum wire finer than any hair, stretched across the eye-glass of the telescope, will blot out Sirius, 6,000 times larger than the sun, and 8,400,000,000 times larger than our globe.

It is a great thing to be "of the truth," to be so in love with it as to be willing that our eyes should be purged of every film in order to gaze upon her radiant form, and to have our feet blistered in toiling up the rugged path in which the heavenly maid walks that she may lure us to the skies. St. Paul in Eph. iv.15 has one expression which shows the very quintessence of Christian candor requisite for realizing in experience the highest spiritual verities, "truthing in love," or "pursuing truth in love." Love is the eye which sees God's truth when the eye of mere intellect utterly fails. There is always a certainty that they who are disposed to sacrifice all to the truth as it is in Jesus, and out of love to Him, will speedily scale the loftiest heights of spiritual knowledge, and daily dwell upon these sunlit summits evermore.

Such are not stumbled at doctrines never revealed to reason but to faith only. Happy are they who early learn to render to reason that which belongs to reason, and to faith that which belongs to faith. Among the latter are all those truths relating to eradication of sin "through sanctification of the Spirit and belief of the truth."

To a person objecting to entire sanctification in the present life because he could not "see into it," excellent advice was recently given in these homely Saxon words, "Get into it and see out." The advice contains a truth that is capable of wide application. Every doctrine which is to be apprehended by faith and not by speculative reason, must be verified by experience before its truth can be realized. Christianity came into the world as an experimental science, saying to every one, "Come and see, test me and prove the truth of my divine origin, taste and see that the Lord Jesus is good." This was the challenge with which the Son of God met all doubters. "If any man willeth to do his will he shall know of the teaching, whether it be of God, or whether I speak of myself" (John vii.17, Revised Version). A right attitude of the inquirer's will is the indispensable condition of his success in his study of the Christian evidences. The culpability of unbelief lies in the absence of this obedient attitude of the will, the disposition to follow whithersoever truth may lead. Hence I preach that there is no such thing possible in God's moral universe as permanent, honest doubt. At some point in the doubter's history, truth has pointed to a path which he was not willing to tread. One refusal to follow his best light has spoiled forever afterwards the plea of honest scepticism. The relation of Christian truth to every human soul is that of a key to a lock. The gospel was constructed by omniscient wisdom to unlock every heart. Wherever it fails, when faithfully applied, to turn back the bolt of unbelief, the fault is not in the key, nor in the original structure of the lock, but in that tampering with the wards which is in the power of every free agent. God never made such a moral monstrosity as an intelligent soul incapable of believing His truth. The aphorism of John Fletcher, "All salvation is from God, all damnation is from man," is really a moral axiom. Unbelief is damning because it has a moral cause, the perverse will. When the will passes into a state of obedience, the soul emerges into the region of light. This law is as invariable as any in the physical world. Whenever there is a "total, irreversible, affectionate self-surrender to Jesus Christ as both Saviour and Lord," the Spirit of truth streams through and through the soul like a pencil of sunbeams, vitalizing, illumining, warming and cleansing. This statement is true in respect to all the stages of spiritual progress. Many have verified it in the joyful experience of the new birth, and many with gladness attest its truth in that spiritual uplift which has followed that all-surrendering faith which has laid hold of Christ as our entire sanctification from inbred sin. That uplift awaits all true believers in the Holy Spirit, the outpoured gift of our glorified Saviour. He is God's elevator, moving from earth to heaven, lifting all who perfectly trust in Him from the low levels of fogs and damps to the sunlit summits of full assurance where the sun shines day and night. This is the "higher life," to which all Christians are commanded to ascend. "Seek the things that are above." When the believer steps into this elevator with perfect confidence in its safety and in the almighty Motor, it is astonishing to what altitudes he will be lifted instantaneously while he does nothing but to trust. St. Paul prayed that the Ephesians "might know what is the exceeding greatness of his power to usward who believe," "the very same power" which God "wrought in Christ when he raised him from the dead." God can do what He will with inert matter, because there is inherent in it no power to resist His fiat. But when the Omnipotent would mould the sinful human spirit into more than angelic beauty, into the beauty of His own moral likeness, He may be thwarted by the obstinate resistance of the free agent. He made man without his consent, but He cannot save him without his consent. When that consent is fully given, and the hand of faith is put forth to appropriate Christ to save unto the uttermost, then is experienced what St. Paul, by a strain of language itself, piling up words expressive of unlimited transforming energy, styles "the exceeding greatness of, his power to usward who believe," because He is able to do "superabundantly above the greatest abundance." (Adam Clarke.)

One effect of this wonderful inward transfiguration is an astonishing quickening of the spiritual perceptions, so that the distant becomes near, the opaque transparent, and the indefinite and incomprehensible becomes clearly defined and easily discerned by the anointed vision. Many are trying to see before they buy of Christ the divine eye salve. Multitudes are applying to spiritual things the wrong faculty of knowledge, reason instead of faith; with results as far from the truth as those which follow the attempt to distinguish between pulverized sugar and fine salt, not by the taste but by the touch.

Even the mystery of the trinal distinctions in the divine nature, although still inscrutable to reason, becomes to the Spirit-baptized person a truth lifted forever beyond the region of doubt. Thus attested Dr. Wilbur Fisk ever after that personal Pentecost at Wellfleet camp-meeting, where he sought and found entire sanctification under a demonstration of the Spirit too great for the strength of the earthly tenement. This is the testimony of thousands who have exercised an all-consecrating trust in Christ for the full heritage of the sons of God this side of glory.

"Get into and see out" is just what the astronomers did in order to get a true view of the solar system. For ages they strove to harmonize the retrograde motions of some of the planets with the geocentric theory, but in vain. At length one of them dared in thought to take his stand in the sun and to look out upon the orbs wheeling through the heavens, when, lo, before his enraptured gaze was a perfectly harmonious system without one backward motion. Get out of the earth into the sun, and the solar system becomes heliocentric. Get out of self into God, and theology becomes christocentric and beautifully consistent. One of the old divines had for his motto, "It is the heart that makes the theologian." Rutherford used to say to students for the ministry, "If you would be a deep divine, I recommend to you sanctification," and to all Christians, "sanctification; sanctification will settle you most in the truth."

The faith requisite to entire sanctification is essentially the same as that which is the condition on which forgiveness of sin is received.

It remains for us to discuss entire consecration, its nature and motives, as preliminary to the faith by which we are sanctified wholly. *Motive* is the word ordinarily used in speaking of the conditions of choice. We call it an *inducement* when it is adapted to excite the sensibilities, and we call it a *reason* when it is addressed to the intellect in the form of argument. The motive to entire consecration includes both, because it is an appeal to all of man's nature back of his will. We might bring out an array of various inferior motives to a perfect devotement of self unto God and His service, if we did not see that all motives to this act which are not comprised in one grand motive are too weak to deserve mention. They are such as these: fear of penalty, self-respect, a full and rounded development of our being by the stimulus communicated to the intellect when the love of God is perfected in the heart, greater usefulness, increased happiness, the honor which comes from God and good men and that greater reward which results from greater godliness. Without delaying to discuss these motives, mostly commendable but all of them combined inadequate, we proceed to present the motive presented by the inspired apostle, "I beseech you therefore, brethren, by the mercies of God." The persons addressed are already Christians, for they are tenderly called "brethren." They are not plied with the threatenings of the law, because "There is now no condemnation to them that are in Christ Jesus." They are no longer "under the law " as the impulse to service. Hence the lash of penalty cannot be wisely applied. It is not in harmony with the diction of the New Testament to address threatenings to the sons of God. This is a servile motive. Children by adoption who hear within the cry "Abba, Father," are on a higher plane. Yet this does not prove that they have reached spiritual perfection. It is the habit of St. Paul to exhort those who have already become sons and daughters to cleanse themselves from all filthiness of the flesh and spirit, perfecting holiness in filial reverence, not in guilty terror (II Cor. vii.1).

"The love of Christ constraineth us." Love responsive to the self-sacrificing love of the Son of God is the only genuine motive to our complete self-surrender to Him, soul, body and spirit. The manward aspect of His atonement had this very design, the believer's total consecration under the mighty impulse of gratitude to his great Benefactor. "He died for all, that they which live should no longer live unto themselves, but unto him who for their sakes died and rose again " (II Cor. v.15, Revised Version). Love, especially love to the unworthy and the sinful, awakens gratitude, except where the noble capacity for gratitude has been utterly blasted by the mildew of depravity. Gratitude finds expression not only in word, but in service and devotion to the benefactor even unto death. The dreary annals of human selfishness in the form of wars and oppressions are here and there lighted up by instances of heroic self-sacrifice of souls struggling to express a gratitude too great for tongue or pen to utter. Hence we solemnly aver that the noblest act of which a man is capable is the total and irreversible consecration to Christ of every atom of his being. When he has done this he will long for an enlarged capacity of loving service and sacrifice.

The writer testifies, after drinking from this spring for half a century, and during the last twenty-seven years drinking to the fulness of his capacity, that he is to-day more athirst than ever for a larger vessel to contain the water of life. Not a few souls can bear witness to this blessed paradox.

Chapter XVI
THE WITNESS OF THE SPIRIT

THIS IS THE DOCTRINE of assurance which Wesley did more to elucidate and to relieve of obscuring misapprehensions than any preceding theologian. He thus describes the *direct witness* of the Spirit as "an inward impression on the souls of believers, whereby the Spirit of God directly testifies to their spirit that they are children of God."

The *indirect witness* is an inference from the discerned presence of the fruit of the Spirit, love, joy, peace, etc., and it follows the direct witness in the order of time, "because," says Wesley, "in the nature of the thing, the testimony must precede the fruit which springs from it." The voice of the Spirit within the believer is to all who know God the most real of all realities. It is sometimes called a seal which secures, authenticates and appropriates.

The Holy Spirit is God's seal. "Ye were sealed with [not by] that Holy Spirit of promise" (Eph. i.13). Another metaphorical designation of the witness of the Spirit is "the earnest of the Spirit." The earnest is derived from mercantile usage traceable through the Romans and Greeks to the Phoenicians, the founders of commerce. It assures the fulfilment of a promise as a part of the purchase money paid in advance to bind the bargain, or as an instalment of a servant's wages paid at the time of hiring, obliging the servant to render the service and the master to pay the rest of the wages after the work has been done. It places both parties in a position to enforce the contract. The buyer, if he does not take the goods, forfeits the money advanced, and the servant who fails to render the service must refund the earnest which he has taken. The master who repents of his bargain must lose the wage advanced, and the merchant who withholds the goods because the market price has risen, or for any other reason, must repay the money advanced. The phrase "earnest of the Spirit " occurs only twice in the New Testament. Grammatically "the Spirit" is in apposition with "earnest," meaning that the pledge consists in the Holy Spirit bestowed upon the believer and dwelling in his heart. "And gave us the earnest of the Spirit in our hearts" (II Cor. i.22). There is no hint here of the time when the full wage will be paid, although in Eph. i.14 it is "until the redemption of the purchased possession." Those who take a narrow view of present Christian privilege and put the fruition of the promises after death interpret the earnest only of the fulness of joy in heaven. But I believe that it is a pledge and a foretaste not only of heaven hereafter, but of a present heaven attainable by faith— even the fulness of the Holy Spirit.

"By mistaking the earnest for the fulness we run the risk," says Joseph Parker, "of stating incomplete truths as final revelations." The earnest of the Spirit is the assurance of the fulness of the Spirit in this life, and in the future life it is a right to drink evermore of "the river of water of life, bright as crystal, proceeding out of the throne of God and of the Lamb " (Rev. xxii.I, Revised Version). The fulness is certainly promised in this life; it is prayed for by Paul for believers, and it was enjoyed by many in the apostolic church, and there have been some witnesses to this experience in every subsequent generation. From its very beginning the normal regenerate life is a continuous progression in spirituality, arithmetical if not geometrical, receiving with its widening capacities richer gifts of the wisdom and holiness of God.

> "New births of grace new raptures bring;
> Triumphant the new song we sing,
>   The great Renewer bless.
> Darkness and dread we leave behind,
> New light, new glory still we find,
>   New realms divine possess."

With respect to the obligation which the earnest of the Spirit lays on its recipient, it has been well said that it is a lien upon the future service of the receiver. If the service be unperformed, the earnest will be withdrawn; whereas if the service be lovingly rendered with the whole might of the heart, the measure of the gift will be filled up even to the sanctification of the whole body, soul and spirit. The Church is in its infancy as to the realization of spiritual blessing, as mankind is in babyhood in its application of electricity to human utilities. To what surpassing altitudes will the individual believer and the Church as a whole be lifted when the gift of the Spirit is fully realized and appropriated.

> "Spirit, who makest all things new,
> Thou leadest onward; we pursue
>   The heavenly march sublime.
> 'Neath Thy renewing fires we glow,
> And still from strength to strength we go,
>   From height to height we climb."

Another very instructive property of the earnest is to

be noted in the fact that beyond the idea of security it implies identity in kind. If the earnest is paid in silver, the whole will be paid in silver. If the earnest is in gold, the wages will be golden. If the earnest in the case of the believer in Jesus Christ is the Holy Spirit, then the fulness of the blessed Comforter will be his portion in this life and his eternal reward. This is the Old Testament promise, "I am thy exceeding great reward." Hence we need not die to know what are the felicities of saints in heaven. They flow from the same fountain from which we are drinking in this world — "the joy of the Holy Ghost." The bliss of the Old Testament and of the New, of earth and heaven, is the same. To all spiritual intelligences God is a satisfying portion.

> "There is a stream which issues forth
> From God's eternal throne,
> And from the Lamb— a living stream,
> Clear as the crystal stone.
> The stream doth water Paradise,
> It makes the angels sing:
> One cordial drop revives my heart;
> Hence all my joys do spring."
> *John Mason*

This doctrine of the immediate contact of God's Spirit with my spirit, without the medium of symbol or sacrament or absolving priest, does not rest upon one, two or three cardinal proof texts, but upon a wide variety of scriptural proofs, such as the communion of the Holy Spirit, the revelation of Christ within the soul, the knowledge of God, the strengthened form of the Greek *epignosis*, clear, certain, thorough and perfect knowledge of Christ, a favorite term with both Paul and Peter, together with *plerophoria*, full assurance, excluding all doubt. Count up the many times in John's first Epistle in which he says "we know," and add the stronger words, "ye all know," instead of "ye know all things" (I John ii.20), found in the Revised Version margin and the text of Westcott and Hort, and our reader will see the broad basis on which this doctrine stands.

The direct witness of the Spirit is intermittent in most young Christians. Before the fulness of the Spirit is received there are only occasional gleams of light through the rifted clouds, followed by sunless intervals when doubts distract and harass the soul. The cry of such Christians when seeking the abiding witness, the indwelling Comforter, is voiced by Charles Wesley, who alone among all the versifiers of the eighteenth century gave due prominence to the Holy Spirit; "the author," says James Montgomery, "of a great number of the best hymns in the English or any other language." The superiority of the permanent to the transient witness of the Spirit is thus finely expressed:

"O that the Comforter would come!
  Nor visit as a transient guest,
But fix in me His constant home,
  And take possession of my breast,
And make my soul His loved abode,
  The temple of indwelling God!"

In another hymn he prays to the Spirit in these words:

"Spirit of love, return
  To every troubled breast,
And comfort us who mourn
  For permanence of rest.

Thou often visitest Thine own;
  But in an hour or day
Our transitory guest is gone,

Our joy is fled away.

"O might we always know
The Father reconciled!
Set up Thy throne below
In each adopted child."

This alternation of experience from sunshine to shadow affords occasion for the temptation to cast away our confidence in Christ and to abandon His service. Many yield to this suggestion of Satan and go back to the world instead of climbing to altitudes above the clouds. Some are told by stationary and retrograde Christians that they will never be so happy as they were when they first entered the kingdom of God. This dismal outlook upon the future intensifies the temptation with which they are wrestling. Hence it is not surprising that not a few young converts turn away from Jesus and walk no more with Him. They should have been told that in the normal Christian experience "it is better farther on." It is to be regretted that there are so few normal Christians who are at hand to give the discouraged convert this word of good cheer. Many professors of faith in Christ are living on so low a level amid the miasmas and fogs that they never have even a glimpse of the sunny spiritual uplands,

"Where dwells the Lord our Righteousness,
And keeps His own in perfect peace
And everlasting rest."

It is a great mistake to bring a young convert into an unspiritual and worldly church. It is like laying a newborn babe on the breast of a dead mother for nutriment and growth. Hence we deprecate the promotion of conversions to increase the membership of a dead church. It is like enlarging a graveyard. A healthful revival always begins, not outside of the church, but within it. Zion must herself travail before living children are born. Some unwise pastors, in their eagerness to swell the number of church members, try to awaken sinners over the heads of a slumbering church, whom they dislike to awaken lest they should be displeased. Men awakened suddenly are usually not kindly disposed toward those who arouse them.

The result of many modern revivals is to multiply the number of those who are strangers to the direct witness of the Spirit to their adoption into the family of God by the new birth. Another result is that those who do receive this divine witness and retain Him intermittently find few to counsel and encourage them when ecstatic emotion subsides and they are called to walk by naked faith alone without feeling.

Our advice to all who have occasional gleams of sunshine through the rifted clouds, with intervals of doubt and incertitude, is, to ascertain the cause of this intermittency, and to remove it as soon as possible. For the cause is not, as some teach, in the sovereign will, but in ourselves. To this declaration the only exception is some physical condition into which we have been brought by divine Providence, such as a prostrated nervous system, or a concussion of the brain, depressing the mind and obstructing conscious access to Christ. The Christian, by thorough self-examination, should assure himself that no sinful act has veiled his inward vision of God. Then he may patiently and believingly wait for the veil to be lifted again, and continue to be lifted so long as he has a firm grip on the promises of God. For where sin is absent the Spirit's witness is intermittent, because faith is wavering. Hence the remedy is a greater familiarity with the Word and a constant personal appropriation of the full heritage of the believer, especially the great gift of the Comforter. When the Third Person of the adorable Trinity is fully received, or, rather, when He fully possesses us, there is no more interruption of His testimony to our sonship to God. For He is now the abiding witness. Ecstatic joy may come and go as the tides ebb and flow, but peace and assurance abide forever, as Miss Havergal so truthfully sings:

> "Like a river glorious
> Is God's perfect peace."

We advise the believer who does not dwell on the bank of this beautiful river to gather together the promises of Christ respecting the abiding of the Paraclete found in His last address before His death, recorded in the 14th, 15th and 16th chapters of St. John, and the numerous references to the same glorious theme in St. Paul's epistles, and especially in the First Epistle of St. John, where the mutual abiding is taught, "God in us, and we in God." In such a spiritual life, filled and interpenetrated by God, there can be no hiatus, no vacuum, and no place for doubt.

Where vital interests are at stake it is very comforting to know that we are on the winning side. Calmness and comfort came to the two hundred and seventy-six storm-driven souls on the coast of Melita when Paul stood forth and uttered the cheering message from God, "There shall be no loss of life among you." This seemed to be a non-forfeitable life-insurance policy, representing the Calvinian assurance of faith, unconditional because it is grounded on the decree of election and the assumed perseverance of the saints. But Paul made an important *addendum* to his prediction. When the tricky sailors were stealing the lifeboat to make good their own escape, that Roman prisoner, who had an angel for a cabin mate the night before, stood up again and said to the military custodian, "Except these abide in the ship, ye cannot be saved." This illustrates the Arminian conception of the assurance of eternal salvation. It rests upon the small word *if*. If the Christian perseveringly believes, he will be saved. Methodists, however, apply the term "assurance" to the consciousness of present salvation. It is the undoubted conviction of deliverance, here and now, from the guilt of sin and from the love of sin. Our doctrine of assurance is grounded on the direct witness of the Spirit, and not on the Word, as some assert, for it cannot certify the fact of my adoption. It is the office of the Spirit to give assurance of this fact by crying in our hearts, not in the Bible, "Abba, Father." But doubtless the inquirer who requests me to discuss this vital theme desires a more exact definition. It is not easy to explain spiritual realities in human language. It is a transaction wholly in the realm of spirit, invisible to the natural eye and inscrutable to the human mind. It is "the white stone and the new name written, which no man knoweth saving him that receiveth it." The direct witness is of the nature of a spiritual intuition, the voice of mercy speaking comfort to the troubled soul.

If you ask for the manner of this divine communication, I must reply, "The wind bloweth where it listeth," The manner of all knowledge is a mystery the attempted solution of which has given birth to all the philosophies, materialism, realism and idealism. In all communications from one mind to another there is the same mystery. The thought in my consciousness is conveyed to yours along a path which the wisest philosophers are unable to map out in their psychologies. Yet the mother looking down with a smile into the eyes of the babe a month old awakens a responsive smile. She has laid a cable to that little island and flashed the message of a mother's love. Cannot God do as much to a lost child seeking His face? Cannot He who made man unmistakably reveal Himself to him? Yes, assuredly. The manner is a speculative question which may be omitted, while we proceed to answer more practical questions.

Do we need any other evidence besides the direct witness of the Spirit to our adoption? Yes, we need the indirect witness, the confirmatory proof of the genuineness of the Spirit's testimony; for a person may imagine some flash of his own fancy to be the voice of the Spirit. This is the way fanatics are made.

What is the safeguard? The fruit of the Spirit perceived as existing in us— "love, joy, peace," and the whole train as in Gal. v.22. These are the marks of the regenerate state, and are needful not only for the purpose just mentioned, but also to sustain the believer when the direct testimony is obscured. There are cloudy days in the spiritual realm, when the sun is veiled and there is no ray of direct light. Then it is comfortable to walk in the light reflected from the clouds. In early Christian experience the direct witness is frequently intermittent. Then the indirect witness is of immense value to keep one from casting away his confidence in Christ. If one says that he has the direct witness of the Spirit to his adoption and continues to commit sin, he shows that he has not that saving faith that gives victory over the world. When Gavazzi, the great Italian orator, was last in America, he preached in my pulpit on justification by faith. His singular pronunciation riveted one sentence in my memory: "If a man says that he is youstified by faith and keeps right on sinning just the same as before, his youstification is a mistake."

The advantages of the direct witness are, salvation from doubt on fundamentals, certainty with respect to adoption and forgiveness, the joy of the Lord and the strength which always springs therefrom. It is the secret of Methodism and the source of her aggressive spirit and power. It gives positiveness and convincing cogency to testimony. Conscious salvation attested by the voice of the Spirit crying "Abba, Father," is a great safeguard against apostasy— 'the greatest next to the Spirit's work in entire sanctification. A sudden conversion, bright and joyful, is a towering monument in the memory. It is a rebuke to the backslider so long as memory is unshaken. A slave lad in the South was under a deep conviction for sin several months. At length his Christian mistress said to him: "Sambo, I think you have experienced religion, because you do nothing wicked; your life is greatly changed." To this the boy made this wise answer: "Not so, Missus. I don't want dat ar kind of religion that I can get and not know it, 'cause I might lose it and not miss it." A Christian life which has no spiritual birthday anniversary is not to be discounted or rated as spurious, for many are converted, especially children, without such a marked and memorable transition; but the ideal new birth of the New Testament, since the day of Pentecost, has a date to it which only the direct witness of the Spirit can impress on the mind.

But this suggests another question which perplexes many: Is it necessary to salvation? We have already hinted that an inference from the marks of the new birth found in us cannot save from doubt. Eternal salvation depends on faith in Christ. "He that believeth has the witness in himself." St. John, whom we quote, does not say whether this is direct or indirect and inferential. Some kind of evidence will follow saving faith. It may not always be joyful, or even satisfactory. It may be weak and only occasional. There are well-authenticated instances where persons have for years doubted their regeneration, and yet have lived on the right side of their doubts by fearing God and working righteousness. They were servants of God, as John Wesley was until he was thirty-five years old, when he emerged into conscious sonship. This he called his conversion, and wrote himself down in his journal as "a child of wrath, an heir of hell," till that event. But he afterwards annotated his journal thus: "I believe not. I had even then the faith of a servant and not of a son." To the passage, which declares that he was not converted himself when he went to convert the Indians, he appended as a note: "I am not sure of this. I was a servant and safe, but knew it not; but now I am a son and safe and know it." His final teaching on this point is this: "I have not for many years thought a consciousness of acceptance to be essential to justifying faith." He ascribes the absence of assurance in exceptional cases "either to bodily disorder, or to ignorance of the gospel promises." These exceptions under Methodist preaching in his day were rare indeed. He says that ninety-nine out of every hundred could tell the day of their regeneration by the Holy Spirit.*

The two witnesses. 1. We are taught in Rom. viii.16 that "the Spirit himself beareth witness with our spirit that we are children of God." The first is the divine testimony in every normal religious experience, a simple, undoubted, satisfactory and sometimes very joyful assurance, like an intuition, by which we are notified as from some outer source, and made to feel that all is blessedly right between God and our own soul, that His wrath is turned away and He loves us. This comes in answer to the prayer of faith, and in direction as if from the God to whom we pray and the Christ in whom we trust. Should a disobedient son speak through a telephone to his distant father asking his pardon, and receive through that wonderful instrument the words "My son, I fully forgive you," would he doubt that his father was reconciled? But the pardoned sinner who hears the Spirit crying in his heart, "Abba, Father," experiences the filial feeling suddenly warming his inmost soul, something the earthly father could not transmit by electricity. This the heavenly Father transmits by the Spirit of adoption.

2. The witness of our own spirit is inferential. We note the marks of the new birth as found in the Bible; then

---

*See Appendix, Note G

looking into our own hearts, consciousness discerns these marks, and thus lays down the premises for our inference that we are regenerated and adopted into the family of God. Thus the second witness is a self-judgment confirming the first.

Both are necessary and both should be constant. But the first is often intermittent in those in whom the fulness of the Spirit does not abide.

Chapter XVII
CHRIST'S TWO RECEPTIONS AND TWO BESTOWALS OF THE HOLY SPIRIT

SECTION 1. THE TWO RECEPTIONS OF THE SPIRIT

JESUS ON THE DAY of His baptism by John received the Holy Spirit in a manner which indicated that it was a permanent and not a transitory gift, for the Spirit descended and abode upon Him. A second reception of the Holy Spirit took place after His ascension (Acts ii.33). The differences of these receptions we may not be able to point out. But since the earthly life of Jesus is an example for His disciples, it is important to know just what the Spirit did for Him and whether we may expect Him to do the same for us.

We now come to the question, What did the first reception or anointing of the Spirit do for Jesus as a man? It certainly was not His entire sanctification, for He was perfectly sinless. It was something more than a visible consecration or setting apart for the work of the world's redemption. God does not do merely spectacular deeds. The form of a dove was designed for human spectators, but the reality, the descent of the personal Holy Spirit and His permanent abiding, was an uplift in the life of the Son of God on the earth and a special enduement for the work of redemption. From that hour He went forth in the power of the Spirit. His perfect manhood needed this enduement for the successful accomplishment of His mission. If this be true, does not every man and every woman need, in addition to perfect purification, the same empowerment for life's mission? For we believe with Dr. Bushnell, that God has a plan for every person's life, a work for every one to achieve. Moreover, we believe that this plan, if realized, will secure two ends, God's highest glory and our highest happiness. What a prerogative of personality it is that I, a creature, may advance the glory of the infinite Creator by reflecting His moral attributes and by giving a race of sinners a more worthy conception of His character! This can be done only by the fulness of the Holy Spirit exalting, intensifying and guiding our mental and moral faculties. Even entirely sanctified souls cannot depend on their unaided natural energies. Such souls are like the telegraph wire along which the lightning can flash, and not like a storage battery of electrical power. By the baptism of the Spirit, Jesus became such a battery. Many a Christian worker has failed to put on power, or has lost both native and divinely imparted power, by erroneously trusting to himself as a reservoir. The truth cannot be too strongly accentuated, that only when the human spirit is indwelt by the divine Spirit does it attain that clear insight, that emotional fervor, that spontaneity and maximum energy of will for which his Maker designed him. It is possible to avail ourselves of a power not of ourselves and to do things impossible to ourselves. We cannot stand in Boston and with the aid of our natural voice converse with a friend in Chicago.

But by utilizing a subtle and mysterious power called electricity I can perform that miracle. My speaking into the telephone and placing the receiver to my ear, thus connecting me with that unknown force, is an act of faith. It is impossible for me by my own energy to transport myself from Boston to New York in five hours. But I can by entering an express car subject myself to a power to do the impossible. This is an act of faith.

"All things are possible to God" and to him who is linked to God. Faith is the link. Hence "all things are possible to him who believeth." Hence I am accountable not only for what I can do, but also for what I *plus* available omnipotence can do. I attain my maximum power and answer the end of my creation only when I am to my utmost capacity filled with God by the fulness of the Holy Spirit. This important truth many fail to realize.

In the reception of the Holy Spirit by Jesus there are three notable stages. The first was the work of the Spirit in the creation of His humanity, in the miraculous conception which obviated the possibility of contracting any transmitted corruption from Adam, for He was the second Adam, the first term in a new series, while He was, by His birth from Mary, within the human family as a kinsman— Redeemer. The fact that "the child grew and waxed strong, filled with wisdom, and that the grace of God was upon him," is a sufficient proof that He was filled with the Spirit, as Luke ii.40 intimates, which in His early years imparted the consciousness of His divine Sonship and redemptive mission.

The second and enlarged reception of the Spirit was at His baptism or anointing for His public office of Messiah. Here was an external manifestation of the Three Persons of the Trinity: the voice of the anointing Father was heard; the anointed Son and the unction, the anointing oil, the dove symbolizing the Holy Spirit, were seen. The abiding of the dove on the head of Jesus is noted by John the Baptist as the fulfilment of a prophetic sign, "the Spirit of Jehovah shall rest upon him" (Isa. xi.2). As the

Son of God He may not have needed this anointing. But as the Son of man, made like unto His brethren to fit Him for His mediatorial work, which included a perfect example for His disciples, that unction was requisite for His complete qualification to be the Saviour of the world. It is worthy of remark that this visible display of the Trinity, and especially this descent of the Holy Spirit, took place while Jesus was praying to his Father probably for the greatest gift that He could send or that men could receive, the long-promised prophetic gift of the Spirit (Luke iii.21).

Henceforth His "commandments unto the apostles whom he had chosen were given through the Holy Ghost " (Acts i.2). His miraculous activity dates from His baptism with the Spirit. "The Spirit of life in Christ Jesus" may be regarded as the source of all His actions, and especially of that wonderful symmetry and balance of character, combining in perfection the most opposite qualities —boldness and meekness, self-assertion with deep humility, piety and impenitence, omnipotence and non-resistance, as described in Dr. Horace Bushnell's celebrated tenth chapter of his "Nature and the Supernatural," in which he constructs an absolutely unanswerable "argument for Christianity as a supernatural institution."

The third reception of the Holy Spirit by Jesus Christ was after His ascension: "Therefore being by the right hand of God exalted, and having received of the Father the promise of the Holy Ghost" — that is, the promised Holy Ghost— "he hath shed forth this, which ye now see and hear" (Acts ii.33).

This final reception of the Paraclete and His bestowment on all believers demonstrates several vital truths:

1. It is a fulfilment of prophecy. It is true that the Old Testament prophets speak so obscurely of the resurrection of the Messiah that the Jews did not, before the fact, interpret them as relaying to that event. Ps. ii.7; xvi.10;

Isa. liii.10; Hosea vi.2). But that glorious event is implied in the clear and undoubted predictions of the ascension gift, the reception of which is so distinctly foretold in Ps. xlv.7: "Therefore God, thy God, hath anointed thee with the oil of gladness above thy fellows." The anointing oil typifies the Holy Spirit. The ascension gifts are more clearly foretold in Ps. lxviii.18: "Thou hast ascended on high,… thou hast received gifts for men;" to the world the spirit of conviction, and to believers the Spirit of adoption and sanctification, the Spirit of love made perfect, and the fountain of joy, an artesian "well of water springing up unto eternal life." We are told in John vii.37-39 that the "rivers of living water" so frequently foretold by Isaiah as breaking out in the desert figuratively describe the Spirit, whose joyful and abundant effusion awaited the glorification of the ascended Christ.

2. It is a vindication of His righteous character. On earth He was accused of sin, of Sabbath breaking, of associating with sinners, of blasphemy, of non-conformity to the Jews' religion. They condemned Him to die with malefactors. What a reversal of that sentence it would be if news should come down from heaven that the condemned culprit of Calvary had been received in the court of heaven and had been crowned Lord of all the heavenly hosts! The descent of the Paraclete promised by Jesus when He should have gone to the Father is a positive proof that He has reached the throne of the universe and has been glorified. The gift of the Holy Spirit is a certificate of His holiness while on the earth. His going to the Father demonstrates His righteousness (John xvi.10).

3. It is a reward for His self-sacrifice. "Looking unto Jesus,… who for the joy that was set before him endured the cross, despising the shame, and is set down at the right hand of the throne of God."

4. As a credential of His Messiahship and supreme divinity. Previous to His resurrection the Spirit had been

bestowed as a personal gift. Now the power to bestow Him upon others, held in abeyance till after His resurrection and ascension, has full exercise— "a blessing so momentous that it may be described as that in which all other blessings are included."

None but God can fathom God. But "the Spirit searcheth all things, yea, the deep things of God. The things of God knoweth no man, but the Spirit of God" (I Cor. ii.10, 11). This omniscience of the Holy Spirit argues His divinity. Hence the power and prerogative of imparting Him demonstrates the Godhead of the Giver. This is the culminating proof of the divinity of our Saviour, even towering above His resurrection from the dead. What scriptural proof have we that the coronation gift, as a credential of divinity, was the Paraclete, or rather the power to bestow Him upon men? In the first place, we have the assurance that the Son would "pray the Father for the gift of another Paraclete" for His disciples. This implies that the Comforter was not then communicable. In Heb. i.8, when the Son of God is anointed above His fellows— all other kings— "he is addressed twice, at least once, in the vocative as God" (Delitzsch): "Thy throne, O God, is forever... Thou lovest righteousness, and hatest iniquity; therefore, O God, hath thy God anointed thee," etc.

5. "Declared to be the Son of God with power, *according to the Spirit of holiness*, by the resurrection from the dead" (Rom. i.4). The weight of scholarly exegesis is that the spirit of holiness is not the personal Holy Spirit, but the divine nature of our Lord. But it seems very much like a Hebraism for the Holy Spirit, whose effusion after Christ's resurrection supplied the most conclusive evidence of His supreme divinity. "The effusion of the Spirit on the apostles and on the Church terminated the controversy whether He was the Son of God. The communication of the Holy Spirit— a gift competent to no created being— proved Him to be the Messiah and the Son of God, ac-

cording to His own claim" (John v.19).* Our position in reference to this text is strongly confirmed by Paul's declaration that a personal Pentecost is an experience necessary to the reception of the doctrine of the Godhead of Christ. "No man can say Jesus is Lord, but in the Holy Spirit" (1 Cor. xii.3).

John implies the same idea in 1 John ii.18-20, where he predicts that *many antichrists,* or deniers of Christ's divinity, will come. Then he says, the same as to predict that the persons addressed would hold fast to that fundamental truth, "But ye have an unction [or *chrism*] from the Holy One," in contrast to the *antichrists* who left Christ and became *antichrists* because they had not the sanctifying *chrism,* the Holy Spirit.

One acquainted with the original tongues of the Bible has a perpetual memorial of Christ's fulness of the Holy Spirit in the Hebrew title "Messiah," and in Greek, "Christ the Anointed." He very early in His ministry makes a brief allusion to the future gift of the Spirit to the individual believer, in the words which Dr. Pope styles "the dawn of Pentecost." "How much more shall your heavenly Father give the Holy Spirit to them that ask him." Matthew reports the same saying of Christ, except that "good things" are instead of "the Holy Spirit." The two reports are harmonized by the idea that the Holy Spirit comprises all spiritual blessings.

6. As a complete endowment of Christ's mystical body, the Church. The reception of the Spirit by Jesus on the banks of the Jordan was for His personal equipment for His earthly mission. His reception of the Paraclete at the right hand of the Father, enthroned as the world's Redeemer, in answer to His prayer (John xiv.16), is for the conditional full equipment of His Church as an army commissioned to conquer the whole world. The condi-

---

*Professor Smeaton Cunningham, "Lectures," 1882, page 72

tion is that faith which bears the fruit of love and obedience(John xiv.15-17). Says Dr. C. H. Parkhurst: "There were no completed Christians till Pentecost, and there can be no completed Christians with the cessation of Pentecost. There was no Church till Pentecost, and a Church without a Holy Spirit is as much a delusion as a Church without a Christ."

SECTION 2. *CHRIST'S TWO BESTOWALS OF THE SPIRIT*

As there were two receivings of the Holy Spirit by Jesus, so there were two impartations to His disciples, one on the evening of the day of His resurrection and the other on the day of Pentecost. The exact import of these two receptions and bestowals has not been revealed. Yet it seems desirable that the two gifts of the Spirit to the disciples should be brought into harmony with each other and with the apostolical doctrine of the offices of the Spirit in the present dispensation. Clearness of doctrine is intimately related to unity of faith and uniformity in practice. We cannot accept the theory that the breath of Christ did not in any sense communicate the Spirit, but rather that it was a symbol and prophecy of the future Pentecostal gift. We prefer to say that something real was imparted, but far less than the fulness of the Spirit. "To understand John xx.22 as the outpouring of the Spirit, the fulfilment of the promise of the Comforter, is against all consistency, and most against John himself; see vii.39 and xvi.7." (Alford.) To understand it rightly, we have merely to refer to that great key to the meaning of so many dark passages of Scripture, the progress of doctrine in the New Testament. Christ's presence in that hour was a slight fulfilment, an earnest, of His manifest coming and permanent abiding in them by His representative, the Paraclete. This corresponds to the witness of adoption as stated in Paul's epistles, especially Rom. viii.16 and Gal. iv.6. It is quite evident that the apostles were previous to this hour in a state of salvation, but as servants rather than sons crying "Abba, Father." In the high-priestly prayer in John xvii they are spoken of as given to Christ, as having kept His word, as having all been kept, except the son of perdition, and as being "not of the world, even as I am not of the world," twice declared. This manifestly demonstrates that they were in a state of acceptance with God, but like all the Old Testament saints, destitute of the gospel blessing of the direct witness of the Spirit to divine adoption, the special prerogative of New Testament believers (John i.12). That the disciples were already born again and were then in possession of spiritual life, may be inferred from the words of Paul, "The natural man receiveth not the things of the Spirit," and the declaration of Christ Himself respecting the Spirit of truth, "whom the world cannot receive, because it seeth him not, neither knoweth him: BUT YE KNOW HIM."

Bengel well says that this bestowment of the Spirit is "the earnest of Pentecost." "It belongs to the peculiarities of the miraculous intermediate condition in which Jesus was, that He, the bearer of the Spirit (John iii.34), could already impart a special *first fruit*, whilst the *full outpouring*, the *baptism* of the Spirit, remained attached to His exaltation." (Meyer's Commentary.)

It is not derogatory to the apostles to say that they were up to this hour servants rather than conscious of sonship to God. Says John Wesley, who spoke from experience: "There may be foretastes of joy, of peace, of love, and those not delusive, but really from God, *long before we have the witness in ourselves*; yea, there may be a degree of longsuffering, of gentleness, of fidelity, meekness and temperance (self-control) (not a shadow thereof, but a real degree, by the preventing [preceding sonship] grace of

God), before we 'are accepted in the Beloved,' and, consequently, before we have the testimony of our acceptance: but it is by no means advisable to rest here; it is at the peril of our souls if we do."

This gift of assurance by the initial gift of the Holy Spirit was very timely. The day of Pentecost was seven weeks distant in the future. Suddenly bereft of the constant companionship of their Teacher and Lord, they needed special strength to keep them from fainting in spirit during this interval. Moreover, they needed the capacity to lay aside their worldly conception of the Messiah's kingdom and to begin to take in the new and spiritual view of that kingdom. The witness of the Spirit would enable the disciples to mount up with wings as eagles, to run and not be weary, and to walk and not faint, during this period of transition and suspense before the Spirit in His fulness should be poured out. "This gift," says Alford, "belongs to the Church in all ages, and especially to those who by legitimate appointment are set to minister in the churches of Christ, not by *successive delegation* from the apostles, *of which fiction I find no trace in the New Testament. That no formal gifts of apostleship were now conferred, is plain by the absence of Thomas,* who in that case would be no apostle in the same sense in which the rest were."

The experts are divided in their decision respecting the tense of the verb *to be* in John xiv.17. Meyer insists that "the preponderance of witnesses favors the future as in our Authorized Version, 'and shall be in you.'" These witnesses include the two uncial MSS., the Sinaitic and the Alexandrine; also the Parisian, the Vulgate, and the critical editions of Tischendorf, McLellan and Dr. B. Weiss. Westcott and Hort put a doubtful present tense, "is in you." The only uncial MS. which has this reading is the Codex Vaticanus; critical editions of Lachmann and Tregelles also have the present tense. But we are inclined to the reading of the future, "and shall be in you." How the Spirit was with the disciples and not in them may be explained by the fact that Christ, whose infinite capacity monopolized the Spirit, was with them, and so the Spirit was with them in His person. But this monopoly Christ did not carry to heaven in His ascension. "He breathed on his disciples, and saith unto them, Receive ye the Holy Ghost." This they needed to sustain their faith in the interval between His resurrection and the full outpouring of the Spirit at the coming Pentecost.

Some writers assert that the work of the Holy Spirit in the human nature of Jesus Christ is the norm or pattern of His work in the believer. This is true only in part. His humanity was endowed at His baptism by the Spirit with strength to do the redemptive work of suffering and death to which He was called (Heb. ix.14). Thus the disciples at Pentecost were begirded with strength to unfold and proclaim the remedial scheme in the face of persecution and martyrdom at the hands of both Jews and Gentiles. But here the parallel ends, for the first great work of the Spirit in men is the destruction of sin, from which Jesus was perfectly free. He was sanctified in the sense of being consecrated, or set apart by the Father, to atone for the sins of the world, but He was never purified from sin through sanctification of the Spirit, because He never sinned. They who urge believers to seek the baptism of the Spirit for service, as Jesus received it, are doing a good service to the Church; but they who proclaim this baptism for entire sanctification first and then as a full equipment for effective labor act more wisely, because the natural and scriptural order is cleansing before filling.

The liberalists make a similar mistake when they sum up the whole duty of man in imitating the example of Jesus. The example of Christ does not include the sinner's first and second duty, repentance of sin and seeking and finding forgiveness and the new birth. A regenerated soul's first need is inward entire purification, then strength for service.

A sinner's first need is newness of life imparted by the Holy Spirit, the Lord of life, before he can walk in the footsteps of Christ. In the plan of salvation there is a divine order which must be followed in order to attain the best results. In this order purity normally precedes power. This proposition implies that purity is not power. Jesus was perfectly pure and sinless during the thirty years preceding His baptism, but there was no miracle, no astonishing wisdom revealed to the people of Nazareth. He was known only as a blameless young man and a good carpenter. But when filled with the Spirit, "Many hearing him were astonished, saying, Whence hath this man these things? What is the wisdom that is given unto this man? and what mean such mighty works wrought by his hands?"

If even Jesus needed "the power of the Spirit," and did not enter on His work till He received it, surely every Christian needs the same power to do the public or private work to which he is called. But let him follow the divine order for its attainment: life before service, and purity before power. We do not deny that there are cases of effective service without newness of life, and the gift of power in the absence of purity. But these are abnormal cases foretold by Christ in Matt. vii.22, 23, "Lord, Lord, did we not prophesy in thy name? and in thy name cast out devils? and in thy name do many wonderful works? Then will I say unto them, I never knew you; depart from me, ye that work iniquity."

Chapter XVIII
THE PARACLETE'S "ECCE HOMO" IN THE BELIEVER

UNDER THIS NOVEL caption the reader is apprised that we will not discuss the supreme folly and wickedness of Herod's act of political expediency when he presented the Son of God to His enemies to be crucified. Nor are we about to criticise Guido's immortal painting of the thorn-crowned head of the Man of Sorrows. Nor have we taken up our pen to review that anonymous book which appeared thirty years ago, so fresh and original in style as to arouse the interest of two continents, yet so theologically indefinite that evangelical writers condemned it as rationalistic, and rationalists condemned it as evangelical. The title which we have chosen for this chapter implies that it is the office of the Holy Spirit to reveal Christ to the believer. We are not now purposing to dwell upon His office of inspiration by which He gave to the whole world an accurate history of the life and works of Jesus and a reliable record of His words. This exceedingly important function of the promised Comforter we pass by in order to amplify upon another function of the Spirit which needs special emphasis because it is more apt to be overlooked and forgotten— the inward revelation of Christ in the consciousness of the adult believer, as distinguished from that infantile faith by which a penitent is born into the kingdom of God. Uncertainty and doubt perplex and weaken immature Christians. Christ is to them an outside and distant person whom they endeavor with painful effort to bring near and to make real. They try to do the orthodox thing, to cherish certain beliefs about Him. But there is no warmth, no inspiration, no enthusiasm, no intense love. Their experience is much of the time dreary, and their Christian service is mechanical and constrained, not free, spontaneous and joyful. What is lacking? Not the new birth, but a definite experience which follows regeneration. The new birth implants love divine. When this love has been tested and strengthened by obedience it is our privilege by faith to have a spiritual manifestation of Christ in our hearts. "He that hath my commandments and keepeth them, he it is that loveth me; and he that loveth me shall be loved of my Father, and I will love him, *and will manifest myself unto him.*" In every generation since the day of Pentecost there have been witnesses to the fulfilment of this promise. They were never more numerous than they are to-day in all Christian lands and in all evangelical churches. They testify to a wonderful clearness of spiritual vision. Truth takes on reality and solidity. The eyes of the heart have been anointed as the recent application of the X-rays to fluorescent spectacles gives to the bodily eyes an amazing power of penetration called the fluorescent bath. Jesus is no longer a distant abstraction, but a person vividly near and real, the one altogether lovely. Love to Him now becomes intense, passionate and all-consuming. His commands are now delightful, and they are unhesitatingly obeyed. "When it pleased God," says Paul, "who called me by his grace, to reveal his Son in me, that I might preach him among the heathen [treated as dogs by the Jews]; immediately I conferred not with flesh and blood." There in Damascus the scales of Jewish prejudice fell off from his eyes, and the Spirit gave them a fluorescent bath by which he could see Jesus, not now in the clouds above, but in his heart an abiding guest. This explains his heroic career of labors, dangers and sufferings cheerfully undergone in attestation of the truth of Christianity.

"We are often where the Ephesians were when they said, 'We have not so much as heard whether there be any Holy Ghost.' What came to them and saved them was the Holy Ghost. What must come to us and save us is the same Holy Spirit. There they were holding certain truths about God and Jesus, holding them drearily and coldly, with no life and no spirit in their faith. God the Holy Spirit came into them, and then their old belief opened into a different belief; then they really believed. Can any day in man's life compare with that day? If it were to break forth into flames of fire and tremble with sudden and mysterious wind, would it seem strange to him— the day when he first knew how near God was, and how true truth was, and how deep Christ was? Have we known that day?

"The Holy Spirit not only gives clearness to truth, but gives delight and enthusiastic impulse to duty. The work of the Spirit was to make Jesus vividly real to man. What He did for any poor Ephesian man or woman who was toiling away in obedience to the law of Christianity was to make Christ real to the toiling soul behind and in the law. I find a Christian who has really received the Holy Ghost, and what is it that strikes and delights me in him? It is the intense and intimate reality of Christ. Christ is evidently to him the dearest person in the universe. He talks to Christ. He dreads to offend Christ. He delights to please Christ. His whole life is light and elastic with this buoyant desire of doing everything for Jesus, just as Jesus would wish it done. Duty has been transfigured. The weariness, the drudgery, the whole task nature have been taken away. Love has poured like a new lifeblood along the dry veins, and the soul that used to toil and groan and struggle goes now singing along its way, 'The life that I live in the flesh I live by the faith of the Son of God, who loved me and gave himself for me.'" (Phillips Brooks.)

Chapter XIX
THE HOLY SPIRIT AND CONSCIENCE

PROF. WHEWELL, IN HIS "Moral Philosophy," asserts that every human volition expressive of a choice has a moral character which would be perceived by our moral sense were it sufficiently keen. This is a declaration that there are no acts morally indifferent, styled by the Greeks *adiaphora,* such as the choice of the color of a necktie, the length of an overcoat, or the kind of food I may order for my dinner at a restaurant. Most of us are so morally obtuse as to see no ethical quality in these choices, and are disposed to call him morbid and impracticable who finds moral obligations in the selection of shoestrings. But we may be doing injustice to those rare consciences which have attained a more subtle moral discrimination than the multitude who laugh at scruples which they cannot appreciate. For it is possible that culture may impart such an insight into the tendencies of apparent trifles as to discern a disastrous moral outcome in the long run.

Examples of this moral sagacity are found in those who first denounce the skating-rink, the baseball team and the students' regatta. If all had been as sharp-sighted as the few, there would not have been so many bitter experiences. If there were an intuitive recognition of poison under all its disguises, nobody but fools would ever touch it. On many subjects there is no such delicate moral intuition in immature and uncultured minds. What safeguard, then, have such persons? Must they all then drink poison in order to find out its deadliness? No. Let the discerning warn the unwary, let the old caution the young, and experience counsel inexperience. Then those who believe may be kept from downfall, for a good moral character is conditioned on faith just as certainly as eternal salvation hinges on a persevering trust in Christ. In the sphere of morals this is the best that can be done for those who have not their external "senses exercised to discern both good and evil." But in the spiritual sphere into which all true believers have been translated, where there are realities too high for the intellect to reach and questions too subtle for so coarse an instrument as conscience to answer, God has provided another umpire perfectly competent for the guidance of the Christian. "Let the peace of Christ arbitrate in your hearts" (Col. iii.15, Revised Version, margin). "Wherever," says Bishop Lightfoot, England's greatest Pauline expositor, "there is a conflict of motives or impulses or reasons, the peace of Christ must step in and decide which is to prevail." This new arbiter is not peace with Christ, or reconciliation, but a far superior and subsequent experience, "the peace of Christ," the unfathomable ocean of His peace poured by the Holy Spirit into your soul in all the fulness of His incoming and abiding. This peace becomes the paramount consideration where there is an internal conflict. Everything which disturbs this profound rest of soul will be instinctively avoided, and every act that weaves the thinnest veil between you and the face of the adorable Son of God you will instantly shrink from. Thus believers who claim their entire heritage in Christ have an infallible arbiter in a sphere far above that of conscience. St. Paul intended something peculiar by the use of the Greek word for "arbitrate," found nowhere else in the Holy Scriptures, styled by Bengel "a remarkable word." Modern science constructs balances so delicately poised as to be turned by the weight of a fraction of a hair. The Christian may so far realize the higher possibilities of grace as to be even better equipped for testing human volitions. Let me illustrate. I am invited to be initiated into a popular secret order. Conscience does not object, but the peace of Christ does. A social club-house is erected in my town, and I am solicited to join. Conscience discerns no evil there, but the peace of Christ declines to enter where Christ Himself cannot be introduced and be assigned the seat of honor. The question of worldly amusements has for centuries been before the court of conscience, and no final decision has been reached. But it is quickly decided by the arbiter which the gospel has called to the judgment seat, "the peace of Christ." All truly spiritual minds all along down the Christian ages present a consensus of opinion on the deadening spiritual effect of the dance, the card-table and the theatre. Because this consensus has been formulated into a rule of life for the benefit of inexperience, a great outcry has recently been made by some who seem to have forgotten that Christian character consists in something more than good morals, and that its essential principle is spiritual life imparted by the Holy Ghost and sustained by converse with the skies. What all truly spiritual minds have found detrimental to the life of Christ in the soul should be avoided by all who aspire to dwell on what Joseph Cook has recently called "spiritual uplands." There are two classes of Christians. One class asks, "Is this amusement or indulgence forbidden? If it is not, I will embrace it." The other asks, "Is it obstructive of cloudless communion with the Father and the Son through the Paraclete? If it is, I will discard it." The one aims at innocence, the other at spirituality. The party of higher aim, even though it should be in the minority in any church, should prevail. Their standard should become universal. Thus will the unity of the body of Christ be promoted, as is implied in the words of St. Paul: "Let the peace of Christ arbitrate in your hearts, to the which also ye were called *in one body.*" Paul asserts his love for the Hebrew nation, his "kinsmen according to the flesh," declaring that his conscience was "bearing him witness in the Holy Ghost." This strong asseveration implies an intimate relation between the Spirit and conscience. We may not be able to give a full and accurate statement of this relation. Among the self-evident truths with which the human mind is originally furnished is the distinction between right and wrong. The power to discover this distinction inheres in every sane mind. On questions relating to immutable morality all such minds agree in their decisions. Such questions are few, and theoretical rather than practical. They are not modified by circumstances. They are such as these: Is it right to hate a benefactor? Is it right to punish the innocent? Is it right to reward the guilty? Is it right to intend injustice to a fellow man? Is it right to violate my own sense of right? to dishonor a parent? to commit adultery? There can be but one answer to these questions. They are addressed to the intuitive sense of right and not to the understanding or practical judgment which modifies the decision. But when we ask the question, Is this accused man worthy of punishment? we have now to exercise our judgment and go through a course of reasoning before we can decide, and two perfectly conscientious persons may disagree in their verdict, because we are now in the region of mutable morality. Most of the moral questions in daily life are of this character. It is not enough to know that one man has killed another. I must take into account the circumstances, whether it was in self-defence when attacked by a robber, or a burglar by night was shot in the act of breaking into the dwelling. This sufficiently illustrates mutable morality.

I can but think that the philosophy of Lotze and others is true, that all the self-evident truths are in the last analysis the activity of the immanent God in the human spirit. Hence the moral intuitions, immutable and invariable, are the voice of the divine Spirit immanent in all men, irrespective of regeneration and the gracious indwelling of the Spirit. There is a sense in which the Spirit of God is upholding nature. Men are not conscious of this immanent substratum of their being. But when the Holy Spirit, as a gracious gift, is bestowed upon the believer, he is conscious of His presence within as was Paul. The effect is manifest not so much in the increase of the power of moral discrimination, though it does clarify the moral perceptions, as in the marvellous addition to the power that impels toward righteousness. For the conscience has a threefold power— discrimination, impulse toward the right, and, after the act, approval or disapproval, according as the act is right or wrong. The gracious work of the Holy Spirit intensifies each of these functions, the second more manifestly than the first, and the third more than the second.

What effect does the fulness of the Spirit have in the decisions of practical questions in the province of mutable morality? We answer, it does not prevent errors in judgment and fallacies in logic. The Holy Spirit renders no one infallible in such matters. Yet He indirectly helps us by delivering us from the dominance of appetites and passions inimical to clearness of intellect and calmness of judgment. By inspiring in our hearts love to our neighbor as to ourselves, He strongly incites us to do perfect justice to him in our decision of questions involving his rights. Still the best of men and women who love God with all their hearts, and their neighbors as themselves, may go astray in judgment without a loss of love. Hence, in applying their intellects to the construction of systems of theology, some have founded Calvinism with its five points, unconditional election, a limited atonement, irresistible grace, bound will, and the final perseverance of the saints; and others equally devout and scholarly have constructed Arminianism with its universal atonement conditionally applied, the free will, entire sanctification possible before death, and the peril of a total apostasy from the highest state of grace. George Whitefield preached the first of these doctrines and John Wesley the last. Both were filled with the Spirit and were burning as bright candles of the Lord. Both were used by the Spirit to preach the saving truths of the gospel in such a way as to save multitudes of souls.

We do not teach that error is as good as truth in the production of holy character. We believe that in both the doctrines named there is saving truth because Christ is at the centre of both as the object of faith; and salvation consists in a vital union with Him and not in opinions about Him. The maintenance of a good conscience toward God from day to day is essential to the life of faith. The believer must aim at, must be satisfied with, nothing less than this. It is within his reach. Even the Old Testament saints had the witness that they pleased God. By a good conscience we mean an unaccusing conscience, not the assurance that we are exempt from errors in practice arising from misjudgments, but the consciousness that our intentions and aims are unselfish and holy. True spirituality cannot exist unless accompanied by scrupulous conscientiousness, the purpose to do right at any cost. If believers live as they should, they will find as the Christian life progresses, the testimony of conscience and the voice of the Holy Spirit becoming identical. As we have before intimated, the conscience is the activity of the Spirit of God, on the plane of nature, as Creator and Preserver. In regeneration and sanctification the Spirit works on the plane of grace, as the Reconstructer aiming to restore what sin had defiled.

It is interesting and instructive to note the relation of the Holy Spirit to conscience in the work of regeneration and sanctification. If man was created to be a temple of God, his spirit must be the holy of holies in which He dwells, and his conscience must be the ark of the covenant which carries His law. Sin defiled that sacred ark and rendered it offensive to the holy God. The scheme of redemption must have direct reference to the purification of the conscience. The writer to the Hebrews intimates that Mosaism "did not make him that did the service perfect, as pertaining to the conscience" (ix.9), and he exhorts the believer to "draw near, having his heart sprinkled from an evil [guilty] conscience" (x.22). The conscience, relieved of guilt through faith in the atonement made by Christ, and ever after prompting to a life of obedience, is the spiritual organ in which the Holy Spirit evermore dwells, keeping watchful guard over the living law in the heart and constantly witnessing to the persevering believer that he is a child of God. Peace, the fruit of the Spirit, can dwell only with a "conscience void of offence." Holiness, the work of the Spirit, is also attested by conscience. "For our glorying is this, the testimony of our conscience that in holiness we behaved ourselves," etc. (II Corinthians i.12, Revised Version).

This is the place to set up safety guards against the danger of a fanatical conscience, which is sometimes associated with extreme and erroneous views respecting the guidance of the Spirit. We lay down the following principles:

1. The Holy Spirit dwelling in the heart does not supersede the activity of our own reason, judgment and moral sense in the decision of practical questions.

2. While the Holy Spirit's testimony to the fact of adoption, including pardon, is direct and infallible when corroborated by the fruit of the Spirit, His guidance in the conduct of life is not designed to be sole and infallible, but in connection with the inspired Word, our own common sense, divine Providences and the godly judgment of Christian people.

3. No guidance is of the Holy Spirit which collides with the Bible inspired by the Spirit. In such collision the Holy Scriptures must be followed in preference to the supposed leading of the Spirit.

4. The *Holy* Spirit, so named because it is His office to create and conserve holiness, never leads into sin, nor to doctrines which belittle sin by denying its exceeding sinfulness and its desert of eternal punishment, or by weakening the motives to repentance.

5. It being the office of the Spirit to glorify Christ, no teaching that disparages His divinity as the only Saviour can come from the Spirit.

6. It being the work of the Spirit to regenerate and to sanctify, the declaration of any substitute for the new birth and holiness cannot be approved by the Spirit of truth, much less can it be inspired by Him.

7. In practical matters, the province of mutable morality, where fallible intellectual processes are involved and erroneous conclusions are possible, it is a species of fanaticism to ascribe such conclusion to the Holy Spirit.

8. There are two classes of people with whom pastors of churches have difficulty. The first consists of those who consider conscience as infallible beyond the sphere of motives, dispositions and principles, and insist on infallibility in all practical questions, the realm of mutable ethics. They demand that the decisions of the intellect in respect to all moral subjects should be regarded as always right and clothed with the authority of intuitive judgments. Just here is found a fruitful source of most dan-

gerous self-deception and of fanaticism in its various forms and degrees.

The second class includes those who make an analogous mistake in respect to the Holy Spirit. They insist that His infallibility, evinced in His direct witness to adoption, be carried into all questions of every-day life, questions involving intellectual research and the practical reason.

These erroneous claims respecting conscience and the Holy Spirit put these two classes beyond the reach of argument, persuasion and advice. If members of the church, they inevitably become dictatorial, censorious and schismatic.

Chapter XX
THE UNITY OF THE SPIRIT

THE APOSTLE PAUL BESEECHES the Ephesian church to be diligent, to be constantly keeping that essential unity which the personal Holy Spirit originates in the true Church of Christ. The element or principle in which this oneness is maintained is peace, "the bond of peace." The exhortation to diligence implies that in keeping this unity human agency must be vigorously applied. Why cannot the Holy Spirit alone continue that unity of which He is the sole author? We answer, that where there is an obedient will He could preserve that concord which He has produced, if it were the province of the divine Spirit to assimilate intellects as well as hearts. Grace does not harmonize divergent reasons and conflicting judgments. We are to think and let think, and accept the honest conclusion within the limits of Christian orthodoxy. We must within this sphere agree to disagree, as did John Wesley and George Whitefield on the five points of Calvinism, while still loving each other. The hearts of Barnabas and Paul were united while a practical question on which they differed made it expedient for them to labor for a season in different fields. The diligent endeavor which Paul urges the Ephesians to make is to be directed against magnifying differences of opinion on minor questions into causes of heart alienation. It requires constant effort to keep this threefold maxim:

> "In non-essentials liberty;
> In essentials unity;
> In all things charity."

The various sects which divide the Christian world can keep the unity of the Spirit and dwell in peace so long as they are filled with true charity. How can this fulness be insured? Can we originate Christian love? Can we love at will? No. But having in the divine promises a sufficient ground for faith in Jesus Christ, we may ask for the presence of the Comforter in our hearts, whose office it is "to shed abroad the love of God," which is always attended by love to all who bear His natural image, and especially to all who bear His moral image restored by the new birth. Here is the real basis of Christian unity. It is spiritual and not ecclesiastical; not theological beyond the basal truths of orthodoxy; not sacramental and ceremonial. The manner and significance of water baptism, the Lord's Supper and the number and gradation of ordinations should be regarded as in the sphere of liberty. Is God revealed in His divine Son, Jesus Christ, the only Saviour, and does He communicate Himself to believers in the personal Holy Spirit, the only Sanctifier? This is a doctrinal basis sufficient for the unity of all Christians. It is not possible to dwell in Christian unity with those who deny these fundamentals. They do not dwell in the same sphere with us, since they disclaim belief in the offices of the personal Holy Spirit and disbelieve in the Godhead of Jesus Christ, through whom we receive the Paraclete, who implants regenerating love and perfects sanctifying love, the element of Christian unity. Yet we should, without regard to religious belief, co-operate with all good citizens to abate and abolish evils which prey upon society, to enlighten the ignorant, to lift up the fallen and to remove snares from the feet of the tempted. While we believe that society can be most effectively regenerated by regenerating the individual, we should, while applying the truth to secure this end, cherish and express a lively sympathy with all who, though they "follow not us," are trying to cast out devils in the name of Jesus regarded as a mere religious teacher and reformer. They are, so far as the moral well-being of society is concerned, our allies in the great battle with the hosts of the evil one, though they are fighting with bows and arrows when they might be firing Remington rifles. But it must be borne in mind that Christian unity, as Dean Alford well says, "is conditioned and limited by the truth; and is not to be extended to those who are enemies and impugners of the truth;" who reject the real Christ and preach a phantom Jesus, and whose morals are as corrupt as their faith is false. To have fellowship with such a man is "to be a partaker of his evil deeds" (II John ix.11).

It is alleged by some that the fulness of the Holy Spirit received by faith in Christ's Pentecostal promise does not unite, but rather divides local churches. This is not true where the entire membership receive their full heritage. The members of such churches are welded together in the closest possible unity, such as extorted admiration even from persecutors. "Behold how these Christians love one another." Such a church is indeed a spiritual brotherhood.

> "One with our brethren here in love,
> And one with saints that are at rest.
> And one with angel hosts above,
> And one with God forever blest."

But where part of a church are only nominal Christians, baptized worldlings, who either never knew the Lord Jesus as their Saviour or have fallen from grace, there arises a division, caused not by the Holy Ghost, but by those professors who resist Him in His work of purification. This is what Christ Himself predicted. The founder of Christianity, in putting down the kingdom of Satan whose works He came to destroy, brought disturbance and division to every family, every synagogue, every city and every social organization, a part of whose members rejected Him while a part received Him as both Saviour and Lord. Real living Christianity is always a disturber of worldliness and sin, bringing a sword on the earth.

It is the mission of the Paraclete to reprove the world of sin, and if the world has been received into the Church it must be convicted of sin wherever it is found. Otherwise the Spirit would be unfaithful to His mission. He did not come down from heaven to promote discord, but peace on the basis of truth and purity. The resisting party desires peace by being let alone in sin. On whom should the blame rest? Who is responsible for the division and contention? Certainly not those who receive the message which is promotive of the object for which the Church was founded. This is to help its members to become Christlike. Those who reject this office of the Spirit to conform believers to the image of the Son of God are the disturbers of the unity and peace of the Church, and not those who live in harmony with the purpose of its founder. It often is true that a part of a church, frequently a small minority, have the scriptural ideal of what constitutes true prosperity and real strength, namely, a firm grip upon

God's promises and the presence in the church of the converting and sanctifying power from week to week; a zeal for the salvation of souls however poor and submerged in vice; a willingness to give for the support of the gospel from love to its author and an abhorrence of worldly devices for raising money by appealing to selfishness, to appetite, to frivolity and doubtful amusements. Christ is dishonored when His gospel is treated as not worthy of support for its own sake. The Holy Spirit is grieved when various sensual lures and baits, often in their character repugnant to the spirit and purpose of Christianity, are employed to support the gospel of Christ. When the spiritual few lift up their voice, protesting against yoking the world and the Church to draw the car of the gospel, instead of cheerful though self-denying gifts, the majority often are disposed to unfavorable criticism of their conscientious and spiritual brethren, creating a chasm between the members. In such a case, which is not imaginary, the Holy Spirit is not the cause of the division, but rather the absence of the Holy Spirit from the hearts of a part of the church creates the schism in the body of Christ, the visible Church. The cure is a universal baptism of the Spirit. There are other occasions for dissensions threatening the unity of the Church. One of these is partialities and preferences for preachers, one running to hear logical Paul and another desiring to listen to rhetorical Apollos, and still another admiring the earnest and impulsive Cephas. The remedy is to turn the thoughts away from the heralds of salvation to the divine personage who is dwelling in the temple of each believing heart. This was Paul's remedy for the strifes and divisions in Corinth. "Know ye not that ye are temples of God, and that the Spirit of God dwelleth in you?" (I Cor. iii.16). When the Church knows experimentally the indwelling Paraclete, dissensions cease and unity is insured.

Above the mists there are altitudes of Christian experience where believers see eye to eye. Intellectual differences which once stood between them like impassable mountains now seem to their downward gaze like molehills. It is possible to dwell amid the Alpine sublimities of truth so long as to drop our small measuring rods and to acquire larger ones commensurate with the grandeurs about us. It is the office of the Holy Spirit to lift aspiring believers to such Pisgah heights as Paul was familiar with when he prayed that the Ephesians "might be strong to apprehend with all the saints what is the breadth and length and height and depth, and to know the love of Christ, which passeth knowledge, that ye may be filled unto all the fulness of God," Wherever this prayer is answered there will be Christian unity.

> Plunged in the Godhead's deepest sea,
> And lost in its immensity."

Trifles will not unhinge and divide a company of such believers.

In His high-priestly prayer (John xvii.) Jesus prays for His disciples, "That they all may be one; as thou, Father, art in me, and I in thee, that they also may be one in us; I in them, and thou in me, that they may be made perfect in one." There are two kinds of church unity — mechanical like the staves of a barrel held together by the external pressure of hoops; and vital, like the roots, trunk and branches of a tree unified by the mysterious inward force which we call life. For which of these did Jesus pray? We find our answer in these words which He had just uttered, "I am the true vine" (John xv.1). He prayed for vital unity, the only oneness worth praying for. This is infinitely superior to that illusory thing after which many are striving, a church unity through an exterior governmental uniformity. Partisan unity is a good machine for developing political power, but it cannot be used by the great unifier, the Giver and Lord of life, the Holy Spirit. It is He who unites all regenerate souls to Christ, and hence to one another, by His creative and vitalizing touch, drawing all into a marvellous oneness, "a oneness spiritually organic, in which each personality, while quite exempt from *invasion*, falls under the power of a divine *cohesion* whose results in spiritual harmony of life and action will develop forever." (Moule.) The invisible church is always one body, of which the risen Christ is the Head. It would be a pleasant thing to have the invisible exactly commensurate with the visible containing all the members of the invisible church and no others. But under the present dispensation this can never be, because the doorkeeper of the invisible is the heart-knowing Spirit, and the doorkeepers of the visible Church are fallible men. This is hinted at very strongly by Christ in the parable of the tares and the wheat growing together until the harvest. He evidently had in mind the visible Church, also, when He compared the kingdom of heaven to "a drag-net that was cast into the sea, and gathered of every kind;... and they gathered the good into vessels, but the bad they cast away" (Matt, xiii.47). Such an instrument the Holy Spirit does not use. He takes the fish individually one by one; and no sorting is required. There is no discount of His results.

There can be no substitute for the Spirit in producing that unity which will endure all the changes and adversities of life, which will gain the approval of God as realizing His ideal of the Church, and which will savingly influence the world in answer to Christ's prayer for the oneness of all His disciples, "that the world may believe that thou hast sent me." This was the power which conquered the unbelief of the persecutors of the primitive Church. "Behold how these

Christians love one another!" This love did not arise from similar intellectual tastes, nor from assent to the same creed, but from the indwelling in their hearts of the same Holy Spirit inciting to mutual love. When love declines through a relaxation of faith and the uprising of selfishness because of the withdrawal of the Spirit from His conscious indwelling, divisions, parties, cliques and sects arise. When we walk along the shore of the sea we observe pools here and there with their inhabitants separated from each other by rocks and stretches of sand, preventing communication between them. This is because the tide is out. But when it again rises and floods the beach the separate pools are swallowed up in the one great ocean. When the Spirit pours floods upon the dry grounds, self is submerged and Christian unity is restored.

The maxim of Protestantism of the low-church, non-ritualistic type is this, "Where the Spirit is, there is the Church." The maxim of the Papist and sacramentarian is, "Where the Church is, there is the Spirit." In the first case the Spirit creates the Church; in the other the Church professedly insures the presence of the Spirit. But He dwells only in hearts, not in sacraments or in organizations. Hence no organization, however apostolic its history and successive in its ordinations, can secure the Holy Spirit. The unity of the Church, the real apostolic succession, is through the Lord and Giver of life, the Holy Spirit. Paul exhorts believers "earnestly to strive to maintain the unity of the Spirit [the oneness which He brings about] in [or within] the bond of peace," *i.e.*, the bond by which peace is conserved, which is love. As Christ came to establish peace on earth, so the Holy Ghost, "another Comforter," came to execute Christ's purpose, not by treaties formed by diplomatists, but by "shedding abroad the love of God" in the hearts of men. Says Chrysostom, "The Spirit unites those who are widely sundered by nationality and different manners." We see this verified as the result of modern missions, by which the Holy Spirit is putting the girdle of peace around our globe.

"We profess to desire earnestly the outpouring of the Holy Spirit, but we shall do well to note that one of the first things which the Holy Spirit will aim to produce in us will be this Christlike love to the brethren. How many brethren in Christ are now effectually separated from you by a high wall of social position, a wall of conventionality that has been reared by Christian pride? Were Christ's mysterious and unfathomable love to them to find its way, perchance, into your heart, how would it laugh at the huge hindrance of this wall, and by a breath cause it to dissolve into the ambient air! This is no hypothesis. In lands where the Spirit of God is poured out we are told of the sudden and beautiful flowing together of social streams that have flowed separately on for generations. Love like that which Jesus manifested to the Samaritan woman and to the woman who was a sinner, has now found new exhibitions of itself." (G. Bowen.)

Chapter XXI
ENLARGEMENT OF HEART BY THE HOLY SPIRIT

IT WAS THE PSALMIST who, according to the Septuagint version, testifies: "I ran the way of thy commandments when thou didst enlarge my heart." In his early spiritual life there was in this Old Testament saint the same straitness, slowness and lack of momentum which characterize young Christians in modern times. His service had been enforced by the law and its penalties. Duty was a word which had not been written over and almost concealed by the superimposed capitals which spell LOVE. But it seems there was a crisis in his religious life where constraint ends and joyous liberty begins; where irksomeness disappears and spontaneity in service is a permanent characteristic. The crisis which separates these two experiences is the enlargement of the heart. This is a figure for what St. John calls "perfect love," and which St. Paul elsewhere describes as "the love of God shed abroad in the heart by the Holy Ghost," though he once, at least, employs the Old Testament phrase: "O ye Corinthians, my mouth is opened unto you, my heart is enlarged." Reverse the order of these clauses, and we have the cause and the effect. A full heart makes an unloosed tongue. The inquiry is all-important, When is this crisis reached? Some say: "Never this side the dying bed." But no Scripture proof of this dismal doctrine is ever given. It is not true that the believing soul must be a partly filled goblet till it is overflowed by the waters of the river of death. Others say: All souls at the new birth are deluged with love to the brim, a love that drives their chariot wheels as swiftly as the mysterious electric current drives our street-cars up and down our tri-mountain city. Such a steady motive power is not the experience of multitudes, yea, the vast majorities who are truly regenerate. Their inertia is great and the impelling power is feeble. Indeed, something worse than inertia is to be overcome; a strong opposition often arises within, which it takes all their strength to overcome. They have not a heart at leisure from itself to concentrate upon the work of God. True it is that a few Christians, like John Fletcher, very soon after their birth into the kingdom, because of a correct apprehension of their privilege in the dispensation of the Spirit, are deluged with divine love and become giants in faith. The mass of believers are mere babes in spiritual development. They see days of great weakness and are often on the verge of surrender to the foe. Some, alas, throw away their arms and run away from the fight and never renew the battle. Others fight all their lives with foes in their own hearts and never overcome and cast them out. They have been told by their preachers that this war in the members is the normal Christian life. Hence, believing their preachers instead of the Word of God, they limit His power by their unbelief, and never gladly run, but always sadly drag themselves along the heavenly way. This large class of Christians need enlightenment and encouragement, and not denunciation. They need to dwell in thought upon "the exceeding great and precious promises," that they may have an experience of the "exceeding greatness of God's power to usward who believe." They need to lock arms with St. Paul and walk through his glorious epistles, and get his large view of the extent of Christ's saving power, since He has sent down the Holy Spirit, the Sanctifier. They should study the new Greek words which Paul coined to express the fulness of divine grace and the wealth of privilege which are the heritage of those who fully believe; such as that translated by "more than conquerer [sic]" (Rom. viii.37); "much more abound" (Rom. v.20, II Cor. vii.4); "and the grace of our Lord abounded exceedingly with faith and love" (I Tim. i.14). Especially should they ponder that declaration of God's ability to save, found in II Cor. ix.8, in which are two "abounds " and five "alls" — "God is able to make all grace abound towards you; that ye, always having all sufficiency in all things, may abound to every good work." They should daily repeat St. Paul's prayer for the Ephesians, emphasizing each petition, especially the ascription at the close, "Now unto him that is able to do exceeding abundantly [*superabundantly above the greatest abundance*, A. Clarke] above all that we ask or think, according to the power that worketh in us" (Eph. iii.20). There is not sufficient familiarity with the promises on the part of professed Christians. While unbelievers neglect the threatenings, believers are prone to neglect the promises of the Holy Scriptures. Again, the growing failure to magnify the Holy Spirit results in constraint and the legal spirit, instead of the freedom of the evangelical spirit, inspiring courage to run through troops of foes. How many so-called evangelical Christians there are whose creed is practically as defective as was that of the first believers in Ephesus: "We have not so much as heard whether there be any Holy Ghost" as receivable into the heart.

This important item dropped out of a Christian's faith palsies his tongue, paralyzes his hands and enfeebles his feet. If he is a preacher, his message will be delivered in the weakness of uncertainty and doubt. Splendid rhetoric and oratorical tones and attitudes are beggarly substitutes for the unction of the Holy Ghost. The anointed pulpit will always be mighty. The Spirit inspires fearlessness, imparts freedom of utterance, enkindles zeal and unconquerable love of souls. All of these are elements of genuine eloquence. They furnish the man, the subject and the occasion.

The formal prayer meeting would be transformed by the enlargement of the heart. Dumbness, the penalty of unbelief (Luke i.20), will find a ready and glad utterance, and the dry harangue will be replaced by the hallelujah.

Let the heart of Protestantism be enlarged by the fulness of the Comforter, and rivers of salvation would flow out unto the ends of the earth, vitalizing those organizations which He can use, and sweeping away those which have been devised as substitutes for His regenerating and sanctifying power.

How intimate is the connection between efficiency and success in saving souls and the fulness of the Spirit, may be seen in the study ot the lives of those among the laity and the ministry who have instrumentally turned many to righteousness. It is an open secret that their suasive power dated from the hour when their hearts were enlarged by the baptism of the Holy Ghost. From this experience in the city of New York, in answer to the prayers of a few consecrated women, Dwight L. Moody dates the beginning of his highest efficiency as an evangelist. This made Mrs. Catharine Booth's preaching so pungent in convicting of sin among the middle and upper classes in the West End of London; while by the same mighty power as a conscious experience, her husband, Gen. Booth, was conquering the slums in the East End of that city of nearly five millions of souls. Dr. Finney, after the Spirit anointed him, was like an electric dynamo from which streams of power went forth whenever he stood up to preach, and sometimes from his speechless presence. Benjamin Abbott, converted late in life, so extremely illiterate that he preached on the "oyster man," misreading "austere man," preached in New Jersey, Pennsylvania and Maryland under the anointing of the Spirit with so great success that thousands were added to the Lord. A layman by the name of Carpenter was comparatively a cipher in the Presbyterian church until he was filled with the Holy Ghost, when he became, through personal effort, the most successful winner of souls in his generation. He drew men to Christ to the number of several thousands as estimated at his funeral. These are a few instances out of myriads in which the baptism of the Spirit has given all the qualities requisite for moving souls from sin unto Christ, love, self-sacrifice, persistence, faith, fearlessness, tenderness and sympathy. We should have mentioned joyfulness as an element of great power in drawing sinners to salvation. Joy always attends the fulness of the Holy Spirit. It differs from all other kinds of happiness which arise from a pleasant environment and depend on things external and hence changeable and transient. The joy of the Holy Ghost is internal, abiding and eternal. The joy of men and women pelted with brickbats and rotten eggs, taking joyfully the spoiling of their goods, has a strange power to convince the persecutors of the truth of the gospel, on the principle that "the blood of the martyrs is the seed of the Church."

Chapter XXII
KNOWING THE HOLY SPIRIT

IN WHAT SENSE may believers know the Comforter? Jesus, who sends Him, assured His disciples that they should know Him because of His intimate relation to them, dwelling with them and ultimately being in them. The indwelling would be true after His future coming. If we fulfil the condition, which is love to Christ certified by obedience, we shall receive the Comforter and shall know Him. Of course we shall know when we receive so important a person. It will be a crisis marking a new era in our lives. It is evident that this is not inferential knowledge, though this is important as a confirmation. It comes from noting the fruits of the Spirit described in the Bible and comparing them with the Christian graces observed in ourselves, love, joy, peace, etc. Knowledge of God in the scriptural sense is assimilative. No man can truthfully say that he knows the Comforter when these fruits of the Spirit are absent. But knowledge of a person includes more than an acquaintance with his works. I had known the military career of Gen. Grant, and had read his brief despatches after his battles, but I had no personal acquaintance with that great soldier till one day in June, 1865, he permitted me to be presented to him and to shake hands with him on the veranda of a Saratoga hotel. I then for the first time knew Ulysses S. Grant.

In like manner we may have such a second-hand knowledge of the Paraclete as we find in the Holy Scriptures and in the testimony of persons filled with the Spirit, while strangers to the personal Holy Spirit. It is one thing to know much about Him; it is quite a different thing to have an intuitive perception of Him, and to feel the thrilling and transforming touch of His hand, and to commune with Him by day and by night more intimately than with any earthly friend. This is the kind of knowledge invoked in the so-called apostolic benediction. We do not understand that in our knowledge of the Holy Spirit we differentiate Him from the Father and the Son, though some eminent Christians testify to an acquaintance with each Person of the adorable Trinity, one in substance, but three in subsistences. If such a knowledge has been given to any believers, it is quite exceptional. It may be universal in the future world; it is certainly very rare in this. In our present state it is enough for us to receive the love of God and the grace of the Lord Jesus Christ, commingled in one blissful stream descending through the channel of the Holy Ghost. A distinctive knowledge of each person would tend to divide the divine substance and to lead to tritheism, three Gods.

In the scheme of revelation the Father revealed Himself in His incarnate Son. After His visible form was received by the cloud which hid Him from the eyes of His gazing disciples on the day of His ascension, the Paraclete was sent down to testify of the absent God-Man, to keep Him in the world's thought and to glorify Him who came to glorify the Father. Hence the Paraclete glorifies both the Father and the Son when He glorifies the Son. Hence Paul's prayer for the Ephesian church, "That the Father would give them the Spirit of wisdom and revelation in the knowledge of him." This and other texts show that it is not the mission of the Comforter to give prominence to Himself, but to Christ, to whom He bears witness. Thus "when a messenger comes to tell a king, when a witness gives a testimony for his friend, neither speaks of himself. And yet, without doing so, both the messenger and the witness, in the very fact of giving their evidence, draw our attention to themselves, and claim our recognition of their presence and trustworthiness. And just so the Holy Spirit, when He testifies of Christ and glorifies Him, must be known and acknowledged in His divine commission and presence." (Andrew Murray.) It is in this sense that we are to have a knowledge of the Paraclete while He holds up the light for us to see the Father in His adorable Son.

The apostles knew nothing of an unconscious incoming and indwelling of the personal Paraclete. Unconscious regeneration in water-baptism and unconscious reception of the Holy Spirit through a bishop's hands in confirmation are doctrines lacking Biblical proof, the only proof possible after the exclusion of consciousness. The philosophy of the mind seems to require that the introduction of another personality to me, a person, must be with my assured knowledge. If a human person enters my library and addresses me while writing these words, I know it. Shall I not know it if a divine person knocks at the door of my heart and, at my invitation, enters? Will not His personal presence be self-evidencing? Will not His testimony to my adoption prove that He is a Person because He has faculties responsive to my own? If He takes up his abode in me, and converses with me and inspires love in me to Him and the other Persons whom He represents, shall I not be conscious of His personal presence? Love is a spiritual energy which goes forth only toward persons, never toward things. We admire pictures and statuary, but we love persons only. "It is because the presence of the Spirit as the indwelling teacher in every believer is so little known and recognized in the Church; and because, as the result of this, the workings of the Spirit are greatly limited, that there is so much difficulty and doubt, so much fear and hesitation about the recognition of the virtues of the Spirit." (Andrew Murray.) This spiritual incertitude, these hazy Christian experiences and weakening and distressing doubts in respect to fundamental— the truth of Christ and personal salvation through Him— are the natural product of nebulous preaching on the subject of the offices of the Holy Spirit. This defective preaching comes from a negative experience of the fulness of the Spirit. Conversions take the type of doctrines. The Wesleys, after a long and painful search, received the direct witness of the Spirit to the forgiveness of sins. They immediately began to preach this doctrine, strange to that era of spiritual death, though shining in the New Testament as clearly as the midday sun. People were converted by thousands, of whom John Wesley testified that ninety-nine out of every hundred could tell the exact time of their saving acceptance of Christ. This is not the ratio of clear-cut conversions with a date among modern Methodists, because the offices of the Holy Spirit are not now so prominently and constantly held up before the people in the ministrations of the pulpit. What is the remedy? Let the pulpit be baptized with the Holy Ghost. Let preacher and layman who desire to know the promised Paraclete and to realize His indwelling, study the teaching of the Bible on this theme, especially the promises in the fourth Gospel. Gather these promises together and study them earnestly, and then turn to the Pentecostal fulfilment in the Acts, and to the full development and application of this doctrine by the apostolic writers, especially John and Paul. Approach these epistles athirst to find the artesian well of "waters springing up unto everlasting life," and to drink evermore therefrom. Study prayerfully and with faith all that the Spirit of inspiration has put on record respecting Himself and His indwelling and blessed work in your heart. Study in dependence on the Spirit, who alone can unlock the Word that He has inspired. Study with a will ready to follow whither the Spirit may lead, and with a complete self-surrender to God and that perfect self-effacement which Paul describes as a double crucifixion, "the world has been crucified unto me, and I unto the world" (Gal. vi.14). Consecration is indispensable to the successful study of this high theme. It clarifies the intellect, dispels prejudices and misconceptions, and unifies and strengthens all the faculties. In this attitude of hearty consent to the leading of the Spirit, obedience to Christ and crucifixion of the flesh, the persevering believer will soon find the Spirit working in him, first as a search-light revealing impurities and mixed motives never discovered before. Then, if the will consents to their removal, the Spirit will entirely cleanse the temple of the heart and permanently fill it with His glorious presence. He will beautify His sanctuary with the entire galaxy of Christian virtues. He will strengthen its walls and make them impregnable to all assaults from without, and He will insure loyalty within by His constant indwelling "who yearneth for us even jealously" (James iv.5, Revised Version, margin). We must remember that in both the natural and the spiritual world knowledge is preceded by faith. We must believe the Holy Ghost before we can know Him. Every altitude of higher knowledge must be the result of a stronger trust. Faith must be the habit of the soul that aspires after constant growth. Faith ever has to do with the invisible and the seemingly unreal. The Paraclete is unseen to the natural eye, and the inner eye of reason does not recognize His existence. Hence faith is the only door for the Spirit to enter and the only atmosphere in which He can dwell. There is no way of knowing the Holy Spirit but by possessing Him and being possessed by Him, just as there is no way of knowing life but by living. In fact the Holy Spirit is the life of the believing human spirit. The spiritual life is as real to consciousness as the natural life.

The declaration of Christ is, "Ye know him, for he abideth with you, and shall be in you." We see no form. We hear no sound. We feel the touch of no hand. The Spirit does not address any one of the five senses when He creates the soul anew. Spiritual things are spiritually discerned by minds quickened into spiritual life by the omnipotent Spirit, the giver of life. In regeneration the Spirit is inscrutable, His act of new creation is to the subject a fact, a something done in an unfathomable depth below his consciousness. This fact is recognized only by its effects. He knows that he is a new man, that he is fundamentally changed in all his tendencies, that he is released from his accusing conscience, that his past sins are forgiven and that he is no longer cowering beneath the wrath of God, but basking in the sunshine of His love. He no longer thinks of Him as a police judge sentencing him to a deserved punishment, but as a loving Father. The filial feeling has been suddenly and mysteriously inspired in his bosom, and he hears with his spiritual ear new words sounding in his heart, "Abba, Father." Almost involuntarily he utters them with his lips. He is conscious of a spiritual transformation. The personal agent he does not perceive. In fact the personality of your most intimate friend you have never directly seen. Personality is spiritual and is recognized only by its effects— words, smiles and other actions. You may therefore know the Holy Spirit's personality by His works in your own consciousness, as certainly as a son may know his father with whom he has daily intercourse. We say this to show that spiritual knowledge has the same certitude as our knowledge of men and things around us.

"It happens sometimes that the indwelling of Christ and God and His Spirit signalizes itself with such an energy in the believer that the human individual life is overflowed and swallowed up by the divine as a river of delight... In other cases it is certified that the walk of the Christian is in heaven actually (Phil. iii.20, compare Zech. iii.7), by the fact that the future glory is not merely revealed to his perception as a subject of hope (I Cor. ii.9, 10), but is given him for a moment to see and share in by way of foretaste."* This is a state of ecstasy, the highest experience of heavenly blessedness and of a knowledge of the mysteries of the kingdom of heaven. The recipe for the attainment of this knowledge is found in Matt. v.8, Luke x.22.

Some may be inclined to ask another question, How do we recognize the Holy Spirit? How do we know that it is He and not some lying spirit who is speaking to us? The *how* of all knowledge is mysterious. The philosophers are not agreed in the method of our knowledge of the external world. Some assert that we know only our own sensations and ideas, and therefore we are not sure that there is a material world external to our minds. These idealists are inclined to apply the same reasoning to Christian experience and to insist that it is all subjective in its origin, that there is no God in it, that all the changes supposed to be wrought by a divine person outside of us, regenerating, forgiving, witnessing, sanctifying and indwelling, are from hidden causes in our own minds. This kind of reasoning would deny the existence of any human personality outside of ourselves, as well as any material existence. It would reduce all phenomena to our own consciousness and ourselves to a string of sensations.

---

*Delitzsch's "Biblical Psychology," pages 418, 419

All these absurdities must follow the admission that all our religious experiences are only varying states of our own thoughts and feelings with no external cause. Such a conclusion we are not prepared to accept. When the morning light dispels the darkness, I know that the sun has arisen, and I do not need a candle to see him rise. So when amid the gloom of condemnation for my sins, while trusting in Jesus Christ, a light suddenly shoots into my mind and a voice within cries "Abba, Father," and the feeling of dread is suddenly changed to filial love toward God, I know that a divine messenger is announcing forgiveness of my sins. This divine sunrise is self-evidencing. I need no rush-light of human philosophy or testimony to certify it. What has taken place is that my dead soul has been made alive. This life has quickened my dormant power of spiritual perception, so that I know by unerring intuition the presence of God the Holy Spirit. "To know the Spirit," says Murray, "is the divine foundation of certainty." Christian experience rests upon the same basis with mathematics and all philosophy—"self-evident truth, the activity of the immanent God in the human soul." (Joseph Cook.)

But we are not left without some light upon the question how we know the Holy Comforter. John says, "Ye know him, for he shall be in you," or as the Revised Version, "He is in you," the future being by prolepsis spoken of as present, as Alford thinks. The abiding indwelling of the Spirit is assumed to be in the consciousness of the believer.

He who knows the Holy Spirit will always have the Spirit's fruit as a confirmation of His inmost indwelling. But the knowledge is not the result of the fruit, but its cause. He must know in order to have love, joy, peace, etc. He knows directly by intuition, and not inferentially. Hence he needs not to be told by some experienced Christian, "This is the Holy Ghost." He needs no such introduction. The Spirit of truth brings His own credentials with Him, which even the most illiterate can read. He may not be able to tell the distinctive marks by which the voice of the Spirit is distinguished from the suggestions of his own heart, but he instinctively feels them. He recognizes the Spirit of God as a solid and eternal reality, while the world with its glitter of gold, and rank, its style, pomp and power, is a brilliant but vanishing vapor. Hence he is ready, if he must choose between grieving the Spirit and the loss of all earthly good, to go to a martyr's death at the stake or block with shouts of joy. If you think I am theorizing, read Ulhorn's "Conflict of Christianity with Paganism" and Fox's "Book of Martyrs."

He who knows the Spirit quickly recognizes the stranger who has the same knowledge, when all the rest of mankind fail to discern the invisible seal of God in his forehead.

He does not look at the denominational badge. He is free from any overweening partiality to some particular earmark when the name of Jesus is on the sheep, for the Spirit of God dwells in all real saints.

"Names and sects and parties fall;
Thou, O Christ, art all in all,"

The explanation of this fact is that the Paraclete is the bond of union, the Spirit of life, connecting each believer with all others by uniting them with our risen Lord. We have in our modern times telephones, which so transmit speech as to bind up into a social union and possible daily converse millions of people separated by hundreds and even thousands of miles. This is possible only by having all the wires meet at a common centre. This centre of Christian union and communion through the Holy Ghost is our glorified and adorable Lord Jesus. The agency of electricity in the social union of mankind is a faint reflection of the agency of the Holy Spirit in the spiritual union of Christians. The wonders of science on the plane of nature are of small account when compared with the wonders of the Spirit on the plane of the supernatural.

That the Paraclete may be received unconsciously is a corollary of the doctrine that He may be imparted by the hands of a bishop apostolically ordained. There is room for great error in the idea that the Holy Spirit is given in the rite of confirmation while the supposed recipient is in utter ignorance of this important event. For neither do the lips nor the lives of a majority of persons confirmed attest any real reception of the Sanctifier. It is in keeping with that baptismal regeneration which produces no change in the consciousness, conduct or character. The Holy Spirit received and not known may withdraw and not be missed. That reception of the Spirit of adoption uttering not the cry "Abba, Father," and certifying His incoming only by what Phillips Brooks styles the myth of apostolic succession, must be a delusion and a snare founded on the false maxim, *Ubi ecclesia, ibi Spiritus,* Where the Church is, there is the Spirit; instead of the converse based on the Holy Scriptures and common sense, *Ubi Spiritus, ibi ecclesia,* Where the Spirit is, there is the Church. Archbishop Whately intimates that he whose hope of final salvation rests on his ability to prove the apostolic validity of the sacraments has a painfully dubious prospect of inheriting eternal life.

Chapter XXIII
THE FREEDOM OF THE SPIRIT

"WHERE THE SPIRIT of the Lord is, there is liberty." The words "freedom" and "liberty" are found in the New Testament, but they do not have the meaning which is attached to them in treatises on the Will. It is a remarkable fact that there is no attempt in the Bible to prove human free agency, as there is no demonstration of the existence of God. Both of these fundamental truths are assumed without proof. Moral obligation implies freedom, and consciousness asserts it. This kind of freedom has been called *formal* freedom, to distinguish it from that *real* freedom which Christ promises: "If the Son shall make you free, ye shall be free indeed." Since this freedom is the gift of Christ, it is evident that it is not an attribute of man in his fallen estate. It belongs only to the true believers in the Son of God. It is not a deliverance from any bolts or bars or yoke of necessity outside of us, but from "the law in our members," in the will itself, a uniform tendency to yield to the sway of the depraved sensibilities which give birth to sin. When conscience forbids what inclination strongly desires and evil habit draws us to, there is a collision of forces which, without the intervention of Christ, the great Liberator, invariably ends in bondage. "O wretched man that I am, who shall deliver me?" This is the universal cry with all thoughtful souls recognizing obligation to the moral law but without help from above to keep it.

"They see the right, and they approve it too;
Condemn the wrong, and yet the wrong pursue."

This produces a degrading sense of servility. One bright moral ideal after another fades away. After each moral defeat the aspirant after true excellence lets down his standard with a self-loathing and wretchedness befitting one who has voluntarily sold himself into slavery. Thus thousands of noble souls who began to climb the mountain with the motto "Excelsior," have begun to descend, having insensibly changed their motto to "Inferior."

There is only one remedy. Some power must enter into them which can harmonize inclination and conscience in such a manner as to enable the man to do just what he delights to do and at the same time to do exactly right. When desire and duty become one, the soul is truly free and truly happy. How is this identity of duty and desire accomplished? The Stoics endeavored to reach the same end by extinguishing the latter, but they failed. God does not lead men up to perfect freedom by mutilation, but by purification. When we desire only God's will, we will delight in His law. There are minds which cannot be subject to God's law. Still they are accountable. They can consent to the reconstruction of their natures by the extinction of carnality and the renewing of the Holy Ghost. They are, through Jesus Christ, endowed with the gracious ability to repent and to receive Him as their Saviour and Lord. This is initial salvation, or prevenient grace. It is for the will to determine whether this shall become real and complete deliverance from the enslavement of depravity. One would suppose that this is the only choice morally possible to a rational being, since all men abhor personal slavery and political bondage. But we need not go far to find abundant proofs that the so-called "natural man" prefers the despotism of sin to the freedom of righteousness. There is no more hopeless condition than delight in spiritual bondage. In a former generation the saddest parents in America were those who, after converting all their possessions into gold to ransom their sailor boy from captivity in Algeria, received back their money from the consul with a message that their son refused to be redeemed because he preferred the society of his barbarian captors to that of his Christian kindred. He had married a Bedouin wife, contracted nomadic habits, and become fascinated with the pleasures of the lawless Arabs. This is a mirror in which every impenitent sinner may see himself. He is redeemed by One who has paid an infinite ransom; yet for the evanescent and degrading pleasures of an hour he scorns freedom and hugs his chains. He persists in this through all his earthly probation. What would the liberalist do with such a being if he were in supreme authority over him? The question is a fair one. Let there be a candid answer. We have hinted at the way of obtaining spiritual freedom. It is only through the power of Christ, the great Emancipator. Our part is an all-surrendering trust in Him. Says Thomas à Kempis: "My son, thou canst not have perfect liberty unless thou wholly renounce thyself. They are but in fetters, all who merely seek their own interest and are lovers of themselves. Keep this short and complete saying: 'Forsake all, and thou shalt find all. Leave concupiscence, and thou shalt find rest.'" This gives God a chance to do some very needful work inside, even to put His law in the heart.

When this is done, the law, instead of a yoke galling the neck, becomes a well-spring of joy. "Thy statutes," says the Psalmist, "have been my songs" — the Ten Commandments set to music! Only those whose hearts are perfected in love shed abroad by the Holy Spirit can ever learn that tune. It is the first rehearsal on the earth of the new song they are singing in heaven, the song of Moses and the Lamb, the law and the gospel harmonized.

Hitherto we have spoken of the negative side of spiritual freedom. There is a positive side. The love of God filling the soul and excluding all antagonisms, guarantees the unfettered action of the higher nature, restores the man to himself, and makes him his own master, because God has now perfect sway over his will. This is the gospel paradox— rest under a yoke; Christ's *doulos* (slave) and the Lord's freeman. The free are exhorted to use their liberty as the bondservants of God. This is because the highest freedom is realized when the heart is perfectly captivated by the divine love and the will is completely enthralled by the divine will. Faber seems to have experienced this paradox which prompted his hymn to the divine will:

> "And He hath breathed into my heart
> A special love for thee;
> A love to lose my will in His,
> And by that loss be free."

But what are we to understand by being free from the law? In answering this question some have fallen into the error of antinomianism, the denial of obligation on the part of the believer to keep the moral law.

1. He is not under the law as the ground of justification, the blood of Christ being his new plea; nor as the motive to service, love to the Lawgiver having taken its place; but he is under the law as the rule of life, although

Christianity puts man's spontaneous obedience in the place of the act legally enforced, his independent decision in lieu of legal necessity. Thus love unconsciously fulfils the law. It implants the principle of obedience in the heart so that it is free, unconstrained and natural. This is "the law of liberty" of which St. James speaks. I do not wonder that he calls it the "royal law," *i.e.*, the king of all laws. For he whom the love of Christ constrains in all his acts obeys the highest law in the universe. This is Christian perfection. This is being free indeed. This is the heritage of all believers. Reader, if you have not received this heritage, the reason is not found in the unwillingness of the executor of Christ's last will and testament, the Holy Spirit, to hand over your portion. You have not fulfilled the conditions of its reception.

We come now to consider spiritual freedom as related to the moral law, and to anchor a buoy over the hidden rock of antinomianism.

The Jews did not make a distinction, as we do, between the ceremonial, the civil and the moral precepts of the law, but thought that all should be honored by obedience with the same pious regard. As with devout Romanists in our times, the neglect of a mere ceremonial requirement was in heinousness equal to the infraction of a command of the decalogue. It is this use of a term embracing such diverse meanings that makes the intelligent reading of the New Testament difficult. It is the purpose of this section to relieve this difficulty as far as possible. It may not be known to many students of this volume that twelve of its books— nearly one half— do not contain the ambiguous word law. These are II Corinthians, Colossians, I and II Thessalonians, II Timothy, I and II Peter, Jude, I, II and III John and Revelation. This is encouraging to those who have sweat in their endeavor to understand St. Paul and harmonize him with James. It may help the reader of the Greek Testament to know that when James uses the word law without the article he designates only the ethical portions of the Mosaic law. It will be of advantage to all Bible students to bear in mind the fact that in the Epistle to the Hebrews the ceremonial part of the law is the prominent idea. It should also be noted that in the other books this term is so often referred to as to show that the writer or speaker has his eye on the ethical part alone as of perpetual obligation, the ceremonial and civil precepts being no longer binding on Christians. It is ethical where it is spoken of as fulfilled by love, as in Rom. xiii.8, 10, Gal. v.14; also where its perpetual validity is declared, as in Matt. v.18; and also in cases where it is equivalent to the principles of right imbedded in the human conscience, as in Rom. ii.14, 15. St. Paul uses "law" in a peculiar sense as a uniform tendency or dominant impulse. The moral law when used as a sword piercing the conscience is the occasion of an opposition so strong that the apostle calls it "another law in my members, warring against the law of my mind." Here we have the bent to sin inherent in human nature in conflict with the rule of action prescribed by reason, Rom. vii.23. On the battlefield of this chapter grace does not appear, nor is the Holy Spirit one of the combatants. In chapter viii.2 He does appear as a conqueror, under the Pauline phrase, "the law of the Spirit of life," the impulse to right action imparted by the Spirit when He breathed life into the dead soul.

But we apprehend that most Bible readers are in perplexity respecting the declaration that believers are "not under the law" and are "free from the law." Is St. Paul referring to the moral law? Yes, to the whole law. Then how can a man be righteous irrespective of law? Does not righteousness imply a standard of right to which the individual conforms? Yes, every true believer enthrones the law of God in his heart and swears eternal allegiance thereto. When St. Paul says that I am "not under the law,"

I am "free from the law," he does not mean that I am removed from the realm of moral law, for it is so imbedded in my mind that its removal would destroy me by blasting the image of God in me. Hence God's law cannot be abrogated in the sense that I need not obey it, but it is abrogated in the sense that it is, through faith in Christ, no longer the ground of justification. Were I shut up to justification only through the plea that I have never transgressed the law of God, I should be in utter despair, for I have violated my own sense of right and can never be justified by the works of the law. Against this plea "every mouth is stopped, and all the world is become guilty before God." But thanks be to God through Jesus Christ, a new ground of justification is presented. If by faith I plant my feet on this ground, and instead of insisting that I have never sinned, I say, I have sinned, but Thou, O Son of God, hast died for me, I will find not legal acquittal but gracious pardon. In this sense I am free from the law. But it is still my rule of life. Grace enables me to obey it in the future so that I may be free from condemnation.

2. There is another sense in which the believer is free from the law. He is delivered from the fear of the penalty of the law as a motive to service. Love to the Lawgiver has taken the place of tormenting dread, so that the believer is no longer servile in his obedience, but free and joyful. Duty, that unscriptural word, is now no longer on the lips or in the thoughts. It is concealed by the word love written over it in large letters. If disquieting fear of the law still vexes the soul in any degree, however slight, it is because love has not yet been made perfect in kind by the exclusion of every antagonist. This is St. John's explanation.

3. This brings us to a third sense in which we are free from the law — as the instrument of entire sanctification. The law has no power to slay our inward foes, to cleanse from depraved tendency. We cannot sanctify ourselves

by the most vigorous application of the law. It is not the province of the law to cure the depravity which it reveals. This is the office of the Holy Spirit, so called because it is His prerogative conditionally to create and to conserve holiness. It is my opinion that no mistake is more common among Christians than the idea of sanctification by the works of the law. For men may be as legal in seeking freedom from depravity as they are in seeking deliverance from guilt. This idea lies at the root of gradualism, or the denial of the extinction of the propensity to sin by the Spirit's finishing stroke. Only those believe in the instantaneous extinction of inbred sin who magnify the office of the personal Holy Spirit, the Sanctifier. "Then will I sprinkle clean water upon you, and ye shall be clean: from all your filthiness, and from all your idols, will I cleanse you. A new heart also will I give you, and a new spirit will I put within you." "This promise," says Henry, the incisive commentator, "signifies both the blood of Christ sprinkled upon the conscience to purify that and to take away the sense of guilt, and the grace of the Spirit sprinkled on the whole soul to purify it from all corrupt inclinations and dispositions, as Naaman was cleansed from his leprosy by dipping in Jordan." Henry interprets this promise as inclusive of both justification and entire sanctification, or the extinction of sin considered as a principle infecting our nature. Thus impersonal law is not abolished, but is transcended, in both justification and sanctification, by the personal Holy Spirit, the Lord of life and author of purity.

Chapter XXIV
TESTINGS OF THE HOLY SPIRIT

THE GREAT CONDITION on which the Paraclete is given to any believer is love to Christ evinced by obedience. He may think that he loves Christ and be sadly mistaken. His Christ may be a false Christ, a figment of his own imagination, a liberalistic Christ who will save all men on their own terms, or a fragmentary Christ with justice and all the sterner qualities omitted. There is many a nominal, but only one real and saving Christ. Hence tests are required to prove whether we are really obedient to the true Christ, whether, in the words of John Wesley, "naked we are willing to follow a naked Saviour." This means whether at the loss of all things— property, friends and reputation— we will follow a pauper Christ with no hope of any reward this side of the resurrection of the just, and possibly a chance for martyrdom. Will we sell all to buy the pearl of great price? Essentially this test is required of all: "Will you hold all else as cheap, yea, worthless, in comparison with Christ?" The literal divesting ourselves of all our possessions which are necessary to give us a foothold of vantage and usefulness may never be required by the Spirit. Christ required it of but one person. If he had obeyed promptly, I doubt not that Christ would have taken the will for the deed and would have made him His steward to hold and administer the estate in the interest of his Master, honoring every draft he should make.

In the nature of the case there are definite limits within which the Spirit applies His tests. He never requires us to do wrong, to violate our own sense of right. To deny this is to open the door for the worst forms of fanaticism and to justify the most flagrant iniquity. It will not do to cite the command to Abraham to sacrifice his son. He may have deemed it his parental right to take the life he had imparted. This instance affords no argument against our position, for the whole transaction, the command and the interposition, are on the plane of the supernatural. Nor does the Spirit require any one to disobey the code of minor morals, good manners.

It should be noted that tests may be presented by Satan when a believing soul is aspiring to receive the fulness of the Spirit— tests repulsive and offensive, in order to discourage a perfect self-surrender to God. At such times a cultivated Christian woman says that she is always confronted with the question whether she will, uninvited and unauthorized, make public addresses for Christ in the waiting-rooms of railroad stations, hotel parlors and steamboat saloons. Her sense of propriety prompts her to say "No." Another well-balanced woman is asked, when in the act of consecrating all to God, whether she is willing to be like some slattern who professes to be wholly the Lord's, and deems it a sin to make her toilet before a mirror. Her good taste says "No." A man of a bilious temperament, subject to wasting fevers, is asked, while in the act of supreme surrender to Christ, whether he is willing to go to the Congo Mission. Knowing his disability and the adverse opinion of medical experts, and not being eager for a martyr's crown in six months, he says "No." In all these cases this negative answer is used by the tempter to shake the believer's trust in Christ and cheat him of his full heritage. What he should do is to put all these questions aside and to promise that after receiving the desired blessing he will follow his best light derived from the indwelling Spirit, the Holy Scriptures, his own God-given common sense, his own abilities, his circumstances, providential openings and shuttings, and the godly judgment of the church to which he belongs. By thus doing he will thwart the adversary and receive the Sanctifier.

Says F. B. Meyer: "Expect the Holy Ghost to work in, with and for you. When a man is right with God, God will freely use him. There will rise up within him impulses and inspirations, strong strivings, strange resolves. These must be tested by Scripture and prayer, and if evidently of God they must be obeyed. But there is this perennial source of comfort: God's commands are enablings. He will never give us a work to do without showing exactly how and when to do it, and He will give the precise strength and wisdom we need. Do not dread to enter this life because you fear that God will ask you to do something you cannot do. He will never do that. If He lays aught on your heart, He will do so uninvited; as you pray about it the impression will continue to grow, so that presently, as you look up to know what He wills you to say or do, the way will suddenly open, and you will probably have said the word or done the deed almost unconsciously. Rely on the Holy Ghost to go before you to make the crooked places straight and the rough places smooth. Do not bring the legal spirit of 'must' into God's free service. 'Consider the lilies of the field, how they grow.' Let your life be as effortless as theirs, because your faith shall constantly hand over all difficulties and responsibilities to your ever-present Lord. There is no effort to the branch in putting forth the swelling clusters of grapes— the effort would be to keep them back."

But we must be discriminating in this matter, and not ascribe to the evil spirit tests which are for our benefit presented by the good Spirit. Says George Bowen: "The Spirit of God sometimes tests the peace of Christians in this way: A man has been for years enjoying a good measure of what he regards as Christian peace. Suddenly he is made to see himself by the light of a most intense holiness, and his former conceptions of his sinfulness and of the evil of all sin are augmented a thousandfold. Straightway his peace is gone. His faith utterly fails. He finds himself sinking in deep waters. The mention of the righteousness of Christ fails to satisfy him. The Christ that he has been looking at all along was one that would save from a moderate amount of sin, such as he then knew of in himself; he has yet to become acquainted with a Christ able and willing to save from such a dire ruin as he is now conscious of. His past peace, his past faith, are now ascertained to have partaken very largely of the nature of delusion. Happy for him that he has discovered the inadequacy of his faith while it is yet the day of grace! Sad, unspeakably sad, is the fate of many whose faith is not thus tested in their lifetime."

The great danger is that Christians will test themselves, not by the Holy Scriptures illumined and applied by the Holy Spirit, but by the average type of Christian character and attainment. This average is usually low, and this kind of testing, "measuring themselves by themselves," tends to a still lower standard quite near to that vague and indistinct line of demarcation which shades off into the world. We cannot believe that God is pleased with an average piety. Stalker says that the Hebrew prophets addressed nations and were satisfied with national obedience, but "Jesus Christ discovered the individual." Hence He can be satisfied only with marked individuality in the development of all the graces of the Spirit.

Let no man deem it profitable to hide from himself the evil lurking in his own heart. The peace thus secured will not long endure. It is an illusion. No one can afford to rest in a treacherous peace. Absolute safety lies in receiving from the Spirit of truth the intense light that He sheds upon sin, the disease, and upon Christ, the unfailing Physician if called in season.

Chapter XXV
THE HOLY GHOST AND SINGING

SINGING IS A delightful part of divine worship. The only singing that pleases God and melts and moves men is inspired by the Holy Spirit. It is the spontaneous outflow of spiritual joy. "Be filled with the Spirit; speaking one to another in psalms and hymns and spiritual songs, singing and making melody with your heart unto the Lord." According to the Revised Version the heart is the instrument of acceptable singing. It is in tune only when at peace with God and filled with His Spirit, the blessed Comforter. Every hymn which is a true vehicle of praise was composed as the outgush of emotions awakened by the Holy Spirit. For as all genuine poetry is the language of the natural emotions, so all the great and imperishable Christian hymns are the utterances of the spiritual sensibilities.

The great poet of Germany, Goethe, near the close of his life, remarked with sadness that none of his poems had been deemed worthy of a place in the Lutheran hymnal. The Holy Spirit was not in that man and hence could not inspire one immortal lyric. It is just the same with song-singing as it is with song-writing. If the Spirit is not in the singer the highest effect cannot be reached. For there are no substitutes for His presence as the soul of sacred music. Science, art, voice culture and faultless instrumental accompaniments are all hollow without the indwelling Spirit breathing upon the finer chords of the soul. When the Spirit leaves a church the singing of the congregation declines. It becomes spiritless, cold and formal. At last "hallelujahs languish on their tongues, and their devotion dies." They send to the opera for a quartet "to praise God by committee," or for a soloist to say "amen" for them in a poor mimicry of the liquid trills and flourishes of a bobolink. A recent writer, Dr. A. J. Gordon, insists that this is a case of simony, the attempt to buy with money inspired song, a gift of the Holy Ghost. There are some very important things which gold cannot purchase: it cannot secure true nuptial bliss, it cannot bribe death, it cannot buy admittance to heaven, nor can it procure a proxy for praising God.

No modern religious movement magnified the work of the Holy Spirit so much as that begun by the Wesleys. Their converts were remarkable for their singing. Why did their singing draw and disarm even their persecutors? Because their hearts throbbed with "joy unspeakable and full of glory." They must sing or burst asunder without vent to their gladness. Make a man happy and he is sure to sing. If he cannot sing, he will learn. If he cannot learn, he will shout, or make what seems to him a joyful sound, though it may be a discord to others not in sympathy with his joy. The Wesleys, brimming with poetry and music, prepared suitable hymns and tunes and carefully guided this devotional exercise. Listen to some of John Wesley's directions: "Suit the tune to the words. Avoid complex tunes, which it is scarcely possible to sing with devotion. Repeating the same words so often, especially while another repeats different words, shocks common sense, necessarily brings in dead formality, and has no more religion in it than a Lancashire hornpipe. Sing no anthems. In every society let them learn to sing. Introduce no new tunes till they are perfect in the old. Exhort every one to sing— not one in ten only. Sing lustily."

When this charge was given, solo singing was not customary in the churches, and hence is not included in Wesley's condemnation. There is now and then a soloist filled with the Holy Ghost, like Mr. Sankey, who sings so distinctly and earnestly as to evince that he has a message from God. But the great majority of them, especially the women, drown the words in their pranks and twists of voice, as if they were simply trying, like acrobats dancing on the top bar of the musical staff, to exhibit their vocal gymnastics, while the people, instead of worshipping God, are staring at the performer with open-mouthed wonder. Nothing more strikingly demonstrates the spiritual decay of Methodism than the substitution of the artistic music of a few hirelings for the hearty and joyful singing of the whole assembly. We are disgusted with the introduction of the misnamed sacred music of a pure and classic type, "which is devouring," says Tyerman, "the very vitals of Methodistic worship, and no more harmonizes with the hymns of the Wesleys than an automatic scarecrow with a living, breathing man."

Our only hope is in the revival of preaching under the anointing, the pulpit magnifying the Holy Ghost and the pews receiving him in Pentecostal fulness and expressing their joy in jubilant songs.

In addition to the Holy Spirit in the heart, the elements of power in singing are, first, numbers to carry the tune so strongly as to override any discords of ill-trained voices and to create a tidal wave of feeling to lift the entire assembly on its bosom and move them heavenward. In the second place, the older the hymn and the tune the richer will be the tender associations enlivening the emotions. There is something very affecting in the thought that our fathers and mothers and our ancestors for many generations worshipped God in the use of the same words and the same tune. In the next place, the tune itself should not be like a jig, light and airy, suggestive of shallowness of feeling, and the words should be filled with such solemn truths as will awaken the feeling of sublimity. It is a marked characteristic of our old hymns and tunes, in contrast with those of modern composition, that they combine these qualities. Grandeur in poetry is wedded to tunes having long, swelling sweeps of melody bearing all hearts upward and almost blending with the heavenly choir around the throne of the Lamb. Again, our older musical compositions, being free from a chorus attached to every verse, can be sung entire with less weariness than attends the constant repetition of the same chorus in treadmill style without any advance in the thought.

The cathedral singing of the Germans is noted for its effect in awakening devotional feeling. Says an American theological professor: "I can never forget a spectacle that I saw in one of the old churches in Nuremberg. The great edifice was crowded, one half of the audience at least standing. The sermon had been delivered in a fervent manner and had apparently much interested the feelings of the audience. Immediately a powerful and well-toned organ sent its peals through all the corners and recesses of the cathedral, and in a moment every adult and child in the vast throng broke forth in praise to the Redeemer, in one of those old hymns, mellowed by time, and which breathe not of earth but of heaven. The effect, at least upon the stranger, was overpowering. Nothing like it ever can be produced by a small choir, however scientifically trained. Its performance must be comparatively dead, because so modern or so artistic and scientific, or because it has been subjected to so many mutations that few can join in it if they were permitted to do so. Music for a popular audience must be simple, and then, especially if a great multitude unite, it will often be affecting and sublime." Dr. Eben Tourjée, the late great American advocate of congregational singing, on one occasion in Germany was so overpowered by the outburst of universal song that he could not restrain his emotions, but rushed out of the cathedral lest he should disturb the worship by his hallelujahs.

Paul intimates that singing psalms, hymns and spiritual songs is the natural expression of the fulness of the Spirit. Song is the outlet of joy. The Holy Spirit diffuses joy, the highest, purest and most enduring, When the Spirit comes into the heart the tongue of the dumb sings. John Wesley emphasized the Holy Spirit as consciously receivable. The people believed and received, and spontaneously burst out in jubilant song. Charles Wesley was moved by the Spirit to furnish hymns adapted to this modern Pentecost. All the Methodists sang, and sang "lustily " too, as they were exhorted to do by that great reformer inspired by the breath of the Almighty to quicken a dead church and "create a soul beneath the ribs of death." But when the Methodists lost the fulness of the Spirit,

"Hosannas languished on their tongues.
And their devotion died."

Then they sent to the opera and hired ungodly minstrels to praise God for them. It was a long stride away from the masses who love to have an active part in worship. Congregational singing is a great social leveller. The ditchdigger with a rich tenor voice feels that he is the peer of the owner of broad acres. The poor man with a large family and small wages can share in such worship and preserve his self-respect. He is attracted to a democratic form of worship. The Holy Ghost never narrows the privileges of the common people.

President Lincoln once said, "We know that God loves the common people because He has made a great multitude of them." It is the desire of the Holy Spirit to regenerate and sanctify this multitude by drawing them to the house of prayer and keeping them there. Satan has competitive attractions, his institutions which put men on the same level, the saloon, the beer-garden, the Sunday excursion, the bicycle outing, the so-called "sacred concert" and the Sunday newspaper. The churches which are wise will popularize their worship and win back the masses who have been repelled by our artistic, exclusive and costly singing which the Holy Ghost has no use for in saving sinners and training them for life eternal. He can carry to the heart only that which comes from the heart. That singing which is the utterance of Christian truth, first through the glowing heart of the poet, and then through the fervid sensibilities of the singers, the Holy Spirit can impress on both those who hear and those who sing. But when the form in which the truth is conveyed attracts attention to itself, whether it be the ornate style of the preacher or the trills and demisemiquavers of the prima donna, standing where she ought not, admiration of the human performance diverts the mind from divine worship and the Holy Spirit is dishonored. It is a professed adoration of God, but a real adoration of man. Over such singing and preaching the Holy Spirit cannot preside. He can use the singing of a godly soloist whose sole aim, like that of the preacher is the impressive utterance of saving truth.

Such a man is Mr. Sankey, the yokefellow of Mr. Moody. But much solo singing, especially of women, is so performed as to convey no truth to the mind, because it distinctly enunciates no words to the ear, in the effort to mount up to the highest notes possible to the human voice and to leap from peak to peak as Byron represents the "live thunder" reverberating amid the summits of the Alps. The hearer has not the words before him, nor has the preacher read them to the audience. If they are not plainly uttered by the songster, they convey no more truth than do the "*do, re, mi*" of the music-teacher. Such singing done softly may soothe while it does not edify. But it is God's purpose not to soothe with sound, but to save with truth. The organ prelude may awaken the emotion of sublimity in minds responsive to melody, but that alone never brought a sinner to God nor helped a believer into his full heritage in Christ. If instruments accompany singing, they should merely sustain the tune and strengthen the weaker parts, but never drown the words in an ocean of sound. Happy is that people who can sing well without an instrument. There is no music comparable to the human voice. Let it be used by as many as possible, even by those who make only discords, if there is only a volume of tuneful sound sufficient to overcome them.

Chapter XXVI
PREACHING IN DEMONSTRATION OF THE SPIRIT

IN THE SALVATION OF souls and their purification and enlargement preaching must always be the most important human agency. The only rival is the press. This lacks personality, one of the two cardinal elements of preaching. The other is truth. Phillips Brooks defines preaching as the communication of truth through personality. Christian truth embodied in a book held in the utmost reverence is not preaching. It lacks the vital element of personality. Truth written across the arches of the sky in letters of flaming fire might inspire sublimity and awe, but it would not attain the purpose of preaching. There can be no substitute for a personal presence endowed with the gift of speech and with the subtle magnetism of an earnest soul fully surrendered to the Holy Spirit as an organ of His suasive power. "On the other hand, if men speak to other men that which they do not claim for truth; if they use their powers of persuasion or entertainment to make other men listen to their speculations, or do their will, or applaud their cleverness, that is not preaching either. The first lacks personality. The second lacks truth." It must be evangelical truth; not its pleasant elements only, such as the love of God and the bliss of heaven, but its alarming verities also. The highest style of preaching is the tender yet earnest and courageous proclamation of "the whole counsel of God, sin, retribution, atonement, repentance, faith, pardon, purity, judgment, heaven and hell." Both of these elements of successful preaching are brought to perfection through the indwelling fulness of the Holy Ghost. What we call unction, that contagious, indefinable state of the speaker's sensibilities combining deep conviction of the truth uttered, strong emotion, religious fervor and melting tenderness, reaches its climax of persuasive energy only under the inspiration of the Spirit of God. This can never be simulated. Vociferation, boisterousness and physical vehemence are clumsy and disgusting counterfeits of genuine spiritual unction, easily detected by an intelligent audience. The arts of the perfect elocutionist, when completely naturalized, may help, as in the case of Whitefield, to widen and deepen the channel through which the warm, liquid stream of power may flow forth into all hearts, but they can never originate that power. It was a capital offence to counterfeit the "holy anointing oil" (Ex. xxx.33) in the Mosaic dispensation. Can it be a venial sin in the more glorious dispensation of the Spirit to stand up in the name of Christ and pour out upon a multitude of immortal souls needing impulse heavenward a wretched counterfeit unction, a mixture of fine prose rhetoric garnished with scraps of poetry and seasoned with the grimaces and gestures of an actor? Did not our Lord Jesus have such preachers in view when He said: "Many will say to me in that day, Lord, Lord, have we not prophesied in thy name? and in thy name cast out demons? and in thy name done many miracles? And then will I profess unto them, I never knew you; depart from me, ye that work iniquity"? (Matt. vii.22, 23). Meyer, the exegete, describes the distinguishing feature in these preachers as "an impure, often fanatical, boldness in the faith, which, though enabling them to perform acts of a marvellous nature, yet fails to exercise any influence upon their own moral life—just the sort of thing described by Paul in I Cor. xiii.2— and the manifestations of which are to be met with in every age, especially in times of great religious excitement." These solemn words of warning of our Lord should be written in large letters over the study table of every preacher, to be pondered in the preparation of every sermon. They are never read by the writer without awakening him to self-distrust and self- examination. This is especially true since reading again and again Stalker's fifth lecture of his Yale lectures, 1891, entitled "The Preacher as a False Prophet," in which he shows "that the true prophets had to face the opposition, not of heathen and not of the openly irreligious among their own countrymen only, but of those who had the name of God in their mouths and were publicly recognized as His oracles. To us these are now false prophets, because time has found them out and the Word of God has branded them as they deserve; but in their own day they were regarded as true prophets; and doubtless many of them never dreamed that they were not entitled to the name. They must have been a numerous and powerful body.

"This is an appalling fact, that the public representatives of religion should ever have been the worst enemies of religion; but it cannot be denied that even in Christendom, and that not once or twice, the same condition of things has existed."

The question, Is my ministry of God's Word in obedience to the Holy Ghost, or is it in the interest of selfish ends? is of vital importance. It is the question whether I am a false or a true prophet. It is, according to Him who is the appointed Judge, the question on which eternal destiny hinges. Hence it would be well to examine such criteria as are at hand to decide this momentous question.

1. The Holy Spirit stands by all the truth that He has inspired. If any vital truth is unaccepted and unpopular and has largely dropped out of your sermons, you may know that your preaching is not prompted by the Spirit of truth. You have no valid reason for thinking that your proclamation of such generally accepted truth as you do preach is a proof that you are thus far submissive to the dictation of the Spirit, for you may be actuated by motives entirely impure and selfish. He is not a herald loyal to his king who proclaims only such commands as please him and neglects every disagreeable order. This would be the ruling of every jurist. A young curate in England was asked what were the favorite themes of his preaching. He replied, "Free trade and the pleasant parts of Christianity." He probably uttered some kind of ethical or economical truth in every sermon. Does this prove that the Holy Spirit had anything to do with his preaching? "How often we ask with real sadness, whence the remarkable impotence of preaching in our time? It is because we concoct our gospels too much out of the laboratories of our understanding; because we preach too many disquisitions and look for effects correspondent only with the natural forces exerted."

2. The Holy Spirit inspires only that ministry which is subordinate to Jesus Christ, whom He glorifies. He cannot be the soul of that ministry which exalts self above Christ. The Spirit's oneness of nature with Him forbids it. There are only two themes of preaching, Christ and self. Most evangelical preachers begin with the exaltation of Christ. But many come to an imperceptible switch from Christ to self, and from that point in their history they use the ministry of the Son of God as a ladder up which they climb to grasp the object of selfish ambition, ecclesiastical promotion, literary excellence, oratory, a college professorship, an editorship, money, social standing, or some other soap bubble. Many are using the gospel ministry as a stepping-stone to something better in their estimation. The Holy Ghost does not dwell in stepping-stone preachers. A true minister filled with the Holy Ghost feels a repugnance to a college presidency or professorship, and he yields to the call only when he is convinced that he can be more effectively preaching Christ in teaching others to preach. It was this that reconciled Dr. Chalmers to the chair of theology in the Edinburgh University. He came to see "that while many were called to catch and salt fish, some men are called to make salt."

3. The Holy Spirit, the successor to Christ in presiding over His Church, has a special sympathy with those whom He designates as His representatives— the poor to whom He preached. He sent to John, His forerunner, this crowning proof of His Messiahship towering above His miracles, "and the poor have the gospel preached unto them." Here is the criterion. You have two ministerial calls; you are free from debt, and have a fair outfit. One call is to a rich and fashionable church with a large salary; the other is to a congregation of laboring people in "a shoe town" on half the other salary. The size of the two congregations and of the two cities is the same. I do not say that the Holy Spirit does not call eminently spiritual men

to rich city churches. Edward Payson was called to such a church, where he thundered and lightened like another Sinai for twenty years against every form of iniquity. The Holy Ghost evidently dwelt in him, and prompted his utterances. When called to more lucrative salaries in Boston and New York he declined, and refused an increase in his salary in Portland. This spirit of self-sacrifice is a sufficient proof of his freedom from self-seeking and his willingness to follow whithersoever the Spirit might lead.

What we do say is that men of great gifts are needed among the poor, and when they are called to minister to them, and gladly accept a call to the rich instead, we are inclined to say that the Holy Spirit does not prefer the rich to the poor, but rather the reverse. A preference of that call which evinces the greatest self-sacrifice, and which brings the preacher into closer sympathy with the least of Christ's brethren, is an evidence that the preacher is a temple of the Holy Ghost.

Says Austin Phelps of the true ideal of a Christian minister: "He should be able to go, without a ripple of difference in his sense of personal distinction, to the Fiji Islands or to the Fifth Avenue in New York." Robert Hall says: "If God should send two angels down from heaven, one to sweep the streets of London and the other to be lord mayor, there would be no dispute between them as to which is the more honorable calling." What in this respect is possible in angels is possible in the entirely sanctified men and women, hundreds of whom are choosing the wretched abodes of heathenism in which to spend, in the name of Christ, lives of uncomplaining privation and toil. When Lorenzo Dow was told of a preacher who had a call to two churches, offering the same salary, and was in doubt which to accept, but finally decided that he was called by the Holy Ghost to the church which added his firewood to the salary, that eccentric but keen evangelist irreverently said: "It was a wooden Holy Ghost."

We are frequently asked whether the preacher should seek after the induement of power as a special gift.

If you are conscious of the indwelling of the Spirit as purifying and ruling with supreme authority, it is very appropriate to pray as Paul did, for utterance and boldness in the proclamation of truths distasteful to the unregenerate and to the unsanctified. If you have not such a consciousness of the presence of the Holy Spirit, it would be more complimentary to Him to ask for Himself first, and for His gift afterwards. The Spirit rarely intrusts His power to those who do not completely intrust themselves to His cleansing and guidance; He does not give His power separate from Himself. Ask for Him for His own sake, if you wish to show Him proper respect as a person. His permanent indwelling is in itself the noblest end at which you can aim; to aim at something beyond Him is derogatory to Him as divine in His nature and equal to the Father and the Son in glory and majesty. Everybody wants power; few want God. It is not a proof of a high state of grace to ask for power, even the power of the Holy Ghost; this is what Simon Magus wanted; the secret motive may centre in the glory of self on the top round of the ladder of ministerial ambition. There is a chance for mixed motives even in a preacher of undoubted piety. Many pray earnestly for power in their work and receive it not, because they do not assume the only posture in which the power can work; they want to get possession of the power of the Spirit and use it as they please. God wants the power of the Spirit to get the mastery of them and use them as He pleases. If they would surrender to the power of the Spirit to rule in them, that power would surrender to them to rule through them. "God gives the Holy Spirit to them who obey Him," and in His abiding fulness to them only. His wisdom cannot intrust power to the disobedient. The more perfect the obedience the larger the power of the Spirit. "If thou wouldst have this power work in thee, bow very low in reverence before the holy presence that dwelleth in thee, which asks thy surrender to His guidance even in the least things. Walk very humbly, in holy fear lest in anything thou shouldst fail in knowing or doing His holy will."

Moreover, remember that the power of the Spirit is never bestowed as a premium to indolence. There is sound Christian theology in the fable of pagan Æsop about Hercules helping the mired teamster only when he put his own shoulder to his wheel. Asking for the Holy Spirit for our own enjoyment may not be a vicious motive. Certainly it is not the highest; this adorable Son of God. God is constantly seeking men and women of such a purpose to clothe them with power, "for the eyes of Jehovah run to and fro throughout the whole earth, to show himself strong [strongly to hold with, Hebrew], in behalf of them whose heart is perfect toward him " (II Chron. xvi.9).

The power of the Spirit may be in exercise while the preacher is unconscious of it. He may not feel it, though sometimes the speaker is aware that a power outside of him has descended upon him, endowing with spiritual might. To this Spurgeon often gave testimony. But ordinarily the Spirit's power, like gravitation, magnetism and electricity, is silent and unseen, giving a penetrating energy to the speaker's words, even when they seem powerless to himself. Dr. Stephen Olin had a marvellous experience of this sort in his ministry in Charleston, S. C. Several persons dated their conversion from an evening sermon of which he was so ashamed that he dared not meet any of his hearers, but retired from the church through a back door into a dark graveyard, and with difficulty found his way to his lodgings. It is to be noted that in God's chosen order of sequences weakness and power coexist in a wonderful way. "When I am *weak*, *then* am I strong." This is Paul's testimony, who also declares that God takes weak things to confound the mighty.

This paradox disappears when we assert that the weakness is only the human side of strong faith in God. It was a favorite remark of one of God's modern sons of thunder, that "there are two persons in the universe to whom all things are possible: one is God, and the other is he that believeth." It has been well said that faith grows strong in the dark. "The Holy Spirit hides Himself in the weak things that God has chosen, that no flesh may glory in his presence."

If there is any sight especially painful, it is that of a professed minister of Christ destitute of power in a world over which Satan has usurped dominion. He ought to be the most wretched man on earth, who knows how wicked and miserable is a world of sinners lost, but has no power to bring any of these palsied souls to Christ, the Healer and Giver of life. "He lays a kind but helpless hand upon the wound. He tries to relieve it with his sympathy and his philosophy. He is the source of all he says. There is no God behind him."

The preacher needs the fulness of the Holy Spirit to make him an open and wide aqueduct for the water of life to flow to every soul with whom he comes in contact. This implies large faith, the door through which God comes into the human soul, and the door of the communication of grace from the believer to the unbeliever. It implies also what John calls "perfect love," with its kindred graces, meekness, gentleness and patience. The altruists of our generation have made the great philosophic discovery that the way to induce love or any other virtue in our neighbor is to exhibit it in ourselves, a principle embodied in Christ's precept, "love your enemies," and in Paul's "heap coals of fire on his head," not to burn him up but to melt him down. Only the indwelling Holy Spirit can transform a man naturally selfish into such a personality.

But the preacher needs the Spirit of God also for the

other element of ministerial success, the truth. He can appropriate its inmost essence only as he is quickened and transformed by "the Spirit of truth." It is one thing to have an intellectual knowledge of Christian theology, but quite another to have Christ, "the truth and the life," incorporated into your inmost self, and "formed within, the hope of glory." The difference between these two kinds of knowledge, the theoretical and the experimental, is the difference between theology and religion, the body and the soul of Christianity. No preacher can have the truth thus wrought into the very texture of his being except by the abiding presence of the Spirit of truth giving reality and vitality to gospel truth. It is because of a lack of this presence that doubt obscures the inward vision, substitutes nebulous language for clear-cut, positive enunciation of saving truth, and makes the sermon a barren literary achievement in the presence of immortal souls fainting and dying of spiritual hunger. "Even spiritual truth is robbed of its power when held, not in the life of the Spirit, but in the wisdom of man. Where truth enters into the inward parts as God desires, there it becomes the life of the Spirit." Many a preacher satisfies himself with the imagination that truth which only touches the surface of the soul, the intellect and reason, will in some way strike its roots into the rock beneath and produce a spiritual harvest. The effect of such preaching is nothing more than that of human argument and wisdom, that never pierces the hearer's heart as with a sword, revealing the sinful spirit to itself.

When several Unitarian theological students came to Father Taylor after one of his mighty sermons in the Seamen's Bethel, and asked him to teach them to preach, the preacher replied: "You must first have the preach in you, then the preaching will take care of itself." We interpret this advice as meaning that gospel truth in its reality and divine substance must be received in the inmost soul and held as an actual possession, the life of the things which others regard as only shadows. The Spirit is the inner life of divine truth. In His teaching He does not employ symbols, words, thoughts, impressions and images like a human teacher or writer. He has the ability to enter the very roots of our life and to secrete the truth of God there as a seed of divine life. Received by faith and watered by prayer, it becomes a banyan tree overshadowing the whole being. Such a preacher will become a Wesley, a Finney, a Moody or a Payson, not in the extent, but in the kind of spiritual success. All we have said about the inability of the unspiritual mind to be a medium of vital truth is sustained by Paul, who says: "No man can say Jesus is Lord, but in the Holy Spirit" (I Cor. xii.3). If I had the ear of every young preacher and of every student of theology, I would endeavor to convince them of the utter incapacity of human wisdom in its very highest development to grasp the real inward spiritual meaning of a divine revelation without the internal illumination of the abiding Paraclete. It is only as both speaker and hearer are spiritual, under the rule of the Spirit, that there can be a successful communication of gospel truth.

"The Holy Ghost, who is in essential and perfect communion with the Father and the Son, reveals unto us eternal realities. He alone knows the infinite love of God with which He has loved us, for He alone can fathom the depth out of which this love proceeds. Thus what the Holy Ghost reveals and imparts is the knowledge of realities which are eternal in God. It is the Spirit Himself who teaches and enlightens. The *truth itself*, the preaching of the gospel, the reading of the Scriptures, *has no inherent power to bring knowledge into the soul*. These are only the instruments, the Spirit is the agent; they are only the sword, the Spirit is the energy, the hand that wields it. They shall be taught of God. God causes the light of the gospel to shine into our hearts. How little we realize this truth, so comforting and full of encouragement! *How apt are we to forget the living Spirit in the gifts and channels which He uses!* How fond we are of placing ourselves in God's place; if not in the Father's, in Christ's; if not in Christ's, in that of the Spirit."* Hence a Christian worker without the Spirit dwelling within him is a cannon without an explosive, an organ without wind, an engine without steam, and a dynamo without electricity. He is a dead man preaching to dead souls. The same truths which he ineffectually utters would convict of sin and bring to Christ if they came all aglow from a soul baptized with the Holy Ghost and with fire. This is not a mere theory. Barren ministries have been made abundantly fruitful by the advent of the Holy Spirit in the preacher's heart.

Says Stalker: "What an audience looks for, before everything else, in the texture of a sermon, is the blood streak of experience; and truth is doubly and trebly true when it comes from a man who speaks as if he had learned it by his own work and suffering." We should bear in mind that truth is in such a form as to reveal itself not merely to the intellect, but to the sensibilities, those allies of true persuasion. Gospel truth is not an abstraction. It has appeared in our world as a person. One man of all the generations has said: "I am the truth." We did not see Him, nor did we hear His voice on the mountain side and on the shore of the sea. But it is no privation. We are more than compensated for our lack of knowledge through our coarse bodily senses. We may know Him through the medium of a finer intuition. It is the office of the Holy Spirit to reveal the Son of God in the preacher of to-day, as He did in the apostle to the Gentiles. This inward revelation is necessary to the highest efficiency. Paul could not be a genuine apostle till he had seen Jesus with his bodily eyes. No man can be a genuine preacher till he

---

*Dr. A. Saphir, "Christ Crucified," page 109

has seen Jesus with his spiritual eyes. This promise, "I will manifest myself unto him," was not limited to the apostles. It belongs to all who believe and obey. This kind of truth, this seeing Christ, takes the chill out of the heart, the doubt out of the mind, and the interrogation point out of the sermon. For some preachers betray such uncertainty that their sentences end with the rising inflection, as if they were questioning their own utterances. "True preaching is a testimony; it offers not things reasoned, in any principal degree, but things given, supernatural things, testifying them as being in their power, by an utterance which they fill and inspire. It brings new premises, which, of course, no argument can create, and therefore speaks to faith."*

The voice of church history attests that without a clear and constant testimony to the divine personality and agency of the Holy Spirit, preaching is fruitless and the spirituality of the Church declines. Vain are the substitutes for the might of the Spirit— splendid architecture, faultless rhetoric and charming eloquence in the pulpit, classical music in the choir and wealth and fashion in the pews. These may produce a delusive appearance of prosperity; numerous accessions of members more eager to get into good society than they are to abandon their sins; large audiences and an overflowing treasury.

We live in a time when a section of Protestantism is fascinated by ritualism with its gorgeous ceremonial, robed priests, vested choirs, lighted candles, smoking censers, stately processions, intoned prayers, pronounced absolutions, and genuflections before the cross. This is a bad sign, indicating a desire to substitute something visible and sensuous for that which constitutes the healthful attraction, the true charm and glory of Christian worship, the presence and power of

---

*Dr. Horace Bushnell

the invisible Spirit in believing hearts. It betokens an interior vacuum which the ritualist is trying to fill with external shows and sounds and shams. The Spirit of truth abhors these substitutes for Himself. Every mind in which the Holy Spirit dwells instinctively turns away in disgust from the chaff of ritualism. In all manner of *Christian* work— not embroidering altar-cloths and arranging pulpit nosegays— the first thing and the essential thing is that we shall be continually receiving renewed induements of the Holy Spirit, styled by the seraphic Fletcher "the quintessence of our holy religion." It might be truthfully styled the Magna Charta of the Church instead of "the myth of apostolic succession" as Phillips Brooks aptly called it. It certainly is "the everlasting sign which shall not be cut off," the only continued miracle, the converting power on earth, instantaneously changing bad men into good men, the thorn into the fir tree, a transformation above the power of nature. The measure of this supernatural power in any local church is not determined by the caprice of an arbitrary sovereignty, but by the human fulfilment of divinely appointed conditions, the utter abandonment of the soul to the Holy Ghost as the Sanctifier and a hearty co-operation with Him as the Reprover and Regenerator. There is no effectual substitute for the Holy Ghost as the Transformer, neither eloquence, nor personal magnetism, nor philosophy, nor even the energy of a purified human spirit, unless it is interpenetrated by the divine Spirit.

There should be a careful study of revival preaching. There can be no genuine revival unless the conditions are fulfilled. The fallow ground must be broken up by driving the subsoil ploughshare of repentance through and through it. Begin at the house of God; there is much fallow ground in God's field, the Church. There are many nominal Christians who do not realize that they are sinners in the sight of God. They are resting in church membership, promptly paid pew rents and weekly offerings, attendance upon preaching and the Lord's supper, and the same general interest in the prosperity of the church to which they belong that is exhibited by liberalists and Romanists. They also contribute their share to the great charities of the denomination. But all these things a person backslidden in heart may do from other motives than pure love to our Lord Jesus. It may be the effect of habit. He may desire to retain the good opinion of the Christian public for purely personal ends. He may be making an ostentatious display of some virtues to compensate for some vices or to cover them up. Professors of Christianity are prone to sophisticate conscience when they are out of the strait and narrow way. They try to make their crookedness seem to be undistorted. Men spiritually dead have been known to simulate great fervor if called on to pray in public. Sometimes an excessive bustling activity in the externals of Christianity is prompted by the consciousness that the inner life has become extinct and the uneasy moral sense must have something to lean upon. What all these characters need is plain and fearless preaching which uncovers their sins and drives them out of all their false refuges. Their sins should be specially detailed. Their sins of omission, which are most frequently overlooked, should be enumerated and dwelt upon. What a catalogue of neglects the faithful preacher might set in array before the members of his church— *neglect of the Holy Scriptures*, which do not feed them now as they once did, but they appear dry and chaffy. Once they fed upon the Word with great delight; it was sweeter than honey. Now the daily paper is sought first in the morning, and on Sundays the Sunday newspaper with all its trash and flummery. Preach a sermon on the Bible so long neglected that damnation could be written on its dusty cover. Then, what a fearful neglect of family religion is prevalent in our churches. In many of our families the altar-stones have fallen down. The morning and evening sacrifice is no longer burned thereon. Business and the railroad train are put in place of God in the morning. The lodge, the club, the social party, the evening newspaper are instead of God at night. What will become of the children who hear not the voices of their parents in home worship?

"Just as the twig is bent the tree is inclined."

Let me testify to the praise of my heavenly Father that the twig of my childhood was bent heavenward by the voice of prayer about my cradle. Two of the four sons of my father were called to preach, and two of my own. Rebuild the family altars and rekindle the fires, and Methodism of the next generation will feel the effect in the conversion of millions of her children.

Preach on neglected communion with God in the closet, where all unworthy motives, such as the praise of men, are excluded. How common is the neglect of that indispensable condition of discipleship— self-denial! The term is rarely used. Many professors know its meaning by the dictionary only. They never have denied themselves a ribbon or a cigar for Christ and for His gospel. They are quite active in the pleasant parts of religion, but they shrink from everything that requires self-denial. That is too humiliating to pride. What they can do as well as not— flowers for the pulpit or a bookmark for the Bible— they are willing to do, but they are not willing to sacrifice any comfort or any convenience for the advancement of the kingdom of Christ. They seem to think that God ought not to ask them to do disagreeable duties, and that He should feel that He was specially complimented by their condescending to take the name of Christians when there were so many high-toned and fashionable people outside the Church for them to associate with. How few the deniers of self at the contribution box! Here and there a widow with two mites, who gave not her surplus but her capital. Preach self-denial as absolutely essential to salvation. Many are utterly negligent of the highest well-being of their fellow-men, a point on which we have been forewarned that the final judgment will turn. They should be convicted of this sin by the faithful preacher. Says Dr, Finney: "If your soul is not agonized for the poor benighted heathen, why are you such a hypocrite as to pretend to be a Christian? Why, your profession is an insult to Jesus Christ."

Preach repentance for the great sin of not believing God, great because it makes Him a liar. This sin, existing wholly in the invisible realm of the spirit, is by the world and the worldly part of the Church deemed to be destitute of any moral quality. The preacher should put forth his whole strength to tear this destructive falsehood out of men's minds, especially out of the minds of professed Christians. These frequently negative [sic] God's promises by their failure to believe, while sinners throw away God's threatenings. Thus the whole Bible is rejected.

Preach repentance for sins of commission, setting forth specifications of transgressions of the moral law as Christ did in His sermon on the mount. Read Wesley's discourses on that sermon as a part of your preparation. I have been painfully observant of the decline of this kind of preaching in the modern pulpit. It is a bad sign of the times. It indicates that a soft theology is superseding the Biblical doctrines of our fathers. In addition to the miasma of liberalism that is in the air, a doctrine is prevalent in certain circles which negatives [sic] the law as binding on believers, and substitutes faith for repentance and holiness. Its teachers emphasize the fact that St. John does not speak of repentance either in his Gospel or in his Epistles. Negations prove nothing. He does not mention hell either. Both of the causes named tend to weaken the motives to repentance. But it is quite certain that it is absolutely essential to the exercise of saving faith in Jesus Christ, and that every genuine revival is preceded by faithful preaching on this duty.

Preaching should aim at definite results. We know of none more significant than radical conversions with a date, although a dateless conversion may be genuine. Yet it is very desirable that the Christian should be able to look back upon a definite emergence into newness of life, and to name the day of his espousals unto Christ. This is a great safeguard against the two doubts in respect to fundamentals: Is Christ the true Saviour? and does He save me? A sudden transition from darkness into the marvellous light by a pardon attested by God's seal, the Holy Spirit, the agent of regeneration and initial sanctification, is a type of Christian experience quite difficult for scepticism to assail with success. It is a monumental proof of the divinity of the gospel.

Such experiences were frequent in early Methodism because the type of preaching was such as to promote them. Clear-cut statements of saving truth produce sharply defined experiences. Hazy preaching makes nebulous conversions. When you stand under an arc-light and look at your shadow how surprised you are at the sharpness of the outline! Every stray hair is individualized. Why? Because every ray of light streams from one point. Our figure hints at pointed sermons. What would come to pass if Methodism had an arc-light in every pulpit? We do not predict that every conversion would be Pauline. They would be more numerous and more genuine, but they would not all be striking, God has a great variety of operations in the kingdom of grace.

Young preachers who have had a signal conversion are apt to forget this. They begin their ministerial life with a distinct view of the mode in which souls come into the kingdom of God, and of the spuriousness, of course, of all incomings which had not all the peculiarities of that mode. But when such preachers have in their pastoral work listened to the experience of some of their very best members, most spiritual and most active, they will find that their regulation mode of conversion is altogether too narrow for the wideness of God's mercy. They will find persons full of faith and the Holy Ghost on whom the Sun of Righteousness arose in a period so cloudy that they cannot tell the day, and hardly the week, when His rays first shone into their hearts. The truth is that God works in the realm of grace as He does in nature, along certain established lines, as that summer shall follow spring, with fixed general features, but in such a way as to admit of a vast and beautiful diversity sometimes more surprising than the uniformity.

Christianity faithfully applied to childhood results in frequent conversions without a date. It is natural that the transition of a little child of eight years from the world to Christ should be without a memorable struggle. Several of my most intimate friends who are adult believers, remarkable for their devotion and about as steadfast in their Christian career as the sun in the heavens, were converted when children, and are unable to celebrate any spiritual birthdays, There would be more of these in the Church to-day as shining lights if the contrast between the quiet mode of their conversion and the marvellous glare of some adults' experiences had not induced them to throw away the little taper which the Spirit had lighted in their hearts. This is one of the evil results of conceiving that God works in only one way. We must respect dateless commonplace conversions, and give the subjects of them our confidence and a warm welcome to the Church, the fold of Christ.

What we have said of conversion is in a less degree true of entire sanctification. This does not usually occur in immature age, and is generally a more signal event in the consciousness of the recipient. Yet there is even here an infinite variety. As to the space of time after justification, God has given us no almanac. While we know the agent, the Sanctifier, we know not the way He will take in any individual case. Many, especially outside of Methodism, have been wholly cleansed from depraved inclinations, and have not known it by the name given by John Wesley. They were athirst after God's fulness, and they received the baptism or successive anointings of the Holy Spirit. They find themselves strong, joyful, victorious over every temptation, and having full assurance of faith. They have all the marks and concomitants of entire sanctification.

In all preaching to believers the aim should be to make the feeble to become as David in strength, and the house of David as the angel of Jehovah.

The relation of this subject to the various moral reforms and attempted social reconstructions is a theme of practical interest on which we would like to dwell. Some preachers of the gospel are preaching sociology. There are well-meaning people who wish to abate and suppress evils which prey upon human society by ignoring the only radical and effectual cure by the new birth. Many of these are philanthropic, but not Christian. They answer very well Father Taylor's description of one of his sons-in-law, when, in reply to the question whether he was a Christian, the old man eloquent replied, "No, but he is a very sweet sinner." The failure of all such reformers arises from their beginning with the mass and not with the individual, and their cleansing of the outside of the cup and platter, and their stopping at the rectification of the outward conduct, leaving the heart, the innermost seat of character, unchanged. They suppress the symptoms without curing the disease. This may not be a blessing, but rather a damage. It has been said that God shows His great wisdom in attaching outward very unpleasant sequences to the evil in men's hearts, sequences in the shape of vices, gusts of anger, pains of body and mind and "woes that follow at the heels of sin." If men could get all their misdeeds out of sight and still keep sin in their hearts shut in from every human eye, it would be the greatest obstruction to their highest well-being. We have all heard of the street angel and the home devil. He is further from the kingdom of heaven than the street devil and home angel. The external purgation of the world by a grand sweep of outward reform without implanting new springs of action in a regeneration of the natural man, if such a reform were possible, would give the race a paradise restored, but a paradise of hypocrites, heavenly in behavior but satanic in principle. This is the aim of all the naturalistic reformers. But the true preacher, who imitates his Master in his method of doing good, perceiving the folly of smoothing up the world in its sin and alienation from God, boldly cries to sinners as well bred as Nicodemus, "Ye must be born again, born of the Spirit." The new birth is the only effectual safeguard of society. This is taught in Old Testament prophecy. "Salvation will God appoint for walls and bulwarks " (Isa. xxvi.1).

If Christianity is going to regenerate society, its heralds must not stop when they have portrayed its vices and crimes. They must lay bare their fountain, the sin of men's heart, the sin of unbelief toward Jesus Christ, and insist on the new birth as the only cure. The Spirit's great office is to "convict of sin, because they believe not in me."

The gospel has a style of address peculiarly its own. It is not the stately and ornate oration of the Grecian rhetor or the Roman orator, but the unpretending utterance of the herald. It is to proclaim words put into the mouth by a higher authority. Hence Jesus Christ does not call His ministers dialecticians, advocates or orators, but simply preachers, proclaiming that the Messiah has come, and exhorting to the reception of His gospel. One of the first evidences of departure on the part of the Church from the simplicity of Christ is seen in the popular favor shown to those who have ceased to be preachers heralding the world's Saviour, and have become orators, using Scripture texts as convenient staples to hang a chain of brilliant periods upon. That is a false and fatal refinement which takes offence at the plain and earnest preaching of Christ. It always indicates that the godless spirit of Grecian culture, which regards Christ crucified as foolishness, has infused its subtle poison into the Church. There is a widely prevalent mistake respecting the nature of sacred eloquence. Splendid rhetoric, faultless gestures, pleasing illustrations, brilliant imagery and flashing gems of poetry often pass for genuine eloquence. But here are only paste diamonds. When your preacher is taking to himself wings and soaring to the empyrean on some grandiloquent passage, and you mentally exclaim or whisper to your neighbor, "O, how eloquent!" real eloquence has not been reached, because you are not swayed by the thoughts and melted into penitence, or lifted out of yourself into the life divine. You are still a critic. True eloquence will always lift you above the critical attitude. You cease to think of the man, his diction, voice and action; you think only of the burning truth which pours forth a molten stream from the furnace of the preacher's glowing heart.

When you look at a picture, if you are thinking only of the paints and how they were laid on, you are gazing at a mere daub, and not at the work of a great master. He does not permit you to think of the coloring or of the artist. He allows you to see nature only, so perfectly has he mastered the art of concealing art. When you retire from the church admiring the preacher instead of crying, "God, be merciful to me a sinner," or, "Create in me a clean heart," you have been listening to a journeyman and not to a master of sacred eloquence. Do you think that Felix sat in wonder at the diction of St. Paul as he waxed warm and his imagination caught fire as he reasoned of righteousness, and Mount Sinai was thrown upon the canvas, and the awful darkness settled upon its summit, and the lightnings and thunderings and the voice of the trumpet, waxing louder and louder, were portrayed, while Felix feels the earth quaking beneath the tread of Jehovah? Do you suppose that he nudged his Jewish wife at his elbow, exclaiming, "How sublime! what a graphic imagination this countryman of yours has"?

Then when St. Paul portrays the tragedy of Calvary, the darkening skies, the rending rocks, the opening graves, and the Son of God bowing His head in death, praying for His enemies, do you think that the Roman governor felt like clapping his hands in applause as at a well-acted drama? When the bold and faithful preacher spoke of temperance to the tippling and licentious sinner on the tribunal, portraying the drunkard's grave of shame and hell of torment, it is not supposable that the royal toper cried out to Lysias, the chief of his staff, "Splendid! splendid! What excellence this Jew might have attained, even rivalling Hortentius and Cicero, if he had been schooled at Rome!" Instead of this, Felix, conscience-smitten at the vivid picture in the gospel mirror of his own dissolute career, is vainly endeavoring to stanch the tears welling up from eyes unused to weep, as Paul, by the dark ghost of what Felix is, flings upon the canvas the bright ideal of what he might have been. When Paul reaches the thirdly of his sermon, the judgment to come, Felix is sitting with downcast eye, and forehead resting on his hand. We may easily imagine what was the course of that high argument. The materials would be chiefly drawn from the moral and religious ideas of the pagan sinner before him: first, an appeal to his own moral sense, the finger point within, directing him to the hour when justice will mount her tribunal and adjudicate the affairs of men; then a corroborative reference to Roman mythology, involving the judicial scrutiny of the shades in the infernal world; and, lastly, the grand concluding argument used on Mars Hill: "But now God commandeth all men everywhere to repent: because he hath appointed a day, in which he will judge the world in righteousness by that man whom he hath ordained; whereof he hath given assurance unto all men, in that he hath raised him from the dead."

Here follow the infallible proofs of Jesus' resurrection, confirming all His claims, especially that of the future judgment of the world. Then the fearless preacher makes Felix see the great white throne, and the awful Judge, attended by myriads of angels, in majesty sweep down from the skies, and hear the trump of Gabriel calling the slumbering dead from land and sea, and the cry of the wicked for the rocks and hills to hide them from the wrath of the Lamb, and the sentence to the company at the left hand, "Depart, ye cursed, into everlasting fire." Felix is no longer the cool critic that he was when he took his seat on the tribunal. Under a tide of religious emotions awakened in his bosom by the faithful presentation of God's truth, he has lost sight of Paul; he has forgotten his Hebrew brogue, his violation of the rules of oratory, or his conformity to them. Matters of greater importance occupy his thoughts. "My sins, my sins; the judgment, the judgment." This is eloquence. Felix does not say it is. Paul may not think that he has been eloquent. But the end of preaching has been attained: a hardened sinner has been awakened and made to tremble before God. This is preaching, "not with enticing words of man's wisdom, but in demonstration of the Spirit and of power."*

There is much preaching which the Holy Ghost cannot use for the conviction and conversion of the unregen-

---

*See Appendix, Note H

erate and the sanctification of believers. It is generally true that the sermon which has most of the Holy Scriptures appropriately quoted in proof of the argument will be used by the Spirit to the best effect.

The themes of the preacher should be the truths which the Holy Spirit enforces upon the world — sin, righteousness and judgment. These momentous doctrines, of which the Paraclete was to convince the world, most intimately pertain to the whole human family and every individual member thereof. To herald these truths is the great mission of the Church till the end of the world. To withhold them is treason to Christ, and a robbery of the Holy Spirit of His own sword, and concealment of the only medicine that can heal a leprous and perishing race.

Do not tone down God's awakening truth. Do not dilute it. Do not destroy its pungency by your modifications. Do not obscure it by your philosophy. As Ann Phillips said to her husband, "Don't shilly-shally, Wendell." Says Channing, "No man is fit to preach the truth who is not ready to be a martyr to the truth." Says the same great preacher of Christian ethics: "One great reason of the inefficacy of the ministry is the want of faith in a higher operation of Christianity in the higher development of humanity than is now possessed. As long as the present condition of the Christian world shall be regarded as ultimate, as long as our religion shall be thought to have done already its chief work on earth, as long as the present corruptions of the Church and the State shall be acquiesced in as laws of nature, and shall stir up no deep agonizing desire of reform, so long the ministry will be comparatively dead." It is the power of the gospel to transfigure human society by transforming human hearts and thus make a new heaven and a new earth, that should inspire the preacher with courage and persistent application of regenerative truth as the Holy Spirit's instrument of this new creation. The world has scarcely begun to feel the power of Christ to save the lost when regenerative truth shall be pungently and generally preached in reliance on the personal Holy Ghost. Do you ask what are regenerative truths? We answer: The idea of a holy God, of sin, of the law, of the atonement, of the day of judgment, of immortality, of heaven and hell determined by the human will. Set the whole firmament ablaze with the glow and heat of these eternal verities, and your preaching cannot be fruitless.

Chapter XXVII
WALKING IN THE COMFORT OF THE HOLY GHOST

THIS IS DESIGNED to be the normal life of the believer. The Holy Spirit has two distinct kinds of activity in His earthly mission. His delightful work is to comfort, strengthen and cheer Christians. His strange work is to convert sinners— I call it strange because it is strongly allied to the wrath of God. It has been well said that judgment is His strange work, in which a God of love finds no pleasure. I cannot think that the Holy Spirit finds gratification in administering rebuke to those who sin against a holy God. It is sad to think that even in the case of many who have been born of the Spirit, He exercises toward them more frequently the unpleasant office of conviction than the pleasant office of approval and comfort. How few disciples there are who know the Holy Ghost in the latter office. What is His comfort? He brings into our hearts, if we fully believe in Jesus, the glorified Giver, above all, the consciousness that we are pleasing the Father by the power of the Son; that we are reconciled children making glad our Father. "How long," asks one, "will Christians introvert the offices of the Holy Spirit, and oblige Him to be in their daily walk more convincing than comforting?" Of what sin does the Spirit convict? Unbelief. It is only because of unbelief that so many Christians, looking back a day, a week or a year, have not the testimony in their souls that their life has pleased God; and so the Spirit is obliged again and again, in fulfilling the law of love by which He acts, to take up His office of convicting of sin. At last many children of God lose all faith in the possibility that they may for any length of time live a life pleasing to their heavenly Father. Then they begin to look in the Bible for a justification of this wretched lowering of the standard of holy living and diminishing of the glorious privilege of living in cloudless communion with the Father and the Son while walking in the comfort of the Holy Ghost. This they find in misinterpreting the seventh chapter of the Epistle to the Romans and a few other perverted texts in Paul's Epistles, and one in I John, "If we say we have no sin, we deceive ourselves." Having dragged the standard down to the low level of "necessary" daily sinning, they have exchanged the comfort of the Spirit for conviction— a worse bargain than Homer speaks of when a certain man exchanged his gold for brass, or "brassed his gold." Where the members of any church that have thus exchanged their gold have become a majority and their influence is preponderating, it is natural for them to delight to see their degraded standard set up in their pulpit. The old standard is now considered as obsolete. It is an uncomfortable rebuke.

Thus, in many instances, the standard is changed. The

wishes of the church mould the preacher. Demosthenes tells the Athenians that they make their orators. They speak what the churches wish to hear. In this way a generation of Christians is born into the church who have never heard of the strange doctrine of walking in the comfort of the Holy Ghost under cloudless skies, victorious over every wilful sin, and delivered from the former intestine war— the flesh striving against the Spirit. This answers our question why so few, relatively, in modern times testify to a continuous walk in the comfort of the Holy Spirit.

But this is a blessing that is not dependent on the majorities. The condition of its existence is not "a count of heads and a clack of tongues." It rests on faith in the promise of our ascended and glorified Christ appearing in heaven for me to-day and sending down the greatest gift that men can receive or heaven can send.

It may be said that "this style of life is practicable for only a very few, such as ministers whose minds are always filled with gospel truth and who are not jostled about in contact with rough men, and for retired old men and women living on the interest of safely invested funds; these, having few perplexities and vexations, may be able to live in serene and uninterrupted communion with God through the conscious abiding of the Comforter. But this is impossible with merchants making hundreds of bargains every day; with operatives in mills, in close contact with many who believe not in Jesus Christ and obey not the moral principles of His gospel; with mothers shut up with a troop of quarrelsome children, and with many other classes of people who have a hard lot in life." Can we quote any instances of walking in the comfort of the Holy Ghost amid such perplexities? We find many such in church history, but we will cite only two, one a clergyman and the other a layman. The record of the first is this: "In stripes above measure, in prisons more frequent, in deaths oft. Of the Jews five times received I forty stripes save one [a hundred and ninety-five]. Thrice was I beaten with rods, once was I stoned, thrice I suffered shipwreck, a night and a day have I been in the deep; in journeyings often, in perils of waters, in perils of robbers, in perils by mine own countrymen, in perils by the heathen, in perils in the city, in perils in the wilderness, in perils in the sea, in perils among false brethren; in weariness and painfulness, in watchings often, in hunger and thirst, in cold and nakedness, by honor and dishonor, by evil report and good report." What is his testimony to his own interior life while running the gauntlet through these perils and sufferings? "I have learned in whatsoever state I am, therein to be content; in everything and in all things have I learned the secret both to be filled and to be hungry, both to abound and to suffer want." From whom did he learn this wonderful secret? Not from the stoics, but from the indwelling Spirit of Christ. For he says, "I can do all things in him that strengthened me" (Phil. iv.11 — 13, Revised Version).

The business of our illustrious layman, that of a premier managing the vast, varied and conflicting interests of an empire of a hundred and twenty provinces, would naturally be regarded as incompatible with a high degree of spirituality. But Daniel, though living in the pre-Pentecostal era and watched by eagle-eyed jealousy, "three times a day went into his chamber, and opened his windows toward heaven, to breathe the heavenly air. The more business we have, the more we want heavenly air." As Dr. Bushnell believes that Socrates and Plato were regenerated "by a special mission of the Holy Ghost," so we believe that Daniel was sustained in his unconquerable fidelity to the God of Abraham by the special indwelling of the Third Person of the Trinity.

We live in an age when liberalists and agnostics covertly undermine Christianity by the insinuation that its principles are ideal and altogether too lofty to be perfectly obeyed by men and women who have been crippled and diminished in their moral capacity by sin. This is the view from the plane of naturalism. The supernaturalism of the indwelling Spirit declares that "where sin abounded grace does much more abound." Glory to God!

The doctrine of Jesus Christ respecting human responsibility is that it is measured by our original talents and favorable or unfavorable environment. Where much is given, much will be required.

The patriarchal dispensation afforded little religious knowledge. Contrasted with our privileges it was as the light of the moon to the sun. We may discover our responsibility in the study of a patriarchal character which adorned the earth more than three thousand years before the day of Pentecost.

The phrase, "walked with God," is in the Bible applied to only two individuals of the human race whose names are known, Enoch and Noah (Gen. v.22; vi.9). "It must be distinguished," says the celebrated commentator, Delitzsch, "from walking before God and walking after God," since both the latter phrases smack somewhat of the constraint of a legal service. Yet they are used to indicate genuine righteousness and blamelessness of life "under the law" — to use a Pauline expression for obedience prompted by fear rather than love. Servility seems to be implied in walking after any one as the servant follows his master. The same feeling is implied in walking before a superior under whose eye we act impelled by a sense of awe and of espionage instead of the gladness and freedom of filial affection walking hand in hand with a loving Father. Walking with a person implies not only a kind of social equality, but the most confidential intercourse, each unbosoming himself to the other in the closest communion. Enoch's walk with God is recorded twice, as something indeed extraordinary, but not impossible to every man in every age. It is put on record for universal imitation, not as a prodigy preternatural and abnormal. It was designed to be the norm or model of every human character. Let us now consider how much walking with God implies.

1. It certainly evinces *perfect harmony.* "How can two walk together except they be agreed?" There was a complete concurrence of the human will with the divine will. Enoch could have used the words of Faber:

> "I worship thee, sweet will of God!
> And all thy ways adore,
> And every day I live I seem
> To love thee more and more."

There are some who insist that this delightful accord of the believer's will with God's will in all the allotments of life, both painful and delightful, is only a beautiful ideal which can never be realized on the earth. It certainly never can be realized on the plane of nature, nor can it be fully experienced on the plane of that initial grace into which we are brought by the new birth. It is possible only to that fulness of the Spirit which sheds abroad the love of God in the heart, filling it to the brim. It is easy for the child who perfectly loves his parents cheerfully to surrender to their commands.

2. Enoch must also have had *perfect trust in God.* If he who comes to God must have faith, much more must he who locks arms and keeps step with Him have the utmost confidence in this divine companion. Mutual confidence is the root of friendship and the indispensable requisite to the true wedlock of two souls. This unquestioning faith settles the question of divine guidance. In Enoch's walk he left to God the choice of the way. Thus he was relieved of a source of much of the perplexity of life — painful solicitude respecting the way he should take at

every crossroad in the journey of life, and often distressing regret for making a wrong choice. Like Enoch we are all strangers on the earth, walking in a path new to us and having many pleasant but fatal by-paths. To those who wish for unerring guidance there is an infallible Guide whose services are gratuitously rendered to complete trust. As perfect love casts out all tormenting fear, so perfect confidence casts out distressing doubt.

3. Enoch must have had *a very joyful sense of security* in his walk with God, being freed from all uncertainties respecting the direction of his journey and all fear of foes in ambuscade. By day and by night he could say to his omniscient and omnipotent conductor, "Where Thou art guide, no ill can come." Complete confidence in Him can walk straight forward regardless of the roar of the lion, the paw of the bear, the tooth of the tiger and the fang of the serpent. Here we have uncovered the secret of the fearlessness of Paul, the courage of Luther, the calmness of Wesley facing furious mobs from one end of England to the other, and the heroism of "the noble army of martyrs" in all the Christian ages.

4. Enoch was characterized by *a holiness so perfect* as to need no finishing touch in death and no quarantine in purgatory preparatory to his introduction into a holy heaven. Perhaps God translated Enoch and Elijah to rebuke the Gnostic error that men cannot be perfectly holy in the body, and that death by separating the spirit from "the vile body" falsely so called (see Phil. iii.21, Revised Version) perfectly prepares the believer for the inheritance of the saints in light. We have searched in vain for any scriptural foundation of this doctrine, which discredits the blood of Jesus Christ as the means of cleansing from all sin, and discounts the Holy Spirit as the agent of entire sanctification in the present life.

5. He who is on so intimate terms with our ever-blessed God will enjoy *the highest possible degree of happiness*.

The fact that this great world is too small to satisfy the human soul demonstrates its likeness to God, inasmuch as it has an infinite capacity which only the Infinite One can fill. Fill this infinite capacity with the illimitable and fathomless ocean, the *pleroma*, "the fulness of him who filleth all in all," and bliss will be supreme and eternal. The vicissitudes of life, from health to sickness, from riches to poverty, from applause to abuse, may ripple the surface of this profound happiness, but they cannot disturb its immeasurable depths. The soul thus drinking from the fountain of felicity is at home everywhere, and sings with Madam Guyon in prison:

"My Lord, how full of sweet content
I pass my years of banishment!
Where'er I dwell, I dwell with Thee,
In heaven, in earth, or on the sea."

What valid excuse have we for not walking with God as closely and as persistently as Enoch walked? Our circumstances are not less favorable. He lived in a pessimistic world rapidly degenerating and soon to be overwhelmed in the deluge. We live in an optimistic world that is on the up grade, steadily rising in moral tone. He lived before the God-Man appeared on the earth and left for our feet a shining path to an open heaven. He lived before the dispensation of the Comforter, who comes to abide in the believer in Jesus Christ. His dispensation compared with ours is as the light of the stars to the cloudless noonday sun.

He was not exempt from toil and care. While walking with God, he did not dwell apart from society, a celibate in monastic seclusion, but begat sons and daughters, bore the burdens of a father in providing for his family and in disciplining his children and commanding them to obey his precepts. It is quite probable that sometimes he had to secure obedience and respect for his authority by the use of the birch.

In no respect was Enoch's environment equal to ours in promoting communion with God. We cannot agree with Delitzsch that He walked in a visible human form beside Enoch three hundred years, a chronic theophany. The writer of the Epistle to the Hebrews enrolls Enoch among the heroes of faith: "By faith" — not by sight — "Enoch was translated." His whole life was a life of faith. There are on the earth to-day many Enochs with whom God is walking and talking. The purpose of this chapter is to encourage many others to spend their lives in this glorious companionship in heavenward travel, "walking in the comfort of the Holy Ghost."

Chapter XXVIII
SPIRITUAL BABES AND SPIRITUAL MEN

THESE CLASSES ARE contrasted in the Epistle to the Hebrews in a manner not complimentary to the babes (iv.12-14).

Men become believers, in the New Testament sense, when through penitent faith they submit to God and receive Jesus Christ as both Saviour and Lord, and realize forgiveness of sins and the filial feeling which cries, "Abba, Father." To be a believer is to have conscious regeneration and the witness of the Spirit. Many are enrolled on earthly records as believers who have no such inward consciousness and witness. These need help which differs from that needed by true believers. Our present chapter is directed to those who are sure that they have been delivered from the power of darkness and have been translated into the kingdom of the Son of God. There are many of these who rest in the fact of the new birth and regard it as the sum total of Christian experience and character. They are spiritual babes, contented with their cradles. Says Dr. Parkhurst, the terror of Tammany, "When a man says that he is satisfied to keep to the rudiments, and that he has no appetite for anything more than the sincere milk of the Word, all depends upon whether he means by that that his one desire is to be religiously fed, or whether it is a confession that he has no Christian ambition, and that he is satisfied to live all his days on religious gruel rather than to have holy gristle wrought into him by the appropriation and digestion of liberal quantities of the gospel's 'strong meat.'" It is a great mistake to regard as a finality the faith which delivers from guilt, and not as a preliminary to the glorious waiting attainments of perfected Christian manhood. To avoid this mistake which dwarfs so many believers we advise an earnest study of the progress of doctrine in the New Testament from the elementary utterances of Jesus Christ about repentance and seeking the kingdom of God up to His last address in which He announces the incompleteness of the gospel and bids His disciples look for another and final stage of instruction under another Teacher whom He would soon send.

Pentecost was the fulfilment of this promise and the completion of that visibly progressive course of doctrine which Christ began to unfold. Now, doctrine is not an end but a means to an end, and that is transfigured character. This progress of doctrine under two teachers signifies that completed Christianhood lies in the dispensation of the Holy Spirit. Says Bernard, "The teaching of the Lord in the Gospels includes the substance of all Christian doctrine, but does not bear the character of finality." When it reaches its highest point it announces itself as unfinished and opens another stage of instruction. In the practical work of salvation there is an exact parallel to this progressive scheme of doctrine. Christian infancy is prophetic of Christian manhood. The movements of still lingering carnality with which the Spirit strives intimate a still remaining work when the flesh shall be crucified and the Spirit shall be the sole tenant of the purified heart.

Hence every believer, while highly prizing the attained experience preached by Jesus to Nicodemus, should move onward beyond the four Gospels into the Acts of the Apostles and the glorious Epistles, if he wishes to appropriate his full heritage in Christ. The alphabet is a necessary beginning of a liberal education, but he who lingers in his primer year after year, and never enters that rich treasury of literature to which it is the key, is no more foolish than the believer who never "ceases to speak of the first principles of Christ," and ever fails to press on unto perfection.

We are aware of the mysteries involved in this subject which we cannot explain. We are glad we cannot; for what man can fully comprehend man may have invented. Hence says Robert Hall, "A religion without a mystery is like a temple without a god." Yet all must admit that the Holy Spirit is not a vague and impersonal abstraction, but a colossal fact in Christian doctrine and an omnipotent personality in the experience of fully advanced believers. There is mystery pertaining to the theology of the Holy Spirit and His relation to the Father and the Son. But a faithful study of the Gospels and of the Acts clearly demonstrates that the Son relegated to the Paraclete that completion of Christian character which it was not His mission to accomplish before His ascension. After His resurrection He gave a foretaste of this completion when He breathed on His disciples and said, "Receive ye the Holy Ghost." Nevertheless they were commanded to wait for the full measure of the Spirit perfecting their character and equipment: "Tarry ye in the city until ye be indued with power from on high." Thus in the new birth there is a capacity for the fulness of the Spirit, and, in all properly instructed believers, a presentiment and a prayer for its glorious realization. To this prayer there should be added an intelligent, persevering and all-surrendering trust in the glorified Redeemer.

We recently heard a preacher declare that the great purpose of the incarnation of the Son of God was to perfect believers by the plenitude of the Spirit. This novel statement does not contradict the Scripture which says that He came "to give his life a ransom for many," for the atonement is only a means to an end, to link unhinged humanity with God. The only link long enough to reach both and strong enough to hold them in blissful and eternal union is the personal Holy Spirit, the original bond between God and men before the rupture wrought by sin. The bridge swept away by that deluge is conditionally restored by the mediatorial work of the Son of God. The condition is unwavering faith put forth by a wholly consecrated soul.

It has been said that doctrine is the skeleton of religion. If this be true, the backbone of that skeleton is the scriptural doctrine of the Holy Spirit. Let every believer secure for his faith this spinal column. The faith of many is weak and flabby because it is invertebrate. In nature only the vertebrates have strength and speed and dominion in their sphere, as the lion and the whale. It is so in the spiritual realm. The lions are few, while the jellyfishes and sponges are many. Here our parallel must end. Things natural have no freedom. A backbone may be acquired in the spiritual realm, but not in the natural. Hence the immense responsibility of every free agent, and his obligation to be conformed to the image of the Son by accepting the offer of the transforming and conforming Spirit.

Some one has suggested that "the lions did not eat Daniel because he was all backbone."

Chapter XXIX
THE SPIRIT PRESIDING OVER THE CHURCH

ALTHOUGH THE HOLY SPIRIT dwells only in the heart, it is the design of His mission that He should preside over one organization. This is the Church of Christ as a visible institution. There is a spiritual body of which Jesus Christ is the head, sometimes called the invisible church, of which we do not now speak. The two will never exactly coincide so long as fallible men admit and discipline the members of the visible Church. Some will be admitted who are wolves in sheep's clothing, and some genuine sheep will be outside of any human fold. It always has been so, and will continue till the infallible Shepherd shall descend and separate this mixed flock to changeless destinies. The kingdom of heaven in its visible, earthly manifestation "is like a drag-net that was cast into the sea and gathered of every kind" (Matt. xiii.47, Revised Version, margin), the good to be gathered into vessels, and the bad to be cast away, "at the end of the world" or age.

Yet it is the desire of Christ that His visible Church should be holy. For this end the Holy Spirit dwelling in holy hearts should preside over the visible organization. Saintly members should exercise control. Otherwise the organization will promote unholiness and not holiness in its members. The temptation is strong to attract men of wealth and social influence. To induce them to become members, the standard of spirituality, and even of morals, is sometimes lowered. They can be retained only by being deferred to and put in authority. Thus the Church becomes worldly. The pulpit must please ungodly men, and doctrines promotive of a deep spirituality cease to be preached.

The Church of Christ, forgetting the prohibition, "Love not the world," has, in some instances, not only fallen in love with the world, but has actually married the world, and it seems impossible to secure a divorce. The protest of the spiritual part of the Church is regarded as a disturbance of the peace of captive Zion. Yet they must protest, or be silently assimilated to baptized worldliness, or withdraw. These are unpleasant alternatives. What is the safeguard? A spirit of humility and faith which leans on Christ alone for success, and esteems the fruit of the Spirit abounding in consecrated mechanics as far more ornamental to the Church than godless millionaires in the pews; a faith which regards a church composed of day laborers, washerwomen and shop-girls, all filled with the Spirit, and, as Father Taylor used to say, "on speaking terms with God," as stronger and richer in God's eyes than a church of the same number of wealthy and fashionable people who are nearer to the world than they are to God. There are illustrious examples of consecrated wealth. Would that the few were more numerous! The few who get through the needle's eye prove the truth of the declaration of Christ, "How hardly shall they that have riches enter into the kingdom of God!"

The presidency of the Holy Spirit in a church, through its most spiritual members, is imperilled by extravagance in the cost of worship beyond the ability of the spiritual worshippers to maintain. This necessitates a deference to rich outsiders, and a resort to various worldly devices and forms of social taxation to fill up the empty treasury. The beginning of the evil is in erecting churches too costly for the members to pay for without long slavery to debt, which in many instances, alas too many, is a long bondage to worldliness. Unconverted men, because of their long purses, are elected as trustees, and schemes of finance for liquidating the debt and paying current expenses are devised which are repugnant to the gospel of Christ, and which dethrone the Holy Spirit from His control of the church by destroying the spirituality of its members. We make no crusade against elegant churches paid for by those who love our Lord Jesus with sacrifices cheerfully laid on His altar. Christianity is not a declaration of war against aesthetics. We do not say, Build as elegant and costly churches as you can pay for without coming under obligation to worldly men, but we do say, Make as large gifts to your local church as you can under the presidency of the Holy Spirit, who also has under His omniscient eye all the other interests of Christ's kingdom on the earth, especially the millions sitting in the darkness of paganism, and prompts all enlightened Christians to evangelize them. The Holy Spirit inspires the missionary spirit, and also general Christian benevolence, which limit and chasten our indulgence of the sense of the beautiful in the adorning of our persons, our homes and our churches.

It is our belief that, in addition to a Pentecostal baptism, two things are needed to restore the control of the Holy Spirit over our churches: first, training in Christian beneficence, or systematic giving, on the basis of a deeper sense of obligation in the matter of stewardship of the

Lord's property. When this has been accomplished, the scanty streams of money flowing into the Lord's treasury will have become steadily flowing rivers. Then, in the second place, worldly men and merely nominal Christians in control of the church must be displaced by men and women filled with the Holy Spirit. Thousands of churches now leaning on the world, imagining themselves too poor to be independent of this corrupting influence, will then be surprised at their own ability to build commodious churches and support worship in a becoming manner.

We are not pleading for an ideal church. Churches governed by the Holy Spirit have existed from the beginning and exist now. They are witnessing, growing, evangelistic and full of the missionary spirit. They have escaped the woe predicted by John Wesley when warning his societies against spiritual decay, "Woe be unto you when rich men become necessary to you!" He had in view the spiritual peril of churches too costly for the societies. His advice to build plain edifices is needed to-day, and always will be so long as there is a tendency to trust more in material splendor than in the power of God. The Christians of the first century escaped this peril by building no churches. There is no account in the New Testament of the dedication of a temple of Christian worship. The disciples in the days of the apostles met for Christian fellowship in some capacious private house. Preaching was probably under the open heavens in a genial climate. The rigorous winter in many countries precludes this method of evangelization. Hence the necessity of buildings.

We confess a strong sympathy with the Plymouth Brethren in their attempt to maintain their worship by receiving the gifts of only those who are professedly regenerate, and refusing the gifts of all others. Their worship is chiefly in private houses. Thus they escape the evils of a worship too costly for their ability. But they are exposed to the danger of constant schism, having no outward bond of union in a temple built by united gifts and sacrifices. When union ceases, the presidency of Him who conserves Christian unity, the Holy Spirit, ceases also. No form of church life is free from perils. Hence the need of ceaseless watchfulness to keep the Paraclete enthroned in the heart and in the Church.

The Holy Spirit will not preside over an organization which magnifies external religious forms and rests in them. So true is this that the term *formalist* signifies "one who does not possess the life and spirit of religion." The Holy Spirit is free and delights in a variety of manifestations in different believers. There should be room in every church for this variety. "Where the Spirit of the Lord is, there is liberty." The converse of this declaration is also true— where liberty is not, there the Spirit does not preside. "There are diversities of operations" in nature, in Providence, in the individual soul, and there must be in the Church if it is indwelt by "the same God which worketh all in all." We believe in the sacraments given for the purpose of holding the person of our adorable Saviour forever in the centre of Christianity, keeping it from becoming a mere system of ethics, after the idea of modern liberalism, deism and agnosticism. We also believe that they are helps to faith, and, in this way, means of grace. But we do not believe that they are the sole method of communing with God. It is possible for us through faith in Christ to have direct and blissful contact of our spirit with the Holy Spirit. This is the central and distinctive doctrine of that modern revival of Christianity called Methodism. The sacraments may be so magnified as to obstruct spiritual communion and foster an offensive and exclusive sacerdotalism. They were never committed to one body of men as a patent right to all the offices of the Holy Spirit.

Chapter XXX
DISHONORING THE HOLY SPIRIT

AS THE MINISTRY of Christ is divided into three parts, the year of obscurity, the year of fame and favor, and the year of opposition, so the ministry of the Holy Spirit has been marked by great contrasts in the estimation of professed Christians. From Pentecost till the close of the apostolic age He was honored with the presidency of the Church, and was everywhere regarded as the heritage of all believers in Jesus Christ. Then there came a gradual spiritual decline in which the person and office of the Spirit went into an eclipse, at first partial, and at last total. He was still regarded as a Person of the Trinity, but one who had accomplished His part in the scheme of salvation as a miraculous factor in the establishment of Christianity and had retired. The Roman Catholic church for fifteen hundred years has in her teachings shut up the Holy Ghost in the age of the apostles and regarded as fanatic and heretic all who profess to know Him as the witness of adoption consciously dwelling within them.

It would spoil sacerdotalism entirely and destroy the

power of the priests if their benighted people should all find out that the gift of the Holy Spirit may be attained directly without the mediation of any man except the God-Man. Those forms of Protestantism which magnify the sacraments as having a saving efficacy in themselves find it extremely difficult to exalt the Holy Spirit as the agent of the new birth and the conservator of spiritual life. We are told by Hunt in his "History of Religious Thought in England" that some Church of England men believed the Spirit gets no nearer to us than the Bible in which He dwells as a source of inspiration; others, that He dwells in the holy eucharist. Warburton, before the time of Lightfoot and Westcott the greatest scholar among the bishops, insisted "that the operations of the Spirit ceased with the apostolic age. Without the gift of tongues and the power to work miracles, the heathen would never have been converted. But when the canon of Scripture was complete, the office of the Spirit was in part transferred to the rule of faith. To talk of the Spirit being now in the world and miraculously changing men's hearts is pure fanaticism." (Hunt, Vol. III, page 279.) This scholar seemed to have no conception of the need of the Spirit to convict of sin, to reveal Christ to penitent faith, to witness to adoption, to regenerate and to sanctify. So great and good a man as Bishop Butler once said to John Wesley, "Sir, what do you mean by faith?" Wesley replied, "By justifying faith I mean a conviction wrought in a man by the Holy Ghost that Christ hath loved him and given Himself for him, and that through Christ his sins are forgiven." The bishop continued: "Some good men might have that kind of faith. Mr. Wesley, I once thought that you and Mr. Whitefield were well-meaning men, but I cannot think so now. Sir, the pretending to extraordinary revelation and gifts of the Holy Ghost is a horrid thing, a very horrid thing." (Hunt, Vol. III, page 289.)

It is surprising that so mighty an intellect as that of

the author of the immortal "Analogy" should fail to discriminate between the gracious operations of the Spirit in the believer and His office of inspiration and the extraordinary gifts, or charisms, enumerated in I Cor. xii. How appalling must have been the spiritual darkness at that time of the mass of Christians both clerical and lay! We who live in a better Christian era have no conception of the eclipse of faith through which the Church of England was then passing while still in the penumbra of Romanism.

But a better era was even then dawning, when the Holy Spirit would be recognized and His offices be honored by vast bodies of believers in all parts of the world. The human instrumentality for the inauguration of this era was John Wesley, whose torch was lighted at the fire burning on the Moravian altar. The Lutheran reformation was theological and ecclesiastical, the Wesleyan was experimental and spiritual. The Spirit, for centuries relegated to the apostolic age, or limited to the sacraments "administered by the priests in the mythical apostolic succession," freed Himself from all these fancied limitations and came into immediate, vital, conscious contact with believing souls, and there stood up a great and valiant army in the valley of dry bones in both England and America. Faith in Christ and reliance on His promise of the Paraclete afforded the conditions of the Spirit's manifestation. The secret of Methodism is conscious salvation through the testimony of the Spirit, the finger of God touching every penitent who surrenders to God and receives His Son as both Saviour and Lord, who expectantly waits for the Dove of Peace to bring the olive leaf of divine peace and afterwards to bring in perfect purity through perfect love shed abroad in the heart. Calvinism in modern times has become so modified as to admit that the witness of the Spirit and His conscious indwelling fulness are the privilege of all believers and not, as formerly, the exclusive privilege of a few favored souls, the "*electi electorum.*" Unmitigated predestinarianism requires uncertainty respecting regeneration and forgiveness as a safeguard to keep the believer from a neglect of watchfulness and from that looseness of living which would naturally follow the doctrine of unconditional election combined with the witness of the Spirit to our adoption as sons of God. Hence the reign of Calvinism of the primitive type has not tended to magnify the Spirit's office of imparting a knowledge of forgiven sin, while its insistence that the Adamic propensity to sin must continue till the soul is released from its earthly tenement is inconsistent with the Spirit's office of entire sanctification. The decay of Calvinism favors the restoration of the doctrine of the fulness of the Holy Spirit as the heritage of all persevering believers.

There is another hopeful sign of the times very favorable to the revival of the doctrine and experience of the Pentecostal gift universally enjoyed in the Christian Church. I refer to the marked change for the better which has recently taken place in scientific minds. These had so long studied matter and its mechanical laws, and so long had they moved on the dead level of naturalism, that they were strongly inclined to reject all the testimonies to conscious movements of the Holy Spirit in the heart as the figments of excited imaginations. But since Balfour and Romaine have demonstrated that there are grounds of certainty in man's moral nature and spiritual aspirations as worthy of confidence as the testimony of the senses and the conclusions of the logical faculty, the arrogance of materialism toward Christian experience has been effectually rebuked.

Thus many obstructions to the free course of the Spirit have been removed from the path of intelligent men and women. What is now needed to complete the restoration of the Spirit is that His divine personality and His gracious offices in the redemptive scheme should be magnified in the pulpits of Christendom. Then will the purified and endowed Church be prepared to meet the hosts of Satan, "terrible as an army with banners."

These words of the saintly Fletcher in his portrait of St. Paul have clung to my memory more than a score of years: "To reject the Son of God manifested in the Spirit, as worldly Christians are universally observed to do, is a crime of equal magnitude with that of the Jews, who rejected Him when manifested in the flesh."

1. The Holy Ghost is dishonored when spoken of as a thing or an influence, and not as a person. This is often done by referring to Him by the use of "it" instead of "he." Our authorized version of Rom. viii.16, "The Spirit itself," has greatly promoted this error. The Revision is correct, "The Spirit himself." Not only does it degrade the Spirit to strip Him of His personality, but it cuts away the ground for that strong faith in Him which is requisite to secure His abiding presence in us and the complete work of His offices. We cannot trust a thing as we trust a person. Indistinct and hazy conceptions weaken faith. When thought of as a power, a principle, an effluence however bright, the Holy Spirit is degraded infinitely below a personality implying intelligence, feeling, will, freedom and a moral sense. Many true believers in Jesus Christ fail to realize the indwelling Spirit because their faith in Him is far less definite than their faith in Christ. This weak faith is because of nebulous conceptions of the Spirit.

2. He is dishonored when regarded as a created person. Some admit His personality, but deny His divinity equal to the Father and the Son in power and glory. In so doing they divest themselves of the ground of the strongest possible faith in the Spirit. The proofs of His divinity are found in texts which ascribe to Him divine attributes, divine acts, divine titles, and associate Him on implied

terms of equality with the Father and the Son, as in the formula for Christian baptism, Matt, xxviii.19, and the apostolic benediction, II. Cor. xiii.14.

3. The Spirit is dishonored when anything is substituted for His offices in the inspiration of spiritual life and the development of Christian character, such as a germ of natural goodness instead of the new birth, education instead of sanctification, culture of the aesthetic tastes instead of the fruit of the Spirit, roundabout inferences that we are saved, neglecting and undervaluing the direct witness of the Spirit "crying in the heart Abba, Father," the pleasures of sense instead of the joy of the Holy Ghost, the honor of men rather than the approval of God. We have already alluded to the disrespect of the Spirit when His witness to adoption is slighted. This is so important that it needs further emphasis. The Spirit is really, though it may be unintentionally, dishonored when His office of witness to the adoption of the penitent believer is dropped out of the sermon and out of the instruction of seekers at the altar. When the office is slighted the officer is disparaged. When the sinner becomes a new creature it is not by a natural process of evolution, or of development from a germ of goodness, but by the will and work of the new-Creator. When it is said that a man may regenerate himself by assuming an obedient attitude of his will toward Christ as both Saviour and Lord, disrespect is shown to the sole author of the new birth. It is true that men have the gracious ability to convert themselves in the literal meaning of that verb, that is, to turn about, to forsake sin, and in penitent faith to look unto God. This is conversion, a graciously assisted human act. But regeneration is the sole work of the Spirit when the term is used in its theological sense. In the same way the Spirit is slighted when His office as God's messenger to announce the soul's adoption is ignored and something else is put in His place. The modern substitute is the Word,

the Holy Scriptures. Written many centuries ago, they cannot certify my sonship to God by adoption. The Bible nowhere teaches that itself is the ground of personal assurance. It distinctly reveals the fact that the Holy Spirit is the direct witness to this all-important event on which eternal destiny hangs. "Because ye are sons, God hath sent forth the Spirit of his Son into your hearts, crying, Abba, Father." The phrase "into your hearts," instead of "into the Bible," denotes a direct, personal certification of adoption. In addition to this, there are found in the Bible, inspired by the Spirit, the marks of the new birth, the fruit of the Spirit. When these are discovered, they constitute an inferential testimony confirming the direct witness of the Spirit. But when the Word is put in the first place, as the ground of assurance, and the Spirit is omitted, or put in the second place, He is dishonored. There is a numerous school of evangelists who are thus constantly ignoring the Holy Ghost in all their teaching of assurance. It is a great error. It leaves the seeker without that satisfactory certification of sonship to God which He in His goodness has provided. "The Spirit himself beareth witness [direct testimony] with our spirit [inferential testimony] that we are the children of God."

This direct contact of the Spirit is elsewhere taught under the imagery of "the earnest," or money paid to bind the bargain, and "sealing," since the seal authenticates, assures and appropriates. The Holy Spirit in the believer's heart is the Father's seal. Let all religious teachers honor this seal. To dishonor it is to encourage a multitude of professed disciples of Christ to go into eternity with invalid title-deeds to eternal life, with no possibility of rectifying the fatal mistake.

4. Ministers of the gospel and other Christian workers dishonor the Spirit when they more earnestly desire His gifts than Himself; when they are more eager to be clothed with His power than to be filled with His presence; when

they prefer popularity to purity; when they rely more on polished rhetoric than on the power of the Holy Ghost; when they are more concerned about preparing the sermon than themselves; when they are more ambitious to please the Church than the Head of the Church; when they subordinate the ministry of the Lord Jesus to themselves and not to the Lord Jesus; when they use the sacred office as a ladder to personal fame or gain, instead of a stairway up which they may lead repenting sinners to the bosom of God. The Holy Ghost scrutinizes motives. He searches not only the deep things of God, but also the depths of man's heart, and He feels aggrieved when He is outranked in man's esteem by anything beneath the sun, yea, beneath the throne of the ascended Son of God and Redeemer of men, whom it is His mission to glorify on earth. Hence the Holy Spirit is dishonored whenever Christ is not exalted as the only Saviour of lost men; when He is displaced in the pulpit by some fad or fancy of momentary interest; when Jesus Christ crucified is regarded as a less attractive Saturday pulpit bulletin than the last international yacht race, or a panegyric on the last humoristic poet of liberalism.

5. Disrespect is shown to the Holy Spirit when the Bible He has inspired is neglected, and religious books and periodicals illustrating, explaining and defending the Book of books find little sale and less attention, while secular and fictitious literature is read with great avidity. It grieves the Spirit to see myriads of people bearing the name of Christ feeding on the chaff of irreligious reading and crying, "Oh! my leanness!" or devouring the poison of the satanic press and going down to a speedy spiritual death as moral suicides, because of the virus of a baneful literature voluntarily poured into their arteries. "As he thinketh in his heart, so is he." But since a man thinks as he largely supplies materials for thought by reading, it is true that as he readeth good or bad books, so is he.

6. When the Holy Spirit moves holy men to write saving truth for the spiritual healing of the nations throughout all generations, and bad men develop a satanic ingenuity in assailing this precious record and in destroying the faith of men in that religion which transforms sinners to saints here and reveals life eternal hereafter, the Spirit of inspiration is not only grieved but is deeply disgraced. It is like some baneful genius destroying in some dark and stormy night all faith in the mariner's compass and causing all the ships, with all their crews and passengers, in all the oceans of the world, henceforth to sail in painful uncertainty, and many of them to drift into ruin. It is one thing to dig down to the foundations of a citadel in order to show their strength, but it is quite another thing to explode a hundred pounds of dynamite beneath them. There is in our times a class of higher critics who are studious to conserve all the truth that the Holy Spirit has inspired. With such He is well pleased. His honor is safe in their keeping. There is a class of destructives who are madly attempting to sweep out of the universe every vestige of a supernatural revelation, and to beat down to the dead level of naturalism every religious truth that stands a foot above that level. The personal Holy Spirit, whose mission it is to conserve and apply saving truth, cannot look upon this attempt with indifference. It dishonors Him to assault His work. In our day this assault is quite indirectly made by some. They are attempting to bring Christianity to this level, not by beating it down, but by lifting all pagan religions up. They admit the inspiration of Isaiah and Paul, but they assert that Plato and Shakespeare are just as much divinely inspired. We have heard one of the champions of "liberal Christianity" read in his Boston pulpit from Job, Plato, Seneca, Cato, and T. Starr King, and then say, "Thus endeth the reading of the Scriptures."

The robber in the Arabian Nights put a chalk mark on a house which contained treasure, intending to rob it in the night. Morgiana chalked all the other houses in the same way, and thus defeated the robber's purpose. One book contains the treasure of heavenly truth for the enrichment of mankind. That they may easily find it, God has put the mark of inspiration upon it. Liberalism is trying to defeat His benevolent purpose by putting a similar mark on all the religious books of the heathen and all the works of genius. The scheme may so far succeed as to mislead and bewilder thousands of souls and turn their feet away from the path to eternal life. Such an act is doing despite to the Spirit of grace.

7. The divine Spirit is dishonored by the unholy lives of those who profess to be regenerated by Him. The Christian professes to be a sample of the new creation. A defective sample discredits its maker. Thus the unworthy life of a man who by profession writes the name of the holy Christ across his forehead for all the world to read brings reproach not only on those who labored and prayed for his salvation, and on the church with which he is united, but also on the Holy Spirit, the Lord and giver of life and the new-creator of souls. Still greater is the dishonor to the Spirit where one professing to be filled with the Spirit, and to be entirely sanctified by His indwelling, is living an unworthy life. The more valuable the coin the baser is the counterfeit. A Christian may become a false professor in two ways— by an untruthful original profession, and by retrogression from a true profession. In either case the Spirit is dishonored. But I speak more especially of the latter. "How is the gold become dim! How is the most fine gold changed!"

Our words may not only dishonor, but distress the Holy Spirit. From Eph. iv.29, 30, "Let no corrupt speech proceed out of your mouth, but such as is good for edifying... And grieve not the Holy Spirit of God," we learn that "worthless" (Meyer), "profitless and unedifying, not necessarily filthy " (Ellicott and Alford) talk is here indicated as painful to the divine Spirit, vile talk being prohibited in v. 4. Empty and trifling discourses, low wit and nonsense, are so opposed to the holy nature and work of the Holy Spirit, who dwells in Christians, that He cannot fail to be grieved thereat. "The chosen expression 'Holy Spirit of God,' renders the *enormity* of such action most palpable." (Meyer.) "The Christian walking in sincerity utters not only no wicked, but even no useless words." (Olshausen.) This does not exclude animated, instructive and cheerful discourse, enlivened by flashes of delicate and dignified wit, but it does mark with the disapprobation of the Holy Spirit the jester, the punster and studied humorist, whose chief end and aim in human society is smartness, facetiousness and drollery.

The universe is rational, and its Creator is rational, and the Holy Spirit, the divine Person through whom He acts on man as a reprover, and in the believer as the sanctifier, is also rational. He can never be pleased with anything irrational, unreal and farcical. Jesus Christ, whom the Spirit represents, took a view of human life and destiny too realistic to admit of those distortions of the truth which are implied in jokes and witticisms. If it is the office of the Spirit to bring us into conformity with the image of the Son of God in moral character, shall we not be assimilated to His sobriety and gravity also? Will not the Spirit chasten and elevate the imagination and make it the vehicle of truth and the instrument of instruction? Will He not in this way sanctify the fine arts and make painting and sculpture, poetry and music, rhetoric and oratory channels of grace to the believing heart? Is it not the mission of the Spirit to harmonize and unify all our faculties so that the aesthetical and the ethical shall both minister to our complete spiritual development? If an affirmative answer is correct, it follows that so much of pleasantry and wit as is needful for human society at its climax the Holy Spirit will sanctify, and all that tends to degrade He will eliminate. Humor without the savor of godliness always tends downward, changing the sublime into the ridiculous, and turning the sacred into the profane. It may be thought that in the form of ridicule it is necessary to castigate folly and refute error. But Jesus Christ, the model religious teacher, did not use it in denouncing the hypocrisies of the Pharisees and in establishing His gospel. Elijah made use of ridicule against the priests of Baal, as did Paul against Christian teachers insisting on circumcision. "I would they would even mutilate themselves" (Gal. v.12, Revised Version, margin). But it is a dangerous weapon of the nature of a boomerang.

8. Next to disrespect shown to the Holy Spirit is disparagement of His work. Almost identical are an author and his book, a mechanic and the product of his skill. Ridicule of the work is derision of the workman. This truth underlies that weighty and alarming utterance of Jesus Christ, "Whosoever shall be ashamed of me and my words, in this adulterous and sinful generation, of him also shall the Son of man be ashamed, when he cometh in the glory of his Father, with the holy angels." The lifeblood of Jesus pulsates in His words, for He says, "The words that I speak unto you, they are spirit and they are life." It was the work of the Son to take His Father's words on one side of the veil, and reveal them unto men on the other side. Hence contempt for the revelation is mockery of the Revealer.

Moreover, it is true that the more excellent the work in the estimation of the worker, the more keenly does he feel dishonored when it is disparaged. A condemned masterpiece is the climax of mortification.

What work on the earth is the masterpiece of the Holy Spirit? Is it not the completed holiness of a soul born with a propensity to sin? We infer this from the adjective "holy," which is a part of the name *Holy* Ghost. He is thus called, not because this adjective distinguishes His nature from that of the Father and the Son, but because it designates His office to impart and to create and conserve holiness. It is true that believers are provisionally "sanctified in Christ Jesus," just as all men are provisionally saved in His atonement. But men are really saved only when through their faith in Christ they are born of the Spirit, and believers are wholly sanctified only when they appropriate this work of the Holy Spirit as the completion of the new-creation of the soul. This is the climax of His activity on the earth. He is the finger of God when He causes us "to know the exceeding greatness of his power to usward who believe."

Therefore it follows that the sin that borders upon the irremissible sin, the blasphemy against the Holy Ghost, is the irreverent and contemptuous criticism of His work in the entire sanctification of an immortal soul. This is a sin to which every generation of Christians is exposed, but more especially that body of believers which is beginning to lean upon the world and to let down its standard of truth in order to court its favor. Then he who would magnify the dispensation of the Holy Ghost, by attesting His power to perfect holiness in the believer, may expect to endure disparaging and captious criticisms which really reflect on the divine author. This is a serious matter. Of the three Persons in the one divine nature, the Holy Spirit is the most sensitive to slights and insults.

Should it be said that the holiest person you have ever met had faults, and was therefore a just object of criticism, we reply that many imperfections in taste, judgment and outward appearance may be consistent with perfect purity of heart.

The only perfect man since Adam was created did not escape the contempt of men.

In the classroom of President Wayland, many years ago, a student arose and put the following question: "Dr. Wayland, don't you think, if Christian people were more amiable, kind, lovely in their dispositions and in their intercourse with the world, if they presented Christianity in its true aspects, don't you think everybody would be so attracted and charmed as to embrace Christianity at once?" Dr. Wayland, assuming an air more deliberate and earnest than usual, replied in substance: "There was once on earth one who combined in perfect symmetry all the graces of Christian character; one who was wise, kind, unselfish, lovely, without fault, absolutely perfect; and what was the result of this exhibition of character in the world? They cried, *Crucify him! crucify him!*"*

Says Archdeacon Hare: "But the Comforter was to abide with Christ's Church *forever*. Hence it has been repeatedly seen that when He was forgotten and His abiding presence and influence were almost denied by those who occupied the chief places in the outward Church, He has manifested Himself to others, who, as of old, have been mocked, and said to have been *full of new wine*, nay, have been persecuted, and even cast out from the outward communion of the Church. This, which had happened before, happened again the last century. The men who were awakened to a deeper consciousness that there can be no Christian life in the soul except through the operation of the Spirit, were, some of them, led or driven to secede from our [Anglican] Church, while others had to endure reproach and scorn within it. On the other hand, the dominant prosaic rationalism laid down that all manner of enthusiasm must needs be foolish and mischievous. One of our bishops wrote a book against enthusiasm, as a quality fit only for Papists and Methodists, evincing no sympathy with the deep feelings and wants which were venting themselves even in their most offensive absurdities; no insight into the manifold causes which helped to delude them; no desire to separate the

---

*See Appendix, Note I

wheat and preserve it from the conflagration of the tares; and no recognition of that which was holy and just and true in their zeal, their energy and their devotion. Folly and fraud were the author's summary sentence; and with these two words, blind as the hangman's rope, he strung together the puppets of straw that he called by the names of Wesley and Whitefield and Zinzendorf, along with others under the denomination of St. Anthony, St. Francis, St. Ignatius and St. Teresa."

Chapter XXXI
THE FULNESS OF THE SPIRIT

IT IS SOMETIMES SAID that Christ's new commandment, "Love one another," is the eleventh commandment. In the same way we have the twelfth in Paul's mandatory precept, "Be filled with the Spirit" (Eph. v.18). There is an error quite widely spread in the Church, that the baptism or fulness of the Spirit is not universally obligatory, but rather that it is an elective experience, a privilege and not an imperative duty. We note that the passive voice, "be filled," implies that we cannot actively fill ourselves, but that the Spirit is present like the atmosphere and ready instantly to fill every vacuum. It is ours to create a vacuum by an unreserved self-surrender to Christ as both Saviour and Lord. This implies strong faith. In truth, faith is man's only capacity to receive God. He cannot enter us through the senses, for they report only material things; nor can the Spirit enter the soul through the reason, which apprehends only relations, not realities. Therefore faith is the only door by which the Spirit comes into the human spirit. Man, a spirit, is an image of God the Spirit. The creature is made for the occupancy of the Creator, and he finds his highest joy only when as a temple he is "the habitation of God through the Spirit."

It is quite evident that purity is a prerequisite to this indwelling fulness of the Spirit. This is the divine order: first cleansed, then filled. All filling presupposes emptying. It is true that the baptism of the Spirit has been sought and received as a full endowment for service. But a careful examination of such experiences reveals the fact of the Spirit's revelation of an inward bias to moral evil, and also of the seeker's full consent to its extermination by the purifying fire of the Spirit before He takes up His abode within. This consent is a part of his irreversible and all-embracing self-surrender to Christ, the great Physician, whose healing power is preparatory to the full endowment with the Holy Spirit.*

Turning to our Greek Testament we note that the command "Be filled with the Spirit" is in the present tense, denoting not a mechanical fulness once for all, but a vital fulness, a constant appropriation and a perpetual reception, a ceaseless drinking and a ceaseless thirst. Hence the paradox of Charles Wesley:

> "Insatiate to this spring I fly;
> I drink, and yet am ever dry."

The thirst is for more of the same kind, not for anything different, like the thirst of a perfectly healthy babe. "But the water that I shall give him shall be in him a well [artesian] of water springing up into everlasting life." The need of an increase of this water is not excluded. Says Calvin: "The Holy Spirit is a gushing fountain ever flowing, so that they who have been

---

*See Appendix, Note K

renewed by spiritual grace are in no danger of becoming completely dry," so far as the supply is concerned. There is danger of a diminishing appropriation till the soul has ceased to drink. Says Bengel, "Truly that water, as far as it depends on itself, has in it an everlasting virtue; and when thirst returns the defect is on the part of the man, not of the water."

"We may insensibly and without raising the suspicion of our Christian friends lose the life of the Spirit, and preserve at the same time deceitful appearances. For when the Holy Spirit withdraws from the soul He sometimes allows the forms which He has created to remain. The oil is exhausted, but the lamp is there; prayer is offered and the Bible read; the going to church is not given up, and, to a certain degree, the service is enjoyed; in a word, religious habits are preserved, and, like the corpses found at Pompeii, which were in a perfect state of preservation and in the very position in which death had surprised them, but which were reduced to ashes by contact with the air, so the blast of trial, of temptation or that of the final judgment will also destroy those spiritual corpses." (Tophel.)

There is a fulness of the Spirit of the emotional kind which is liable to great fluctuations. It is genuine but not deep. It does not have permanent and staying qualities. It is often received amid the tidal wave of the faith and sympathy of a multitude, and begins to decline when the social magnetism is dispelled by separation from the jubilant throng in the temple or camp. The Spirit seems to pervade only the upper and more easily reached currents of the soul; the depths of the being, the inner life where the will dwells and character has its roots, have not been reached. Their experience is like what Fletcher calls "a land flood," a spring freshet, and not a river steadily flowing from springs so deep as not to be affected by summer's drought and winter's cold. Corresponding to the stony-ground converts to Christ, who receive with joy the word into the shallow soil and immediately send up a flush of green which as quickly withers away, is a class of Pentecostal professors whose uneven ecstatic experiences are a stumbling block to many Christians and a great hindrance to the experimental reception by the mass of believers of the most precious truths of the gospel, especially *the* promise of the Father and of the Son, the gift of the Comforter. Whenever He is deliberately received in the fulness of His offices and the permanence of His indwelling, men of power are raised up, and anointed women go forth to successful labor in the harvest fields of the world.

Many a professed Christian now a cipher in influence would become mighty in advancing the kingdom of Christ if he were filled with the Pentecostal gift. "The apostles were good men before the baptism of the Pentecost. But how dull of apprehension were they though they listened to the instructions, not of a prophet who was of the earth, therefore earthly and speaking from the earth, but of Him who was from heaven and above all, and who spake the very words of God. How little they saw the glory or felt the power of the truth they heard! Yet they knew more, believed more, loved more than all the rest of mankind. They possessed truth which flesh and blood had not revealed unto them, but the Father in heaven. 'I am the way, and the truth, and the life.' But when the Holy Ghost fell on them what a glorious transformation! It was as if meridian day had burst upon them from the obscurity of an eclipse. As with tongues of fire they spoke forth the wonders which, though they knew them before, they till now had not known. God had passed before them and proclaimed His name, shown them His glory. The Spirit had taken the all-glorious beams that blaze from the face of Christ and had carried them deep into their hearts. The chambers of their inner being had become all luminous, and every ray of light there glowed with a dissolving, melting warmth. The fountains of the great deep of their sensibilities were broken up, and floods of happy tears were shed over a thousand remembrances of their beloved Lord. His instructions, His miracles, His holiness, His love, His majesty, His sufferings, His resurrection, His seat at His Father's right hand, His whole manifestation and work stood before them in a new and resplendent light and bathed in glory." (John Morgan, D. D.)

Chapter XXXII
THE UNCLAIMED DEPOSIT

THE SCOTTISH BANKERS HAVE recently reported that the unclaimed deposits in their banks amount to forty million pounds, equal to nearly two hundred million dollars. For several generations depositors have suddenly died, and their bank books have been lost through casualties on the sea or land, and their kindred are ignorant of the treasures rightly theirs. Many of them are doubtless in great need through what Socrates called "myriad poverty," and are fighting desperately to keep the wolf from the door. If some philanthropist should get the names of these lost depositors and search out the legal heirs to these millions of money and persuade them to enforce their claims, he would be a benefactor indeed, worthy of a marble or bronze statue erected by their willing hands.

This suggests the vastness of the spiritual deposits made by our Elder Brother, Jesus Christ, awaiting every child of God when he presents and proves his claim. Many of them are spiritual starvelings in hunger and distress, going about in rags, crying, "Oh! my leanness, my leanness!" when they might be feasting in a palace, clothed in white linen, each having a purse well filled with "gold tried in the fire." For Jesus Christ became poor that we who believe in Him might become rich. President Wayland, in his "Political Economy," defines riches as the abundant means for gratifying desire. Man's deepest desires are rooted in his spiritual nature. He desires unfailing happiness. This in the presence of a holy God must come from likeness to Him, so that we perfectly love what He loves and perfectly hate what He hates. This likeness dwells only in the sphere of love filling the soul to the very brim, that perfect love which casteth out fear. The origin of this love is not a fountain in the lowlands of nature; it is supernatural; it is a stream pouring down from the uplands of heaven.

"The love of God is shed abroad in our hearts by the Holy Spirit given unto us." Therefore the gift of the Holy Spirit Himself abiding in the believer is the true riches, the source of supreme felicity, wherever He is received as the indwelling Comforter. This gift is on deposit for every believer. But many do not claim this heritage of blessing, and others have not really heard the good news of the great deposit in their name. For there are many spiritual babes in God's family to whom, as they emerge from their minority, we must unfold their wealth of Christian privilege. For the gift of the abiding Paraclete is to those only who already love our Lord Jesus Christ and prove it by obedience (John xiv.15, 16). Even to such persons this gift does not come as a matter of course. He comes only to those who so earnestly desire His presence as definitely to ask, and to persevere in asking, till they consciously receive this divine Person. Hence much of gospel preaching has for its proper object the incitement to seek this greatest gift which God can now send or believers receive. If the pulpit theme is prayer, there can be no real prayer unless the indwelling Spirit Himself "makes intercession for us." For He is "the Spirit of grace and supplication." If the subject of the sermon is singing as a part of Christian worship, the argument is incomplete without the exhortation to "sing in the Spirit." Does the Christian aspire to real freedom? He will find that where the Spirit of the Lord is, there, and there only in the wide universe, is real liberty. If the believer is weak, the faithful preacher will say that the only way for him to be strengthened with might is "by the Spirit in the inner man." If the preacher divulges the secret of true happiness, he will speak of "joy in the Holy Ghost." If the doubting soul needs assurance of sonship to God, the only voice which truly cries "Abba, Father," in believing hearts is that of "the Spirit of his Son." Without the cry of the living Spirit within, the written word is not a sufficient ground of assurance. Would you know where God's temple is? "Know ye not that ye are the temple of God, and that the Spirit of God dwelleth in you?" Would you have the whole galaxy of Christian virtues adorning your character? The Holy Spirit is the divine decorator, supplying "love, joy, peace, long-suffering, gentleness, goodness, faith, meekness, temperance." If the believer, conscious of sonship to God, is wrestling with inward hereditary evil, that propensity to sin which theologians call original sin, and is desirous of deliverance and of a full preparation for life everlasting, let him seek perfect cleansing in the only way it can be found, "through sanctification of the Spirit and belief of the truth." Would he have an inward revelation of the Son of God in all His loveliness, such as Paul had, let him study Christ's words respecting "another Comforter:" "He shall glorify ME; for he shall take of mine, and show it unto you; " not to your bodily eyes, but to your spiritual perception, thus fulfilling the promise made by Jesus, not only to His twelve apostles and the disciples who heard His words, but also to every believer through all the coming generations, "I will manifest myself unto him."

We have thus described this treasure on deposit for you, my Christian reader, with a definite purpose. Is it up to this hour, in your case, an unclaimed deposit? If it is, it may be because you have greatly undervalued it under some misconception of its transcendent excellence. Divest yourself of unworthy prejudice; lay aside the error which blinds you to the glory of the gospel of the Comforter. Ask God to help you to study "*the* promise of the Father" with anointed eyes and a heart open skyward. Then will spiritual hunger, which is itself one of the beatitudes, be awakened, and faith to appropriate your now claimed deposit will spring up in your aspiring soul.

But if the study of the Holy Scriptures does not overcome your spiritual inertia and banish the prejudice which may be eclipsing this subject, listen to the testimony of those who have been to God's bank and in the name of Jesus Christ have boldly claimed this their deposit. Testimony is the prime thing in our courts and in all trade, social intercourse and medical science. It has its place in Christianity. "With the heart man believeth, and with the mouth confession is made unto salvation," both initial and complete. Listen, therefore, with candor to the testimony of victorious souls, and you will find by what they conquered. You will conquer by the same sign. In the same field where they sought and found a treasure which makes them spiritual millionaires there is a lot reserved for your pickaxe and spade. Dig and become rich. A pauper in grace reflects little credit upon the Saviour who "is able to do exceeding abundantly above all that we ask or think, according to the power that worketh in us, unto him be glory in the church by Christ Jesus throughout all ages, world without end. Amen."

Chapter XXXIII
RIVERS OF LIVING WATER

IT IS VERY RARELY that we find a saying of Jesus Christ, the great teacher, with an apostolic note subjoined. This unique combination is one of the priceless jewels in John's Gospel (vii.37-39). Christ was at the feast of tabernacles. "At every day of the feast, at the time of the morning sacrifice, a priest brought into the forecourt, in a golden vessel, water from the spring of Siloah, which rises within the mount on which, the temple stood, and poured it, mingled with sacrificial wine, into two bowls which stood upon the altar and in which there was an opening by which it made its escape." Meanwhile the priests sounded trumpets and clashed cymbals, and the words of Isa. xii.3 were chanted, "With joy shall we draw water out of the wells of salvation." Just when the people were exhibiting great joy at the sight of this symbol Jesus stood forth and with a loud voice cried out to the vast multitude: "If any man thirst, let him come unto me, and drink. He that believeth on me, as the scripture hath said, out of his belly shall flow rivers of living water." Upon this John thus comments: "But this spake he of the Spirit, which they that believe in him should receive: for the Holy Ghost was not yet given; because that Jesus was not yet glorified." This explains why Jesus used the future tense, "rivers of living waters shall flow." The ceaseless Pentecostal fountain was yet to be opened for earth's thirsty millions.

It is commonly thought that when Jesus uttered the words, "Come unto me, and drink," He meant but one act— believe on me; that is, to come is to believe, and to drink is to believe. But there is a beautiful shade of difference. Christ used no tautology. To come to a fountain does not quench thirst. This represents the direct act of saving faith, not satisfying, but painful from the strenuous effort. But drinking is a fit emblem of the reflex spontaneity of assuring faith grounded in the Spirit's inward cry, "Abba, Father." This is not a single effort, as saving faith is, but a continuous and joyful appropriation. We come to the fountain once; we drink always and without conscious volition. The first act is saving faith, the second act, or series of acts, is the faith of assurance. In fact, the water will once for all be received into the inner nature, will be immanent in the believer, and will attend him in every stage of his being, even to eternity— "a well of water springing up unto eternal life." Says Tholuck, "This eternally upspringing water expresses that death not only does not interrupt this *life*, this communion with God, but that it rather brings it to perfection."

In John iv.14, Jesus declared His gift of water would be a self-dependent spring within the heart; but at the feast of tabernacles He went far beyond that in saying that the inner fountain should pour forth, not brooks, but rivers, Amazons, abundantly quenching our thirst and refreshing others. This interpretation avoids the error that one Christian can impart the Holy Spirit to another. He may by his testimony and conduct awaken thirst in his neighbor and lead him to the spring where he may himself drink. One may be a channel for the water of life to flow to another.

The conditions on which the living water, the Holy Comforter, is given are clearly set forth in John xiv.14-16, the last address of Christ before His crucifixion. It has been very appropriately called "the heart of Jesus." The conditions are love to Christ evinced by obedience to His commandments and asking in His name. The Paraclete is the greatest mediatorial gift. The words "in my name," as the condition of prevailing prayer, distinctly reveal the mediatorial office of the Son of God in the establishment of His Father's kingdom. No man can wilfully ignore the Mediator and then prevail in his prayer to God for the gift of the Comforter. Hence many fail to receive the well of water, the Pentecostal gift; some because their theology is so meagre that it affords in the unity of the divine nature no place for the Mediator, and others because He is rather a name, an orthodox formula, than a living person in whom they trust with a faith equal to that exercised toward the heavenly Father. Such equal reliance the Son claims when He says, "Believe in God, and believe in me." Before He finished the discourse which opens with these words He completed the prayer taught to His disciples at the beginning of His ministry by adding "in my name." It is this completed prayer, offered in faith by a soul filled with ardent desire, which opens wide the portals for the incoming of the Comforter, and unseals the fountain henceforth eternally springing up in the hidden depths of the believing soul.

Many excellent Christians fail to receive the fulness of the Spirit because, like the woman at Jacob's well, they do not know the gift, or rather, as Campbell translates it, "the bounty, the liberality of God," that disposition of mind from which the best gifts flow. "If thou knewest, thou wouldest have asked." Our asking is limited by our knowledge. Ignorance of God's large-heartedness asks only small favors. Hence a better knowledge of God is requisite for spiritual enlargement. There must be a more thorough acquaintance with His character as revealed in His word and in the testimony of those who are dwelling in the higher altitudes of grace. Knowledge excites desire. The merchant who artistically arranges his goods in his windows acts upon this principle. To awaken a spiritual appetite God sets forth in revelation His showcase of exceedingly great and precious promises. In this display of priceless jewels is the Kohinoor diamond of the Holy Scriptures, "the promise of the Father," towering above all the other promises as indeed "a mountain of light," an ornament for the crown of every "king and priest unto God," who claims his full heritage in Christ.

Jesus said to the woman, "If thou hadst asked, I would have given," showing as invariable an order of sequences in the spiritual realm as in the material world. He answers all true prayer that reaches His ear, and is waiting for more. To bestow the Comforter is His highest delight. He is more willing to give the Holy Spirit "to them that ask him" than earthly parents are to give good gifts unto their children.*

---

*See Appendix, Note L

Chapter XXXIV
THE EXTRAORDINARY GIFTS OF THE SPIRIT

IN THE OLD TESTAMENT we read of extraordinary gifts of the Spirit entirely different from the graces of the Spirit. Bezaleel was endowed by the Spirit of God "to devise cunning works in gold and in silver and in brass" for beautifying the tabernacle. Samson when the Spirit came upon him became preternaturally strong, and both Balaam and King Saul were seized by the Spirit, who constrained them to prophesy, although they were utterly destitute of grace. From his birth, John the Baptist was filled with the Holy Ghost rather as an outward gift than as an inward Pentecostal grace. This Old Testament endowment of the Spirit did not render him sinless from his birth, but it inspired in him a vivid sense of Israel's apostasy and of his own vocation to preach repentance of sin as a preparation for the coming of the Messiah King. He was endowed with a dauntless courage to rebuke sins, even in the court of the king, and an irresistible eloquence, not of the polished Grecian, but of the rugged Hebrew type, to sway the multitudes toward righteousness. He was greater than Abraham, the founder, than Moses, the lawgiver, than David, the warrior king, of the Hebrew nation, and yet less than the least in the kingdom of Christ. Although these least had not the showy gifts of the Spirit, they had what is far better, the Comforter in their hearts crying, "Abba, Father." The filial feeling, with the assurance of forgiveness, is the distinguishing New Testament grace, together with the Pentecostal fulness of the Spirit as the Comforter and Sanctifier.

It is natural that extraordinary gifts should flow forth from the Holy Spirit in New Testament times, to signalize the beginning of His distinctive work as the Paraclete. When the Son of God by the incarnation came into the sphere of matter, it was to be expected that His miracles would be in the realm of things sensible. But the Comforter marked His entrance into the human spirit by miracles in the sphere of mind, the word of wisdom, the word of knowledge, faith, as a charism, miracles, prophecy, discernment of spirits, tongues and interpretations. The only exception is healing, which Bengel suggests has continued to the present time as a specimen of the other gifts, just as the portion of manna laid up in the ark was a proof of the ancient miracle. In order to the intelligent discussion of this charism it will be necessary to describe another with which it stands in immediate connection, the gift of faith. This differs from common or saving faith, called the grace of faith, in the following particulars:

1. The grace of faith is grounded on the general promises of the Bible, while the gift of faith rests not on the written Word, but on the assurance inwrought by the Holy Spirit "that the prayer will be answered and the work accomplished." (Whedon.)

2. Hence the grace of faith, when exercised in prayer for temporal blessings, is always accompanied by the

condition "If it be Thy will." The gift of faith is the assurance beforehand that it is God's will to bestow the thing desired.

3. Saving faith is morally obligatory upon every soul having a knowledge of its object, Christ, and the absence of such faith is the ground of condemnation (John iii.18). Miracle-working faith, a special gift, is required of no one, but is bestowed sovereignly by the Holy Spirit, "severally as he will." Hence there is no more culpability for the absence of this faith than there is for a lack of the gift of tongues.

4. The grace of faith is designed to be permanent, and is as indispensable to spiritual, as breathing is to natural, life. Faith as a charism is not permanent but occasional. St. Paul sometimes had it and could heal (Acts xxviii.8), and sometimes he had it not and could not heal, as we infer from II Timothy iv.20.

5. The grace of faith transforms the moral character. The charism of faith has no such effect any more than any other extraordinary gift of the Spirit. Balaam and King Saul prophesied under the power of the Spirit, and both died accursed of God. There is at least one man in the flames of hell to-day who was once commissioned to work miracles. Compare Matt x.1-4 and xxvi.24, John xvii.12. Jesus Christ intimates that Judas will have plenty of company from the ranks of Christian ministers who in theory acknowledged the Lordship of Christ, after the strictest orthodoxy, and in the exercise of their profession cast out devils and did many mighty works (Greek, miracles), but had not that grace of faith which works by love, purifies the heart and brings its possessor into vital union with Christ. "The distinguishing feature in those men is an impure, often fanatical boldness in the faith, which, though enabling them to perform outward acts of a marvellous nature, yet fails to exercise any influence upon their own moral life— just the sort of thing described

by Paul in I Cor. xiii.2, and the manifestations of which are to be met in every age, especially in times of great religious excitement." (Meyer.)

If the Greek reader will scrutinize this Pauline text he will find that Paul's form of hypothesis (*can* with the subjunctive) assumes the condition, faith without love, as *possible* with some *present expectation* that may be realized. In other words, men may have a mountain-removing faith in unregenerate hearts. A character as paradoxical as this may exist.

"In the exercise of His sovereignty the Spirit may give power of service even to men who are not converted. Or rather, there are men to whom He comes who resist His saving power and welcome His working power... As there was Balaam in the Old Testament times, so there are to be found now those who preach the gospel to others and yet themselves are castaways." (Dr. John Robson.)

"It is certain the faith which is here [Matt. xvii.20] spoken of does not always imply saving faith. Many have had it who thereby *cast out devils* and yet will at last have their portion with them. It is only a supernatural persuasion given a man that God will work *thus* by him at that hour." (John Wesley.)

The doctrine of the extreme faith-cure advocates, that the atonement of Christ covers sickness as well as sin, and that deliverance from both is through faith, rests chiefly on Isa. liii.4. It is true, as they claim, that the Hebrew word for "sorrows" is usually translated "sickness." This is sustained by Matt. viii.17, "Himself took our infirmities, and bare our sicknesses." Let us examine these texts. Isaiah gives a prophetic picture of the Messiah while in the flesh on earth as a man of sorrows, despised, afflicted, erroneously esteemed smitten of God, oppressed, brought as a lamb to the slaughter and wounded for our transgressions. In the middle of this catalogue of humiliations, sufferings and insults, having no reference to His miracles, occurs the phrase, "carried our sorrows," a phrase in perfect accord with the list of disabilities and abuses above described. To make the passage harmonious both the translators of the Authorized Version and the revisers have employed the word "sorrows" instead of "sicknesses." In this they have given the mind of the Spirit in His portraiture of the shady side of the Messiah's earthly life. But should we put "sicknesses" in the place of "sorrows" ("he bore away our sicknesses") we have only a description of the miraculous cures wrought by Christ during His abode on the earth, but no promise of their continuance afterwards. He is not now under chastisement, standing dumb before the judgment seat and bruised for our iniquities. The whole dreadful catalogue of human sufferings is past forever, and with it the painful strain of His tender sensibilities and sympathies with human suffering with which He was brought into constant contact in His ministry of bodily healing. The question now arises, What is the significance of Matt. viii.17, "Himself took [away] our infirmities and bare [away] our diseases"? It cannot mean that He took the leprosy, the epilepsy, the fever, the blindness upon Himself to defile and corrupt His body, but that He miraculously removed them to attest His Messiahship and His divinity. But since His ascension He gives a higher kind of proof of His Godhood through the transforming power of the Holy Ghost transfiguring sinful souls, the converting power, the only miracle designed to be repeated down to the end of time, "the everlasting sign which shall not be cut off; instead of the thorn the fir tree, and instead of the brier the myrtle;" instead of the sot the saint, instead of the rascal the righteous, the one transformed into the other in the twinkling of an eye by the new birth through the Holy Ghost. Read I Cor. vi.9, 10: fornicators, adulterers, abusers of themselves with *man*kind, thieves, drunkards and extortioners, as vile a gang as ever were photographed for a rogues' gallery: "such were some of you," the Corinthian church, "but ye are washed, ye are justified in the name of the Lord Jesus, and ye are sanctified by the Spirit of our God." These are the "greater works" than bodily healing, yea, than raising corpses to life. With far less strain of the Scriptures one might prove that the atonement exempts the believer from physical death. For we read that the purpose of Christ was "that through death he might destroy him that hath the power of death, that is, the devil," that He "hath abolished death; and whosoever liveth and believeth in me shall never die." "This is the bread which cometh down from heaven, that a man may eat thereof and not die." An extremist might insist on the literalism of these texts and teach that faith can ward off death. If it is said that believers do die, we reply that believers are sick also. If faith is not designed to prevent death, it is not designed to prevent consumptions, fevers and plagues, the sappers and miners of death.

The eager desire of some Christians to secure the extraordinary gifts of the Spirit is not an evidence of spiritual progress, but rather of spiritual retrogression. The disciples of the eccentric Edward Irving, the modern Catholic Apostolic Church, imagine that they have "obtained the gifts" by restoring the elaborate ecclesiastical organization outlined in Eph. iv.11, apostles, prophets, evangelists, pastors and teachers. Their success has not made a deep impression on either the world or the Church. One branch of the Second Adventists believe that they have by faith been endowed with several of the gifts of the Spirit, such as tongues and interpretations. A large number of Christians of various churches are diligently inculcating the doctrine that every kind of sickness will invariably be cured by the grace of faith possible to all Christians, and that the absence of such faith is a species of unbelief, constituting a grave defect of the spiritual life. We believe that this hankering after these gifts is undermining the spirituality of those who indulge in it, and we commend to them the grand aim set before us by St. Paul, "I show unto you a more excellent way," LOVE. The church in which the gifts were specially manifest is the most undesirable of the New Testament churches. I would not swap off for it the poorest one of the fifteen churches of my pastoral life. "Indeed, I should loathe to minister to such a sorry set of Christians as were the Corinthians with all their miracles and tongues. Wrangling about Paul, Apollos and Cephas, running after false teachers, full of envying, strife and division, harboring an incestuous person without discipline, degrading the Lord's supper into a feast of appetite, giving to Paul constant sorrow and anxiety, the Corinthians needed miracles to give them a respectable title to a Christian name; and they so abused miraculous gifts by jealousy and contention that they turned their Sabbath assemblies into cabals of men and women shouting, singing, praying, prophesying, pell-mell, without decency or order."* From such a style of Christianity "Good Lord, deliver us," and lead us into the heritage of I Cor. xiii by "the more excellent way."

The proof text for faith cure most frequently quoted is James v.14-16. The first of these verses is often cited as though it read thus, "Is any sick among you? Let him call for the elders of the church; and let them pray over him, anointing him with oil in the name of the Lord, *and he shall be healed.*" But the words in italics are not Scripture. The healing does not follow the anointing and praying as a divinely ordained sequence, but it follows the prayer of faith. We contend that the context, especially the classification of the healing with the miracle-working faith of Elijah, proves beyond dispute that James is here speaking of charismatic or extraordinary faith and not

---

*Dr. J. P. Thompson

of the grace of faith. Wherever the former is bestowed the healing will take place. Whenever it is withheld because divine wisdom sees that death or continued sickness is better for the accomplishment of God's purposes, no healing will ensue. This was just as true in the days of St. James as it is now, that faith for a blessing contrary to the divine will is an impossibility. There may be attempts to believe and efforts resembling faith, but true faith for a thing not in the divine will cannot exist.

About the use of oil recommended by James there are two opinions: (1) That it is sacramental, because the anointing is to be in the name of the Lord. But this does not make it a sacrament, since all the activities of Christian life are to be "in His name." Moreover, there is no indication in primitive history that oil was used sacramentally. In the consecration of kings and priests it was used as a symbol of the Holy Spirit. But James could not consistently be enjoining the use of a symbol after the thing signified, the Pentecostal gift, had actually descended. In the progress of revelation there is no such anomaly as a retrogression from the antitype to the type. (2) That olive oil has sanative qualities. The Orientals used it medicinally, anointing the sick and wounded. Hence the seventy disciples sent out on the trial mission were directed to anoint the sick as a salutary and approved medicament (Mark vi.13). If we translate the injunction of James into modern language it would be, "Use the best approved means, quinine, aconite, etc., and pray and call upon the church, represented by the elders, to invoke the divine blessing upon the remedies."

Before we leave this text in St. James we call attention to an irrefutable proof that the faith in the phrase "prayer of faith " is not the grace of faith which anybody can exercise, but a special gift sovereignly bestowed. James says "the effectual prayer... availeth much." This translation, as Dr. Whedon observes, "is almost a tautology," the effectual prayer produces an effect. The Revised Version endeavors to obviate this difficulty thus: "The supplication of a righteous man availeth much in its working." But the old English annotators, Benson, Bull, Hammond, Macknight, and the German Michaelis and the modern Dr. Whedon insist that the original for "in its working" is passive, signifying "inwrought."* The prayer is a special exercise supernaturally inspired, and the faith is not the common grace of faith required of all, but the extraordinary gift of faith inwrought by the Holy Spirit, as it is classed with the nine charisms described in I Cor. xii.8-11, which are distributed by the Spirit "to every man severally as he will." Hence failure in the faith cure is inevitable in every case where the prayer of faith is not energized or inwrought by the Holy Spirit. There were probably such failures in the days of James in the case of those who did not by prayer seek to know the will of God before calling for the elders. In all cases where the gift of faith preceded this call there could be no failure.

The relation of this subject to the work of the Holy Spirit is very intimate. "Likewise the Spirit also helpeth our infirmity [singular number, Revised Version]; for we know not how to pray as we ought; but the Spirit maketh intercession for us with groanings which cannot be uttered." Here the infirmity is ignorance of what lies in the divine will. Is it pardon, the new birth, entire sanctification, the fulness of the Spirit or grace to help in time of need? No Bible reader need be in perplexity respecting all these spiritual blessings. "He that spared not his own Son, but delivered him up for us all, how shall he not also with him freely give us all things?" This text (Rom. viii.32) following so soon after that which emphasizes our ignorance of what is best for us and our need of a divine teacher (verse 26), is in seeming contradiction to it, and it can be

---

*See Gal. v.6, margin

harmonized in no other way than by understanding that the "all things " which are promised "with him" are spiritual blessings, while the things in respect to which we are ignorant whether we should pray for them or not, are temporal blessings, relief in want, deliverance out of peril, ease when in pain, and restoration from sickness.

Chapter XXXV
BLASPHEMY AGAINST THE HOLY SPIRIT

THIS IS A DOCTRINE which rests on the following undisputed proof texts: Matt. xii.31, 32, Mark iii.28-30 (in which the Revised Version has "eternal sin"), and Luke xii.10. Orthodox theologians disagree about the meaning of John xv.22-24, Heb. vi.4-6, x.29, II Peter ii.14 and I John v.16.

Respecting the nature of this awful sin there are two opinions which divide the Christian world. One was maintained by Chrysostom, that this sin is the assertion that the miracles wrought by Christ through the aid of the Holy Spirit were done through the agency of the devil. Universalists and all who teach the doctrine of eternal hope advocate this view because it seems to limit this sin to the contemporaries of Jesus Christ.

The other theory, championed by Augustine, defines this sin as the obstinate impenitence of the sinner till the end of life while inwardly approving Christian doctrine as divine, yet, against his own convictions, opposing and blaspheming or slandering Christ and persevering in this deliberate contempt till the close of life. Hence this sin is possible in the present time. This is a subject on which we are not disposed to dogmatize. Yet it is a part and an important part of Christ's teaching and should not be withheld from the hearers of the gospel.

The most solemn and awful demonstration of the personality of the Holy Spirit is inferred from the fact that the only irremissible sin is found in some offence against Him. There could be no such pre-eminent offence against an impersonality, an influence, effluence or attribute. That such an offence is possible is implied in the warning given by the tender and merciful Son of God. Our subject does not require us to answer the question, "What constitutes this sin?" Yet since there is much inquiry we will modestly express our opinion. We agree with Julius Muller that the unpardonable sin is not an isolated sin, but sin in its full development.* This is nearly the same as Joseph Cook's definition, "Any sin that involves final impenitence." It is a result of a series of acts of known sin, the outcome of a course of deliberate rejection of light and defiant repulse of the Holy Spirit's warnings in that great debate upon the subject of duty and destiny, a question which every soul in probation must answer for itself alone. He who persistently gives the wrong answer will come into a state of matured enmity to God and a "hatred of recognized eternal holiness." His irreversible choice is, "Evil, be thou my good. "It, not God, closes the door of repentance. For such are the laws of man's moral nature that he can finally and eternally shut up his personality against grace and irreversibly expel the Holy Spirit whom he once received.

We must bear in mind that the dispensation of the Holy Spirit is the highest possible expression of divine mercy. God's mercy endureth forever, but man's ability to appropriate that mercy is for a short time. A man who by abuse of his body has entirely wasted its power

---

*"Christian Doctrine of Sin," ii, pages 418, etc.

of nutrition by assimilating food may starve in a house full of bread. There will be bread and to spare after the last returnless prodigal has refused his Father's tenderest and most persuasive invitation. At the funeral of every lost soul the Father, the Son and the Holy Spirit will head the procession as the chief mourners, preceding the earthly kindred. There is nothing capricious or arbitrary on the part of the Holy Spirit in leaving a human soul to its deliberate self-determined destiny. He is not a judge, but a helper, and He ceases to help when character has become fixed in sin. All sin tends towards final permanence in sin. Can a man once truly regenerated fall into sin and take on this final permanence? Find your answer in I John v.16, which plainly implies that "a brother" may "sin unto death" and put himself beyond the reach of prayer. Study Heb. vi.4-8 and Julius Muller's weighty remarks thereon. The convert from Judaism who after Christian enlightenment and partaking of the Holy Ghost returned to Judaism must pronounce Jesus a false Messiah and the Holy Spirit an illusion in order to be received into the synagogue.

The fact that the Holy Spirit is the last test of orthodoxy throws much light on the subject of the irremissible sin. Human history has had three dispensations— that of the Father, the test of which is the worship of one God; that of the Son, the test of which is faith in Him as an infallible teacher, imitation of His perfect example, reception of Him as atoning Saviour, and obedience to Him as an invisible king, the God-Man. The last and highest test of loyalty in those who have stood the two former tests is the Holy Spirit, the substitute for the personal presence of our risen Lord Jesus. To receive Him is a more difficult test, for the following reasons: 1. The Spirit is perfectly abstract and colorless, beyond the reach of the senses. 2. He is destitute of the interest which attaches to the incidents of a bodily history. 3. His presence addresses no natural faculty of mental perception, and His work in the application of redemption is internal and mysterious. 4. He cannot be discovered by any process of reasoning. 5. Faith in Jesus Christ, resulting in newness of life and imparting the power of spiritual intuition, is the only avenue through which He can be known and received. Receptivity must first be unfolded from a capacity existing unused in the natural man, before the Holy Spirit can be apprehended as a glorious and blessed reality. For the reception of the fulness of the Spirit there must be a large capacity produced by a strong and mature faith. 6. Such a faith is possible to those only who make "a total, affectionate and irreversible self-surrender" to Christ, consecrating to Him our good things, our possessions, our social standing and influence and all our powers of body and mind. When we received Christ we abandoned our evil things. This is an act less difficult than laying all our good things on the altar of Christ. Hence the greater severity of this last test. For this reason many fail to enter consciously into the dispensation of the Holy Ghost. They receive Christ, but remain spiritual babes, many of them so weak and prone to sin that Paul cannot call them wholly spiritual, but rather carnal (I Cor. iii.1). In view of this fact, John Owen in his "Pneumatology" utters words of deep solemnity: "Wherefore the duty of the Church now immediately respects the Spirit of God, who acts toward it in the name of the Father and of the Son, and with respect unto Him it is that the Church in its present state is capable of an apostasy from God… The sin of despising His person and rejecting His work now is of the same nature with idolatry of old, and with the Jews' rejection of the person of the Son." Hence the Paraclete as a specialty claiming the new prominence of the day of Pentecost has become the touchstone of true piety and the article of a standing or falling Church. The words of

Fletcher are very similar to those of Owen: "To reject the Son of God manifested in the Spirit, as worldly Christians are universally observed to do, is a crime of equal magnitude with that of the Jews who rejected Christ manifested in the flesh."

"A parable may help to show the relation of the three Persons of the Trinity to man's salvation. A father wishes his younger son to be educated for a certain profession. The elder brother of that son, who has learned it himself, gives all the books and apparatus necessary for acquiring a knowledge of it. And they together engage a teacher to teach the younger son the knowledge required. And it is evident— and this is the point of the illustration— that the final success of the plan of the father and elder brother depends on the success of the teacher whom they appoint. It is manifest, too, that it is only at this point that the younger son can yield to or resist the efforts of his father and brother. He may speak with the greatest respect and affection of both, but if he refuses to be taught by the teacher he will remain ignorant of the science which they wish him to learn. On the other hand, he may speak most rebelliously of both, but if he submits to the teaching of the teacher they have appointed, he will end by learning the profession they wish. Thus resistance to the father and elder brother may be atoned for by submission to the teacher they have sent, but resistance to the teacher cannot be atoned for by any nominal submission to the father. By its very nature it will prevent his son learning the science."

It is evident in the last supposition that the obedience will be only "nominal," not real, while the younger son is defeating the cherished purpose of those to whom he presents a professed submission. Men cannot resist and grieve the third Person of the Trinity and at the same time be acceptably serving the other two Persons.

Another comparison has been used to illustrate the

same truth. The Father is like a physician who by his wisdom has discovered a cure for a deadly disease. The Son is like another physician who by his skill prepares the medicine thus discovered. The Holy Spirit is like a third physician who goes about administering this medicine to the dying. Here again it is manifest that it is only by the work of the third physician that the work of the other two can be made effectual. They may have finished their work and done it perfectly, but if the sick refuse to take the only remedy from the hands of the third, their resistance cannot but be fatal to them. They may profess to admire the wisdom of the discoverer of this infallible specific for their disease and the skill of the compounder, but this will not heal them. They must render equal honor to the practitioner who applies the medicine, by submitting to all his directions.

Among those who refuse to obey the Holy Spirit there may be great moral diversities, a pure outward life or gross immoralities, but they are all alike in their destiny, after a persistent rejection of the agent appointed to heal them through regeneration and entire sanctification by the Holy Spirit. They must all abide under the wrath of God evermore.*

---

*See Appendix, Note M

Chapter XXXVI
THE HOLY SPIRIT THE CONSERVATOR OF ORTHODOXY

THE TERM "ORTHODOXY" signifies right beliefs in respect to fundamental Christian doctrines. These are, the supreme divinity of Jesus Christ, the divine personality and the work of the Holy Spirit, the threefold personality of the one divine substance, the substitutional atonement, justification by faith, regeneration and sanctification by the Holy Spirit,— both rendered necessary by original sin (a tendency toward sin born in fallen man),— the future general judgment of the race, assigning some to eternal rewards and others to endless punishments, according to the permanent character voluntarily chosen in this life, the only probation. This, as I understand it, is the substance of orthodoxy.

In all ages of the Church it has been an important question how to preserve evangelical truth in the belief of those who profess faith in Christ. Recent events in the history of theological seminaries have intensified the interest in this question. A favorite method is to require the theological teachers to subscribe at stated intervals to a well-defined formulary of doctrines. But the Holy Spirit has not emphasized any portion of the Bible as a shorter catechism embodying the substance of revealed truth. If men draw up these creed statements in the heat of theological controversy, we are not sure that they have excluded all error and included all saving truth. Church history shows that men who have totally fallen away from a prescribed standard of doctrine may, under a temptation to retain their place, continue to reaffirm their adherence thereto by putting their own definitions into the terms. As the forms of liberty survive the spirit, so the orthodox creed may long outlive the spirit of orthodoxy. Required subscription to minute, ironclad statements of doctrine has been the cause of much contention, and a wedge for dividing the body of Christ. Language may be so twisted and words so defined that uniformity of belief cannot always be insured in this way. Hence the most poisonous liberalism may be taught under the forms of evangelical truth. It is my purpose in this chapter to show a better way, the New Testament way, of conserving orthodoxy; a way that always succeeds whereever it is faithfully followed.

The fulness of the Holy Spirit in pastor and people will always insure a correct theology. St. John in his First Epistle, ii.20-27, regards the anointing or full baptism of the Spirit as the great safeguard against being drawn away by the falsity of antichrist. Says Dr. Whedon: "The word 'Christ' signified anointed, as chrism signifies oil, or the anointment. Here the unction or chrism is used in contrast to the antichrists, who became such because they had no such sanctifying chrism. As long as we possess the holy chrism, we will adhere to the holy Christ." St. Paul also implies the same truth when he positively asserts (I Cor. xii.3) that "no man speaking in the Spirit of God saith Jesus is anathema; and no man can say Jesus is

Lord, but in the Holy Spirit." We are to understand that in translating the Old Testament into Greek, Latin and English, the word "Jehovah" was very unfortunately rendered "Lord." This was because the Hebrews had for more than a thousand years ceased to pronounce the word, and had substituted "Lord" for it in all their public reading of the Scriptures. Hence the title "Lord," in Jewish conception, meant "Jehovah." Thus the angels (Luke ii.11) announce to the shepherds, "For unto you is born this day in the city of David a Saviour, which is Messiah, Jehovah." This is the real import of the celestial message when fully expressed in the Hebrew form of thought. "No man is able to say that Jesus is Jehovah, but in the Holy Spirit." This means that no man, however highly cultured, can have an inward realization of the supreme Godhead of Jesus, but through the illumination of the Holy Spirit giving an experimental realization of that truth. Thus it pleased God to reveal His Son in Paul. Unregenerate men may be trained from infancy in the catechism to assert with the lips the supreme deity of Jesus, but it is like the talk of the educated parrot till the Spirit of truth, or the Spirit of reality, makes the dogma which has been drilled into the intellect real to the heart. This truth, though not conflicting with reason, is so far above reason that no person on the plane of nature, unaided by the Paraclete, can ever have a satisfactory realization of it. The natural man cannot receive the things of the Spirit, and he discredits Jesus when He says, "I and my Father are one." Therefore this doctrine of the Godhead of Christ, which is fundamental to the evangelical system, is preserved and rendered vital in the Christian consciousness only by the Holy Spirit. This basal element of Christianity may well stand for the sum total of evangelical truth.

This brings us to our theme— the Holy Spirit in the believer preserves, vitalizes and makes real to the consciousness all the essential truths of the gospel. The spirit of inspiration has recorded these truths in the Bible; but if He had not made them real and living in the Christian experience, they, and the Bible too, would have perished long ago. History is full of instances of essential truth dropping first out of experience, then out of the creed. Thus justification by faith in Jesus Christ disappeared from the Roman Catholic Church and left the world in darkness for a thousand years. Fewer and fewer experienced the conscious pardon of sin as witnessed by the Holy Spirit, till finally there were not witnesses enough left to keep the precious truth from going into oblivion. Luther first experienced and then boldly restored the lost doctrine. Thus the doctrine of entire sanctification was lost during many Christian ages, and was restored to the modern Church by the great spiritual awakening called Methodism, the largest effects of which are not found in the census tables of the various Methodisms, but in the spiritual impulse given to our entire Protestant Christianity.

Church history demonstrates that so long as the Church is filled with the Holy Spirit her grasp of all cardinal Christian truth is firm and unwavering. Mr. Spurgeon once made this remark: "Doubts about the fundamentals of the gospel exist in certain churches, I am told, to a large extent. My dear friends, where there is a warm-hearted church you do not hear of them. They do not come near, it is too warm. I never saw a fly alight on a red-hot plate." A heresy in respect to saving truth never yet lighted on a red hot body of believers. But again and again it has alighted on denominations which have cooled off in zeal and have fallen into spiritual decay.

The Holy Spirit not only put on record the facts of Christ's life, but He conserves all the facts in Christ's history, since His death. Rationalism admits His death, but denies His resurrection. A risen Jesus is scoffed at on the platform of every convention of freethinkers. To them He is as dead as Julius Caesar, and rules the world only from His tomb. The historic proofs all go for nothing so long as they, by their unbelief, exclude from their hearts the Spirit, whose office it is to make real to the heart what is shadowy and visionary to the intellect. Dwelling as they do on the low plane of naturalism, with its uniform laws, they are incapable of receiving the truth that the crucified Jesus is alive. Pentecost proves that Jesus has ascended and mounted the Father's throne, a glorified man. All modern believers who have had a personal Pentecost are convinced by this overwhelming proof. The Spirit takes the living and glorified Jesus, and shows Him unto them. This proof has all the cogency of an intuition. To those destitute of the Spirit it is all moonshine — the vaporings of a distempered imagination. Let the sceptic candidly weigh the historical proofs of the resurrection of Jesus, and he will be astonished to find them a Jacob's ladder with which to climb up to a spiritual experience in which it will be impossible to believe that Jesus is still in the tomb. The resurrection of the dead soul to newness of life by the Holy Spirit is a mighty confirmation of Jesus' resurrection from the tomb. Ask any young convert living with the Spirit's testimony in his heart, whether Jesus is dead or alive, and he will joyfully answer: "I know that He is alive, for He saves my soul." The ascension of Jesus through the heavens to the highest place the universe affords is a fact not of reason, but of the gospel record made real to believers by the Holy Spirit. The apostles who saw Him ascend may have had perplexities and intellectual difficulties about what had become of their Master above the clouds, whether His body had been etherealized and dissipated through space, or whether the whole scene was an optical illusion, or as the Germans say, a kind of scenic withdrawal into invisibility. Such sceptical suggestions may have haunted their minds during that ten-days' prayer meeting after the ascension, severely testing their faith. But when the Spirit came down with His gift of fiery tongues and of inward purification, purging the disciples' eyes from every film, and filling their hearts with joy, the lost Jesus was suddenly found. He did not stand forth in bodily form in their company, saying "Peace," but stood forth a glorious, undoubted and bright reality. He had promised that when He had reached the throne He would send the Comforter, and now the downcoming of the Paraclete demonstrates that Jesus is glorified. Who would be knowing anything about Jesus Christ to-day, after eighteen hundred years of absence from the earth, if it had not been for the Holy Spirit, His successor on earth? His very name would have been forgotten by mankind. The absent and the dead soon pass out of mind. There was a time when Alexander the Great was on the world's tongue. He died, and men ceased to speak of him. So it was with Julius and Augustus Caesar, Napoleon in Europe, and with Washington, Lincoln and Garfield. Why are men talking of Bismarck and Gladstone, of President McKinley and Queen Victoria? Because they are alive and conspicuous figures in modern politics. Why do men and women, friend and foe, keep talking, writing and printing the name of Jesus Christ? Why does every infidel convention, every assembly of liberals, discuss Jesus of Nazareth with so intense interest? Why not let Him sleep undisturbed in His tomb in Jerusalem? Why is His religion a live question in circles of highest intellectual culture in the nineteenth century? Because Jesus Himself is alive in the nineteenth century, and reports Himself to the world's consciousness, to the sinner's fears and to the believer's hopes, through the Holy Ghost sent down from heaven. Just in proportion as the world has listened to the voice of this heavenly messenger has the world received her Saviour and Lord, and just in proportion as the Church has been filled with the Holy Spirit has she firmly held the truths of orthodoxy. But whenever the

Spirit has ceased to sway her, and she has fallen into a decay of her spiritual life, she has relaxed her grasp upon the fundamentals of the gospel. Study the history of Romanism, and see if her departure from the saving truths of Christianity to the doctrines of men was not through a long period of spiritual decline and worldliness. As the fourth centennial of Luther's birth has just passed and our minds are specially turned toward Germany, we trace with sadness the blighting rationalism in that land of the Reformation to its source, and we find it to be a church spiritually dead, a Lutheranism losing the spirit of Luther, which was the Spirit of his Master, and trusting in the sacraments for salvation. The Anglican Church has travelled the same road from spirituality through formalism to ritualism on the one hand, and to liberalism on the other. But we need not cross the Atlantic to find exemplifications of the truth of our theme. Study the history of theological thought in New England since the landing of the Pilgrims. They were brimful of the Holy Ghost, holding evangelical truth so firmly that exile in a savage wilderness was cheerfully chosen in preference to a surrender of one saving truth of the New Testament. But unwisely limiting the right to vote in town-meeting to church members, for political power unconverted men crowded into the church. These soon got into the pulpits, for the pulpit was in high honor and afforded a good salary for life, levied by a lawful tax upon the property of the town. Preachers generally preach what the people delight to hear. A church declining from a high spirituality did not like to hear of the exceeding sinfulness of sin and its dreadful punishment in hell fire, the necessity of repentance, the new birth, and sanctification of the Spirit. So the pulpit furnished the pews with good moral essays on the beauty of virtue, and as a result every distinctive truth of the gospel was neglected for a generation in many pulpits. To be silent on any doctrine for a generation is to root it out of the faith of the Church. Then came Whitefield sounding the trump of a spiritual resurrection, shouting to preachers and people on Boston Common words which seemed then most radical and revolutionary, "Ye must be born again." Forty thousand in New England believed and were born of the Holy Spirit. But many churches shut their doors against this God-sent apostle of a spiritual Christianity, and the preachers went on reading their moral essays. There was no difference in the printed creeds of the spiritual and unspiritual churches. They were all alike Congregational. But the spiritual preachers preached the creed, while the mere moralists ignored it for another generation. At last the day came for drawing the line between spiritual death and spiritual life, when, lo, it was found that that line was the exact demarcation between orthodoxy and heterodoxy, between the Evangelicals and the Unitarians. Then the fact was made public that a majority of the old Puritan churches in eastern Massachusetts had been so long without the Holy Ghost that they could not say that Jesus is Lord: they repudiated the corner-stone of orthodoxy, the supreme Godhead of Jesus Christ. Still they taught that He was in a degree divine, the most exalted creature in the universe, far above archangels, cherubim and seraphim, and next to the throne of God. They held to the miraculous basis of Christianity, the supernatural birth of Christ, the work of the Holy Spirit in regeneration, the inspiration of the Scriptures, the resurrection of the dead, the general judgment and eternal punishment. William Ellery Channing, when teaching school in Richmond, Va., came to the conclusion, and records it in his journal, that he could no longer worship Jesus Christ. What follows this denial of supreme worship to the Son equally with the Father? The very moment he and his adherents stepped off from the Rock of Ages, the Godhead of Christ, they found their feet on an inclined plane of ice, sliding, sliding, sliding, down, down, down, finding no logical stopping place till they have reached bald and bare deism, a cold and misty pantheism merging into blank atheism disguised with the euphonious name of "agnosticism." Let us show you the logical steps down this stairway from Puritan orthodoxy to atheism. First, a spiritual decay in the churches till the Holy Spirit no longer reveals Christ in the heart, and His supreme divinity is repudiated. Second, if Christ is a creature He cannot make a substitutional expiation for sin, so the atonement drops away; for a creature, whether man or archangel, can do no more than his duty; no merit of his can be the sinner's plea. Hence, in the third place, there is no justification by faith, for this rests on the atonement. If there is no pardon of sin through faith in the only Saviour, then follows, as a fourth step, salvation by works, every man his own saviour. Next, sin is viewed as a mere incident in the natural unfoldings of a finite being, the tumbling down of an infant taking its first toddling steps in probation, a childish disease like the chicken-pox, to be outgrown by intellectual and moral development. Hence there is no need of regeneration. All men are born pure as Adam in Eden. Original or birth sin is a blot on the character of a good God; all men are born with a germ of goodness in them, which only needs culture to develop into Christianity. As there is no need of regeneration and sanctification, the Holy Ghost, as the personal Regenerator and Sanctifier, is a superfluity. He is degraded from a person to an influence or an attribute. Thus far the inspiration of the Bible has stood unquestioned. But now this is sifted to the bottom and reported to be a mass of chaff. Theodore Parker, the advance destroyer of orthodoxy, made the brilliant discovery that the Bible is a superfluity, man being by nature furnished with a set of moral judgments and religious intuitions, a great deal better than God's Word in the form of a book, and that the volume which is the ultimate authority with the Christian is no more inspired than "his grandfather's old musket" which did good service at Lexington. The next doctrine to be thrown overboard was eternal punishment. There are two ways of disposing of this exceedingly disagreeable item of orthodoxy. The Universalist thinks that God is too good to damn him, and the Unitarian thinks that he is too good to be damned, so that both rid themselves of this unpleasant doctrine, the one on the ground of God's benevolence, and the other on that of man's goodness. Thus we see that in the space of about seventy years Puritan churches which began by neglecting to seek the work of the Holy Ghost in personal experience, have slidden rapidly down to atheism, till at last professed Christian ministers, without any shock to their own consciences or the moral sense of their churches, step out of their pulpits into Thomas Paine Memorial Hall, to give countenance to the infidels in heaping abuse upon Jesus Christ and His Church.

The Godhead of Jesus Christ protects all other vital doctrines, the personality of God and the dignity and the worth of man and the true estimate of sin. Admit that the supreme God stooped to the amazing condescension of taking man's nature and dying in our behalf, and you give to man a value, and to sin a significance, utterly beyond all computation.

Deny the incarnation of God in man, and you tear away from him his patent of nobility issued by heaven itself, and you leave him a highly developed tadpole, an educated and trained monkey evolved into a man void of immortality. In the same way the cross of Christ is the only correct measure of sin. If Jesus is God in human form, His death as the sin-bearer gives sin a tremendous significance. Otherwise it is a mere trifle, and its eternal punishment is offensive to reason and disgusting to the delicate moral sensibilities of our refined civilization. But what was the first step which led down from Puritanism to atheism? It was the attempt to build up a Church without the Holy Spirit in conviction for sin, in regeneration and sanctification. I have now shown by historical examples in both Europe and America that an orthodox creed must perish when the spiritual life dies out of a denomination. I might show that the Unitarian or "Hicksite" Friends originated in exactly the same way. History is philosophy teaching by examples. Like causes will continue to produce like effects. It will be true of the existent evangelical churches that the speculative age will succeed the spiritual if we suffer the spiritual era to depart. Then heresies will swarm into the vacuum left by the Holy Ghost. I fear that other denominations by their neglect of the Holy Spirit are stepping out upon the inclined plane of ice. The liberalistic drift of Andover is no surprise to me. Years ago I announced to the public that the Holy Ghost was not receiving His due honor in the preaching and theological thinking of New England scholars. As a proof I cited the "Bibliotheca Sacra and Theological Review," published at Andover, thirty-six volumes, 1844-1879, containing one thousand two hundred and fifty articles by three hundred contributors, as not containing one article on the personality and offices of the Holy Spirit in the salvation of men. This indicates a corresponding silence in the pulpit during the same period. As a result of this long neglect of the Spirit, a plentiful crop of speculative errors in respect to fundamental truth will soon spring up. The same causes are at work in other evangelical denominations. The theological thought of Methodism (M. E.) as reflected in her *Quarterly* for the last fifty years, has not one article on the Holy Spirit, save one on the sin against the Holy Ghost and one on "The Holy Spirit as a Factor in our Intellectual Life." It has been the boast of Methodism that she has conserved her orthodoxy by her spirituality and intense evangelistic zeal. Happy would it be for herself and for Protestantism, of which she is becoming the leader, if this boast of no doctrinal schism could continue another one hundred and forty years in the twenty-seven Methodisms represented in the London Ecumenical Conference. We quote from the address of the bishops of the M. E. Church in 1880: "It has been the honor of Methodism to have maintained from the commencement of its history the doctrines of the Church in their purity and efficiency. The controversies which have arisen have had reference to questions of church policy, but not to questions of doctrine. Its ministers fully accepted the teachings, and were almost universally faithful to their vows. We regret to say that in some quarters a spirit of latitudinarian speculation has been introduced into the Church, and occasionally ministers have claimed the right to preach doctrines which are not in harmony with our articles and standards." What is the cure? Not new articles added to her creed, not ironclad tests of orthodoxy to be subscribed by her theological professors, but the universal baptism of the Spirit.

Twenty-seven years ago I was closeted alone with a distinguished judge in Syracuse to draft the charter of a Christian university. The first draft would have suited a Mohammedan or a Buddhist institution, for there was no allusion to Christ. At my suggestion the adjective "Christian" was inserted before "learning." The jurist was then asked whether an evangelical interpretation to "Christian" could not be incorporated into this charter of the university, so that it could be forever held for orthodoxy as found in Methodistic standards. The case of Harvard College was cited as having been wrested from the Evangelicals, by whom it was founded, and turned into a propagandist of liberalism. Never will the reply of the judge be forgotten: "There is no safeguard possible. Harvard went over to Unitarianism because the Church herself apostatized from the faith. You cannot, by legal documents, prevent a denomination from drifting away from its creed. If Methodism backslides from orthodoxy, she will carry her universities with her." The lawyer taught the preacher an important lesson, which he has exerted himself to teach to others ever since. Orthodoxy can be conserved only by the Holy Spirit abiding in the consciousness of the individual members of the Church. Then, and then only, are we safe. But if our piety declines with our growth and popularity; if we begin to glory in our millions of members and twice ten thousand churches and hundreds of academies and scores of colleges; if we admit to our communion our well-behaved children without a radical, spiritual change of heart, and are satisfied with a decent morality only and a reverential attendance upon Sunday worship and the sacraments, and do not insist on the new birth, the witness of the Spirit and the fruits in a holy life, Methodism will inevitably lose her hold on the most vital Christian doctrines, and will tumble at length into the slough of liberalism. Toward this calamitous end, look at the decline of the class-meeting and the attempt to abolish probationary membership, which is fostered and tested by this peculiar means of grace; also the wholesale reception into full membership in some parts of our country of seekers who have not yet found satisfactory assurance of a change of heart. We should remember that the Methodist Episcopal Church South has already gone this length, and the signs of the times indicate that the mother of Episcopal Methodism is fast following in the footsteps of her retrograde daughter. How are we to interpret the wide-spread resort of our churches to worldly devices for raising money, devices which appeal to love of self instead of love to Christ who bought us with His blood? Do not the least objectionable of these commercial expedients, those which avoid the statutes against gambling, indicate a drying up of the streams of Christian beneficence consequent upon the decline of a spiritual life? So it seems to the author. Was there not a time when Methodism loved God so ardently that she gladly poured out her money for His cause without the premium of an oyster supper or pincushion? Many of my readers can remember the time when church fairs and festivals for ecclesiastical revenues were monopolized entirely by denominations which slightly emphasize heart religion. From her lofty spiritual height Methodism once looked down upon these things with abhorrence.

Do not stigmatize the writer as an alarmist if he points out to you manifest symptoms of doctrinal decline following upon the heels of confessed spiritual decay. The pulpit is the best place to feel the pulse of a denomination. Preachers are human and are inclined to abandon preaching truths distasteful to their audiences. What are the truths which once rang out in every Methodist pulpit, but have now fallen into neglect and are not preached at all, or are passed over like a slurred note in music? The helpless depravity of the natural man and his need of the new birth in order to be saved; the witness of the Spirit of adoption directly to the believer. In every church under my care I find many who confess ignorance of the meaning of the phrase "the direct witness of the Spirit." They say that they are resting on an inference drawn from the marks of regeneration recorded in the Bible and observed in their own hearts. They are strangers to the direct contact of God with the soul, upon which Wesley insisted so fully, frequently and emphatically, and which was the distinguishing feature of early Methodism and her secret of power. They say that the modern pulpit does not insist on this experience as the privilege of every believer. Thus many are left at ease without that heart knowledge of God which is eternal life. Hence the rarity of the radical Wesleyan type of conversion at our altars, so generally witnessed fifty years ago.

Wesley records the fact that ninety-nine per cent of those converted at his altars received the direct witness of the Spirit to their adoption into the family of God. In fact, there seems to be much less prominence given in our pulpits to the personality and distinctive offices of the Third Person of the Trinity in the plan of salvation than formerly. This is both a cause and an effect of the spiritual decline of the Church. If the Holy Spirit is the source of spiritual life, the more clearly He is presented to the faith of believers the more firmly will He be grasped, the more transforming will be His influence and the more abundant His fruit. Where do we look for the least zeal for Christ, the least ardor of Christian love, the least self-sacrifice for the promotion of the gospel, the least travail of soul for the conversion of sinners, the fewest conversions to Christ, the least interest in missions, the least joy in Christ, the least deadness to the world, and the least spirituality? It is where the least is said about the Paraclete, the peculiar and distinctive work of the Comforter. The unity of the Godhead without any such distinctive presentation is preached in the Mohammedan mosque, in the Jewish synagogue and the Unitarian and Universalist churches, with no spiritual fruit. The results are nearly as meagre in those Methodist churches where the Holy Spirit has been largely eliminated from the preaching. The same effects follow the same causes under whatever denominational name. Those denominations which emphasize the work of the Spirit are more spiritual and aggressive, while those which slight the Spirit are in turn slighted by Him, and become dead, worldly and stationary, or rather declining and on their way to the graveyard. It is vain to say that there is in the neglect of the Holy Spirit a compensation, inasmuch as the love of God is the more highly exalted and the Father more perfectly honored when preachers, neglecting the Third Person of the Trinity, give prominence to the First and Second. This is a very great fallacy. It is the office of the Spirit to take of the things of Christ and show them unto us, to testify of Christ. "He shall glorify me." He is the looking glass which reflects the image of the invisible Jesus. Remove or veil the mirror, and there is no vision of the Son of God; and where the Son is dimly seen, the Father is vaguely apprehended. Where the Holy Spirit is not exalted, Christ is not magnified. This lessening emphasis of the Spirit's work is leading our people into several grave misapprehensions respecting the spiritual life. One of these is that the office of the Spirit is limited to the beginning of the life of God in the soul; that He is needed only to convict sinners and convert penitents, and then may be dispensed with. The process by which this error is inculcated is this:

A revival is desired. An evangelist is sent for. His preliminary work is to prepare the members of the church to be channels of the Holy Spirit. They are all set to praying for His outpouring. Prominence is given to Him chiefly as the agent in conversion. The evangelist is dismissed after his work is done, and the Holy Spirit is dismissed also, as being no more needed till the time comes round for another revival. This sad mistake arises from the fact that the Spirit is made prominent only in the initiation of the spiritual life. In the advancement and sanctification of the believer He is not necessary. The young convert either hears nothing said about entire sanctification as the distinctive work of the Spirit, or he hears it vaguely preached as the result of growth. So growth takes the place of the Sanctifier, and He is left with nothing to do. So with all the fruits of the Spirit. The convert is told that if he would have joy he must seek it in doing every duty. Thus duty, a term used only twice in the New Testament, and then having no reference to the Christian life, usurps the place of the Paraclete, the wellspring of perennial joy. If the convert is troubled with doubts, instead of being pointed to the fulness of the Spirit as the source of assurance, excluding all doubt, he is told that doubts trouble everybody, and that there is no effectual remedy; but that which comes the nearest to the perfect cure is to plunge into Christian work so earnestly as to forget your doubts. Thus the Holy Spirit is insensibly supplanted. What will be the outcome of all this? The fervent and highly spiritual era of Methodism will pass away; then look out for the speculative era to come; the era of doctrinal disintegration, theological confusion and schism on dogmatic grounds.

Again, the law of God and His wrath against sin, the sanctions of the law, the eternal punishment of the finally impenitent, are not so plainly, boldly and earnestly preached as formerly. The law is still the schoolmaster, or child-leader, to bring men to Christ. Where the law is not preached through deference to long-pursed impenitent pew-owners, there are no conversions, and the preacher has to send for some evangelist to come and preach the same unpalatable truths the pastor has kept back; and sinners hear and are pricked in their hearts, and cry for pardoning mercy till they find salvation. There was no place for evangelists in Methodism fifty years ago, because every preacher preached the whole gospel, thundering the terrors of the Lord into the ears of slumbering sinners. How rarely do we now hear a sermon on the second coming of Christ and the day of judgment!

> "Day of judgment, day of wonders;
> Hark! the trumpet's awful sound,
> Louder than ten thousand thunders.
> Shakes the vast creations round;
> How the summons
> Will the sinner's heart confound!"

This style of preaching is out of fashion in our pulpits, just as though the everlasting gospel of the changeless

Christ were subject to the caprices of fashion, fickle as the winds. Jesus addressed sinners' fears, uncapping the pit of woe, bidding them gaze upon the undying worm, the unquenchable fire, and the smoke of the torment ascending up for ever and ever. Sin and the penalty have not changed. Human nature and the motives which influence it are the same in all ages. Who then has changed? Modern Christians are not, through the fulness of the Holy Spirit abiding in them, brought into such sympathy with Jesus that we realize these great truths as He did when He warned men to flee from the wrath to come. The penalty of the broken law is not preached in liberalistic pulpits, and, as a natural consequence, there being no schoolmaster to lead Christward, nobody is converted. Ought we not to expect the same barrenness to attend similar soft, sentimental and velvety preaching in so-called evangelical pulpits? The modern treatment of sin is alarmingly superficial. It is treated as if consisting wholly in the act; the state of heart behind the act is ignored. The doctrine of original sin, a poison stung into humanity by the sin of Adam and curable only by the radical purgation of the believer's soul, body and spirit, through the Holy Ghost in entire sanctification, after the new birth, has quite generally dropped out of our pulpits. How few preach about sin in believers, repentance in believers, and bring our church members under conviction for clean hearts, attainable now by faith and faith only in the blood of sprinkling which sanctifieth the unclean! In how few pulpits do famished Christians hear of the great salvation, Christian perfection, or the perfect holiness of believers, insisted on "clearly, emphatically and explicitly," a work described by Richard Watson as distinctly marked, and "as graciously promised in the Holy Scriptures as justification, adoption, regeneration and the witness of the Spirit." Why has the doctrine styled by John Wesley "the grand *depositum* committed to the people called Methodists," ceased to be heard in a majority of our churches, clearly unfolded, bravely defended, and faithfully urged upon all believers with its unanswerable array of scriptural proof? Is it not because the general tone of spirituality has sunk to so low a point that few believers in the pulpits and in the pews are thirsting after full salvation? This silence on a vital doctrine has almost wrested it from the Church providentially raised up for its promulgation. And this silence in turn is the result of the lack of the general diffusion of the Holy Spirit through our ministry and membership. Doctrinal errors must follow. The advance guard of the coming host of heresies is already visible— the denial of the resurrection of the body, of original sin, of the personality of Satan, of entire sanctification after justification, and of this life as the whole of probation. What the main army will be we know not, except that it will be marshalled by antichrist. To be forewarned is to be forearmed. If I have any special mission in the afternoon of my life between this and sunset, it is to show to the Church the grave perils which will inevitably follow the abandonment of an intense spirituality and the neglect of the doctrinal truths which inspire this vigorous spiritual life. If the warning is heeded, doctrinal defections will be checked, and all our members will have an experimental realization that Jesus is Jehovah. Then will the weak ones become as David, and David as the angel of Jehovah in valor and strength. Then there will be at least one denomination that the devil will not laugh at and the world spit upon. It was Whitefield who wisely said that he "had rather have ten members wholly consecrated to God and filled with the Spirit, than five hundred that the devil laughs at in his sleeve." The world has an instinctive fear of the man who intensely believes the whole Bible from cover to cover, who is dead to the world and alive to God in every fibre and atom of his being, with every capacity filled and every power energized by the Holy Ghost. "Give me a hundred men," says Wesley, "who fear nothing but sin, and desire nothing but God, and I will shake the world; and I care not a straw whether they be clergymen or laymen; and such alone will overthrow the kingdom of Satan and build up the kingdom of God on earth." He got his hundred men, and he shook the world with an earthquake mightier than can be produced by a million of easy-going nominal Christians afraid of the Holy Ghost and apologizing for their own distinctive doctrines.

I wish I had power to reach every Methodist on the round earth. I would say, cease living on the heroism of your fathers, quit glorying in numbers, sacrificing to statistics and burning incense to the general minutes; down upon your knees and seek and find for yourself the secret of the power of the fathers, a clean heart and the endowment of power from on high, then arise and unfurl the banner of salvation free and full and a common-sense theology, the beauty of which, as Joseph Cook says, is "that it can be preached." Then, in double-quick time, charge upon the hosts of sin and conquer the world for Christ. A Brahmin recently said to a Christian, "I have found you out. You are not as good as your book. If you Christians were as good as your book, you would in five years conquer India for Christ." Come, Holy Spirit, and so cleanse and fill us that we may be as good as our book!

Glory be to the Father, and to the Son, and to the Holy Ghost, as it was in the beginning, is now and ever shall be, world without end. Amen.

Appendix

Note A

The office of the Holy Spirit is not independent, but ministerial. He ministers Christ to men. He makes His words living and real to believers. He is not the revealer of new doctrines, but the inspirer, inciting men to record Christ's words and deeds, and so guiding their minds and refreshing their memories as to secure a truthful narrative.

Bishop Webb calls attention to an inevitable sequence of the recent dogma of "infallibility." By declaring that the Holy Spirit, through one earthly voice, from time to time, makes fresh revelations of doctrines to be added to the creed, the Roman Catholic Church has placed the Holy Spirit in an office which is not His, the office of a revealer of new truth, instead of His taking the things of Christ already revealed and applying them to believers. We are aware of the reply that the Pope does not reveal, he only, under the illumination of the Holy Spirit, gives a new interpretation to the Holy Scriptures; that he is supernaturally endowed with insight to discover in Gabriel's salutation to Mary, "Hail, highly favored, the Lord is with thee: blessed art thou among women," the doctrine of her immaculate conception, a doctrine never named till after a thousand years, and then universally rejected.

Note B

The orthodox doctrine of the Trinity is that the three Persons are by nature equal in power and glory. Theologians call this the *essential Trinity*, which may be represented by three stars on the same level.

But the Scriptures speak of the Persons as performing different offices in creation and redemption. In creation the Father is the principal, and the Son and the Spirit are agents. The First Person creates through the Second and the Third as agents coequal to each other, but in function subordinate to the First Person. This is called the *economic Trinity*, which may be represented by two stars on a level, with one star above them.

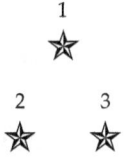

In the work of redemption there is a different relation of these Persons. The First is said to send the Second, and both of them to send the Third. This may be represented by placing the stars thus:

This is called the *redemptional Trinity*. The Father sends the Son, and the Father and the Son send the Spirit. This functional Trinity the Greek Church denies, but admits the essential Trinity and the economic Trinity. It denies the *filioque, i.e.*, that the Holy Spirit proceeds from the Son.

Note C

The Doctrine of the Spirit

The Holy Spirit is a *divine Person* distinct from the Father and the Son. It is hazardous to attempt the definition of the term "Person" as applied to the Trinity. All the mystery in the doctrine of the Triune God is wrapped up in the definition of "Person." It is a Latin word for the Greek *Hypostasis*, the English *subsistence*. Yet Dr. Barrow defines it as "a singular, subsistent, intellectual being," and Bethius as "an individual substance of a rational nature." While both definitions may be true, they lean strongly toward tritheism, the doctrine of three Gods. It is sufficient for our purpose to say that it is a self-conscious agent in the Trinity that says *I* and me (Acts xiii.2). The proofs of the personality of the Holy Spirit are found (1) in the personal pronoun *he*, John xiv.16, 17, 26, xvi.7-14; (2) Personal faculties and offices are ascribed to Him, such as searching, knowing, teaching, guiding, speaking and grieving; (3) He is the object of faith, obedience and worship, being co-ordinate with undisputed Persons in the baptismal formula which is the final revelation of God, Matt, xxviii.19; (4) He is the subject of benediction; (5) There is a sin against Him which is irremissible.

The Divinity of the Holy Spirit

1. He bears divine names and titles: *God*, Acts v.3, 4; *Lord*, II Cor. iii.17, 18 (Revision).

APPENDIX 323

2. Divine attributes are ascribed to Him. He is *omnipresent*, Ps. cxxxix.7, I Cor. iii.16; *omniscient*, ii.10; *omnipotent*, xii.4-11. *Wisdom*, Eph. i.17; *goodness*, Ps. cxliii.10. "Let thy good Spirit lead me," etc. (Hengstenberg.) *Infallibility*, compare Mark xiii.31 with Acts i.2.

3. Divine works are attributed to Him, as *creation*, Ps. civ.30; xxxiii.6, "the breath of his mouth" is His Spirit; Job xxvi.13. *Inspiration*, II Peter i.21, Mark xii.36, Acts i.16, iii.18, xxviii.25, Heb. iii.7. The *resurrection* of Christ, Rom. viii.11, I Peter iii.18, compare Acts xvii.31.

4. He abides in the spirit of the believer. It is a prerogative of God alone to dwell in His creatures. To no other beings or persons is it ascribed in the Bible.

5. A very strong proof of a negative kind is found in the fact that He is never mentioned among creatures. When created spirits are enumerated, such as angels, archangels, thrones, principalities, powers, cherubim and seraphim, the climax never ends with the Holy Spirit, as we should expect if He is both a person and a creature.

"What do we understand by the personality of the Spirit? Let us here first ask, What do we understand by human personality? It is something more than individuality. We can apply the term individual to any member of any species of the lower animals, but we cannot apply to it the term person. What is it that raises human individuality into personality, while individuality is the highest that we can predicate of the lower animals? Obviously, that while in the latter the individual is entirely subordinate to the species, among men the individual may rise above the species. He has intellect to understand, and the will to control and guide his instincts, while the animal is entirely subject to them. The stronger and more pronounced these higher qualities are, the greater, we say, the personality is. Personality is thus the highest form of life with which we are acquainted, and if we apply the term to the divine life it is simply because we have no higher term by which to define it. It enables us to understand what it is as little as animal individuality enables us to understand what human personality is; but as we may define personality as human individuality, so the distinction of persons in the Godhead may be expressed as divine personality. That, no doubt, transcends human personality infinitely more than human personality transcends the individuality of the brute creation. But it is the only term we have to apply to it, and it enables us in some measure to understand the relation in which we stand to them." (Dr. John Robson's "Holy Spirit, the Paraclete.") Lotze, the German philosopher, insists that the Infinite is the only perfect personality. Small, sceptical philosophers are so shallow as to assert that personality is impossible to the Infinite.

"Rev. J. H. Evans, an acceptable minister of the Church of England, became Sabellian, *i.e.*, came to deny the distinction of Persons in the Trinity so emphatically as to publish his denial in a book. The fascination of his new opinions so blinded his mind that he did not for a time perceive its practical effect. As he did not deny the work of the Spirit upon the heart, he did not for a time suspect that the Holy Spirit was dishonored. But his own soul suffered and there was a very manifest withering in his ministry. Inquiring for the cause, and finding that he had denied the real glory of the Holy Ghost in the economy of redemption and had reduced the Son of God to an unsubstantial shadow, he collected all the copies of his book which he could secure and consigned them to the flames with every mark of contrition. After his return to sound Trinitarian views, scarcely ever was there in London a more blessed ministry than his." (Prof. Smeaton's "Doctrine of the Holy Spirit," page 350.)

Arianism, which teaches that both the Son and the Spirit are creatures, destroys the foundation for eminent spirituality, which is produced by the indwelling Holy Spirit, the gift of the ascended Christ. To make Him a creature is to question His ability to impart so great a gift. To regard the Spirit as a creature is to cheapen the gift itself and thus to weaken the motive for seeking His presence and work in the heart of the believer. Neither Sabellianism nor Arianism, modern Unitarianism, is productive of deep spirituality. This statement is confirmed by the history of the Church.

"Has not the denial of the *filioque* (and from the Son), which withdrew the Greek Church from the ground occupied in Athanasius's time by the whole Church in the East and West, operated to the deep injury of vital religion in the East? Has it not tended to subvert, in the general sentiment of the Greek mind, the deep ground on which the Lord Jesus, as mediator, acts as the dispenser of the Spirit and as baptizer with the Holy Ghost and with fire? Has it not operated in an unsalutary way, in raising a barrier between the living Head of the Church and His people, considered as the habitation of God in the Spirit, and on the whole spiritual life of the Greek Church? Our conviction is that it has done so. So calamitous, indeed, have been the practical results of denying the essential relation of the Spirit as the Spirit of the Son, that we cannot fail to perceive them. The Spirit, economically considered, is largely dispensed from the Son. And the Greek Church has become much of a fossil, untouched by any of the reformations or revivals that renovated the Western church." (Professor Smeaton.)

"If the *Holy Spirit* is dwelling in you at all, He is there as a Person in all His majesty and glory and strength; in all the infinite resources of His deity. As to His gifts,— His grace,— there may be given to you, "by measure," more or less (Eph. iv.7, I Peter iv.10); but the *Holy Spirit* Himself, inasmuch as He is a Person, is not with you at all unless He is in you in all the fulness of His divine personality, in all, the majesty of His Godhead." (Bishop Webb.)

In answer to the objection that we should expect to be conscious of this majestic presence, Bishop Webb replies: "It is partly because in mercy He withholds the signs of His presence. You know how dull we are, — how *rude* to Almighty *God*; therefore, in very mercy, He does not come before us face to face, lest we should look into His face and turn our backs upon Him. He deals with us with a holy reserve, lest "we should lose our souls; for a terrible condition follows when the glory of *God* is revealed and then rejected." "Now have they both seen and hated both me and my Father." "The ways of the *Holy Spirit* are like the ways of *Christ*, ways of gentleness (Ps. cxliii.10, Rom. viii.14, Gal. v.18, Eph. iv.30)."

Note D

Says Dr. J. M. Buckley, editor of the *Christian Advocate*:
"Even from the evangelical churches the sense of sin in large measure departs. Modern penitential grief is often hardly worthy of a higher description than pensiveness, and the joys of the new creation are as feeble as the grief over sinfulness is diluted. The penalty of sin inflicted by the righteous indignation of a personal *God* gives place to vague or limited notions of the natural consequences of sin. Without once being stirred or hearing anything to make them wretched on account of their sins, to-day it is possible for the worldly minded, and even the vicious, regularly to attend service in many churches that were founded on the doctrine of the *Holy Ghost*.

"The condition of the Church of England immediately prior to the rise of Wesley, and the state of many of the German churches show how any form of error in doctrine or life may coexist with liturgical uniformity and artistic, musical, elocutionary and scholastic excellence.

"Every age has its peculiar battle. That of the next century is to be more subtle than any which has preceded it. As the nations are fighting more and more by diplomacy, and less and less on blood-stained fields, so the conflict between the kingdom of grace and that of darkness will be less violent, but more perplexing and dangerous.

"Strides in this direction have been made within fifteen years so rapid that there are already hundreds, and will soon be thousands, of churches in America as absolutely devoid of the *Spirit* of *God* in the New Testament sense as they would have been if they had been originally intended as literary and social clubs. This will be compatible with an increase in numbers, and statistics will be rolled up and published, as they are now, which no more indicate moral forces than would the roster of an army that should include invalids and babes.

"The churches are pursuing a course which shows how little confidence we have in the power of *God*. Our methods of securing accessions proceed increasingly upon the kindergarten principle, which, however useful for infants, promotes rather childishness than a childlike spirit in adults. We are willing to turn over the reformation of drunkards to quacks with secret remedies. We make few direct efforts to save hardened sinners, and send forth few laymen or ministers competent to grapple unbelievers and overcome them, not by argument in the plane of polemics, but by the irresistible force of personal testimony to the power of the *Holy Ghost*.

"The conclusive proof, which can leave no one familiar with the history of early Christianity, of early Presbyterianism, early Quakerism or early Methodism in doubt as to the force and danger of these tendencies, is the disuse of church discipline and the prevalence of theories that it is superfluous and beyond the just powers of the Church, except in cases of public scandal. To this may be added the feverish anxiety of many clergymen to maintain the appearance of influence and popularity by hastening to discuss whatever may attract a passing crowd.

"The need is not for great men to turn back the tide of evil and swell the tide of good, but that every one, small or great, who knows his sins forgiven, and is absolutely certain that he is under the power of an endless life, should cry aloud and spare not, so testifying that men will ask a reason of the hope that is within him, and find him ready with meekness and fear to give an answer."

Says Archdeacon Hare:

"When the Spirit of God came to convince the world of sin, what was the sin He began with? If any of us had to convince a person of the sinfulness of the world, how should we set about it? We should talk of the intemperance, and licentiousness, and dishonesty, and fraud, and falsehood, and envy, and ill-nature, and cruelty, and avarice, and ambition, whereby man has turned God's earth into a place of weeping and gnashing of teeth. These, however, are not the sins of which the Spirit of God convinces the world; because all these might be swept away, and yet, unless far more was done, the world would continue just as sinful as before. All these sins, this terrible brood of sin, were indeed to be found in every quarter of the earth, so far as it was then peopled, in our Lord's days, no less plentifully than now. They had swollen themselves out, and rose up on every side in the face of heaven, like huge mountains; they flowed from country to country, from clime to clime, like rivers; they spread themselves abroad like lakes and seas, lakes of brimstone and Dead Seas, within the exhalations of which no soul could come and live. Whithersoever the eye turned, it saw one sin riding on the back, or starting from the womb, of another. This was the Babel which all nations were busied in building, — and confusion of tongues did not hinder them, — a Babel underground. They went on digging deeper and deeper, until its nethermost story well-nigh reached to hell, and was only separated from it by a thin, crumbling crust. Nevertheless the Spirit of God, when He came to convince the world of sin, and to bring that conviction home to the hearts of mankind, did not choose out any of these open, glaring sins to taunt and confound them with. He went straight to that sin which is the root and source of all others, want of faith, the evil heart of unbelief. *'When the Comforter is come, he will convince the world of sin, because they believe not in me.'*

"Now this is a sin, which the world till then had never dreamed of as such: and even at this day few take much thought about it, except those who have been convinced of it by the Spirit, and who therefore have been in great measure delivered from it. For those who have spent their whole lives in thick spiritual blindness, and whose eyes are still dark, cannot know what the blessing of sight is, and therefore cannot grieve at their want. They alone who have emerged into the light can appreciate the misery of the gloom under which they have been lying. Thus, until we have begun, to believe we cannot know what unbelief is, its misery, its sin, its curse. Want of faith is a sin of which no law accuses us... Laws, inasmuch as by their nature they deal only with that which manifests itself outwardly, in deed or in word, take no cognizance of the sin of unbelief. Conscience, which only sounds when some positive sin is trampling upon it, is silent about this. Hence our need that the Spirit of God should graciously vouch safe to convince us." ("The Mission of the Comforter.")

Note E

Being led by the Spirit is a sequence of regeneration, and is therefore an evidence that this momentous change has been wrought. "For as many as are led by the Spirit of God, they are the sons of God."

This does not imply that every thought is suggested by the good Spirit, for we are still within bowshot of the devil, who may inject thoughts into our minds, and it is our business to acquire keenness of spiritual perception sufficient "to discriminate between good and evil" (Heb. v.14). The leading of the Spirit implies the weakness of a child needing a strong support, and an ignorance of the way of life through a thousand snares and pitfalls requiring guidance. We are to surrender our wills, affections and inclinations so completely as to desire to do nothing for merely selfish ends, but only for the glory of God, so far as we can under the illumination from above, confirmed by its accordance with the written word of God, which is ever to be a light to our feet. When a Christian finds himself following the Spirit to the neglect of the Holy Scriptures, he is in danger of getting into the devil's snare of fanaticism. The bones of many an unwary pilgrim are scattered about that fatal pitfall.

Note F

Bishop Foss on Entire Sanctification

In an address delivered to a class of young ministers about to be admitted to the conference, Bishop Foss said: "I take it that every Christian minister of the Methodist Episcopal Church recognizes that it is needful we retain and, as Methodist ministers and preachers of the gospel, preach the truths of the New Testament as taught by our church, and that silence for six months together on what the church believes and teaches on the subject of perfect love is just paving the way for irresponsible teachers to come forward and take the work out of our hands. If we are Christians after the New Testament type, let us preach those doctrines which, as a church, we believe are contained therein; and I think that upon the doctrines of perfect love and the cleansing from all sin by the blood of Jesus, it will be done in much the same way as John Wesley and Richard Watson preached them. Don't let people listen to you for six months and then have to ask what you mean upon these questions. Having taken your ordination vows, preach perfect love as the Bible puts it, and it won't hurt much if put exactly as John Wesley teaches it.

"Lead the people up always to a higher life. If you do this, you will take the wind out of the sails of those who teach it in other ways. God bless them in so far as their work is right; but let our own hearts be warmed and our minds fired upon this question, and we shall lead the people to the heights and depths, and to know the love of God, which passeth knowledge."

WHAT METHODISM MIGHT HAVE DONE

Under the above caption that excellent journal, the *Michigan Advocate*, publishes a very significant article as follows:

"Though not a Methodist himself, the late Dr. Dale of England was a great student of Methodism, and a great admirer of many of our doctrines and usages. In 1879 he preached a sermon before the Wesleyan conference at Birmingham, which produced a profound impression. Among other memorable utterances he declared that 'if Methodism had carried out its doctrine of entire sanctification in public as well as in private life, it would have effected the most profound and beneficent ethical revolution modern history has known.' It seems to us that this statement is irrefutable. The world has need of a great church that dares to hold up boldly the very highest standard of righteousness, and to proclaim the glorious possibilities of divine grace in renovating society and in purging the hearts of all men from the power and guilt of sin. In some degree Methodism has done this, but not in the highest degree. Since the death of Wesley in England, and of Asbury in America, our official deliverances upon this subject have been comparatively few and far between, and to some extent in an apologetic tone. Of late years neither our board of bishops nor the general conference has uttered a full, clear and ringing note upon this central idea of Christianity. The whole glorious subject has been left too largely to the tender mercies of a few specialists, who have distorted it and misled many an earnest soul. It is a theme which should shine out from the church itself, from its official deliverances, from its conference sessions, from its regular pulpits, from its camp meetings and conventions, and should be held in correct relation to other doctrines, explained, commended, enforced, illustrated and practically exemplified by bishops, presiding elders, pastors, local preachers, official members, leagues, Sunday schools, missionary societies, in a word, by the complete and undivided church. Had this been done through all our past, and were it done to-day, the 'profound and beneficent ethical revolution' would be tremendously under way, and society the world over would be reaping the gracious benefits of a higher spiritual ideal and a loftier moral standard. It was as a worthy object of endeavor, a sweet and attractive ideal, that Mr. Wesley himself most loved to present this doctrine. After giving the scriptural account of a perfect Christian, he was fond of saying: 'By these marks the Methodists *desire* to be distinguished from other men; by these we *labor* to distinguish ourselves.' He held up the ideal and urged his followers to do their best in striving to attain to it. To this method there can be no reasonable objection in any unprejudiced mind."

"Why is it," says Beck, "that people lay stress, almost exclusively, with a view to faith in Jesus, on this, that He bears the sin of the world, and neglect so much the other point, that He is able to baptize with the Holy Ghost? The apostles, on the contrary, lay stress on this gift of the Spirit as the source of a new life, a new disposition and walk, in which both the impression and the expression of God's law are to be seen. The apostles and the prophets also treat the matter in its ethical aspect, whereas the traditional treatment represents the gift of the Spirit chiefly as a seal of forgiveness and adoption, and holds that from the joy of gratitude for this— that is from a mere psychological factor— the new life and strength are to spring. This view we find in our best authors. The Scriptures, on the contrary, lay stress on the new-creating and satisfying power of the Holy Ghost as the principle of all Christian disposition and personal activity (Rom. viii.2). Christ's sin-bearing only prepares the way for the coming of the Spirit (John vii.39, Gal. iii.13, 14); it is the foundation, but not the whole." The answer to this question of Beck why sin-bearing is exalted above Spirit-baptizing is; because (1) Most of the preachers are experimentally ignorant of the baptism of the Spirit; (2) They treat the pardon of sin as the principal benefit of Christianity; (3) Much of the prevalent preaching is either on the evidences, ethics or elements of the gospel, and little on its deeper experiences and higher life. It is therefore natural that the pulpit should be more largely stored with bottled milk than with "solid food," and that there should be many sermons on justification and few on sanctification.

SANCTIFICATION BY THE SPIRIT NOT IN THE INTERMEDIATE STATE

Bishop Webb, who strongly advocates the advanced doctrine of sacramentalism, teaches that regenerate souls who have failed of sanctification by the Spirit before death will be entirely purified in Paradise. "Dear brethren, for progress in *holiness* it is not necessary to assume a time of pain and agony. Souls may and will expand in the Paradise of *God*, in happiness and brightness, in light and refreshment. Progress in knowledge would imply progress in holiness. There is no necessity to assert the dogma of purgatory."

When discussing the agency which will produce this holiness, our good bishop, whose theme is the Holy Spirit, finds no proof text for an after-death purification by the "sanctification of the Spirit," but he intimates that "progress in knowledge and holiness may possibly be learned from those who have gone before, or from the angels, or perhaps from some more direct action of Christ, and from the Holy Spirit. Some kind of sacramental action upon the soul that has been cleansed will still proceed in the near presence of Jesus Christ, 'for to him that overcometh will I give to eat of the tree of life, which is in the midst of the paradise of God.'"

On a subject of so great importance it is better to imitate God's perfect silence in the Holy Scriptures than to mislead any soul by our "perhaps" and "possibly."

"The life of faith— progressive, increasing faith— is a motion in a straight line and not in a closed curve; it is not like an Irish penance around a sacred well, where one makes progress with the final result of being where you started, and perhaps ready for another revolution, as, indeed, it must appear to some Christians whose circle is a week and whose starting point a Sunday. Neither is it like the pilgrimage up Pilate's staircase at Rome, in which the pain of going up on one's knees is only varied by the discomfort of coming down again and finding ourselves just about where we were before, as it must appear to some good people who live the up-and-down life. It is an upward and onward life; on our knees, if you will, but upward and onward, and like the stairs in Ezekiel's vision, still upward. And the Scriptures encourage us forward, bidding us leave the word of the beginning of Christ and go (not crawl) on unto perfection." (J. Rendel Harris.)

Two Eminent Witnesses to Entire Sanctification

Dr. Wilbur Fisk, the charming, inspiring and subduing preacher, the founder of institutional education in American Methodism, a man combining the distinctive charms that endear to us the beautiful characters of Fenelon and Channing, Jonathan Edwards and John Fletcher, lived more than a score of years in the faith and exemplification of the sublime doctrine of Christian perfection as taught by Jesus Christ, St. Paul and St. John. He prized that great tenet as one of the most important distinctions of Christianity. With John Wesley he deemed this fundamental truth— promulgated as a distinctive blessing almost solely by Methodism in those days— to be one of the most solemn responsibilities of his church, the most potent experimental proof of the divine origin of the gospel. When he received the baptism of this great grace, his purified heart could not sufficiently utter its thankfulness that he had been providentially kept within the church which clearly taught this pre-eminent doctrine, and that he had not yielded to the temptation to unite with other communions which offered larger salaries and higher social standing.

His experience, which left its radiant impress on his daily life, was signalized by an overwhelming effusion of the Holy Spirit, depriving him of physical strength for several hours. It occurred at a camp meeting at Wellfleet, on August 10, 1819. As he was passing one of the Boston tents a lady invited him to stay in that tent. She then told him that on the way down an assurance had been given her that Mr. Fisk would receive the blessing of a holy heart at that meeting. "Her words thrilled through me in an indescribable manner. I wept, I trembled, I fell. But Satan drew a veil of unbelief over my mind. They prayed for me, but all was dark, my heart was harder than ever. Thursday morning we had a familiar conversation concerning heart holiness... I preached that day with considerable liberty; felt my mind more and more given up to the work, but thought if I had been through such struggles, and had obtained what I was seeking, much more remained to be endured. And I felt willing to endure anything.

"About the setting of the sun, word came that souls were begging for prayers in Brother Taylor's tent [the celebrated 'Father Taylor' of the Seaman's Bethel]. I went immediately in, and behold, God was there. We united in prayer, when one after the other to the number of four or five were converted. We rose to sing. I looked up to God, and thanked Him for answering prayer, and cried, 'Lord, why not hear prayer for my soul?' My strength began to fail while I looked in faith. 'Come, Lord, and come now. Thou wilt come. Heaven opens, my Saviour smiles,— glory! glory! O glory to God! Help me, my brethren, to praise the Lord.' The scene that was now opened to my view I can never describe. I could say, 'Lord, Thou knowest that I love Thee! I love Thee above everything... Bless the Lord, O my soul, and all that is within me praise His holy name.'" When he knelt to offer this prayer he was in the very act of guarding against strange fires such as produced bodily exercises of which he had grave doubts. Then it was that he was smitten to the earth by the mighty power of the Holy Ghost filling all his being. When he had so far recovered his physical strength as to be able to be taken to his own tent, there was held another season of holy communion. Being unable to stand, he was supported by ministerial brethren. His language and whole appearance had something in them more than human, indicating that his soul then glowed with ardors of love allied to those of angels.

From this period Dr. Fisk dated his experience of perfect love. Before that he had passed through seasons when he doubted the fact of his acceptance with God, his personal interest in Christ, and even the truth of Christianity itself. When in later years a young minister consulted him concerning just such doubts, Dr. Fisk told him that he had been delivered from such things forever at the Wellfleet meeting. They could no more dwell in the presence of the full development of the life of perfect purity, perfect faith, perfect love, perfect humility and perfect assurance than darkness can dwell in the presence of noonday.

In his subsequent description of his experience in a letter to his sister, he says: "In the work of sanctification upon the heart there appear to be two distinct stages: one is to empty the soul of sin and everything offensive; and the other is to fill it with love. 1. The strong man armed is bound and cast out. 2. The stronger takes possession. God was pleased, however, in my case, to empty and fill in the same moment." ("Life of Wilbur Fisk," by Dr. George Prentice, pages 44-54.)

Stephen Olin stands forth with commanding prominence in the history of the American pulpit. It is thought by many that he was intrinsically the greatest man, taken "all in all" that American Methodism has produced. It could be said of him as Rowland Hill said of Chalmers, "The most astonishing thing about him was his humility." He was the best example we have personally known— the writer was with him for six years— of that childlike simplicity which Christ taught as the essential condition for entering the kingdom of heaven, and Bacon declared to be equally necessary to those who would enter into the kingdom of knowledge. Like Dr. Wilbur

Fisk, he was a personal example of St. Paul's doctrine of "Christian perfection," as expounded by Wesley. At first he entertained doubts respecting it; but as he advanced in life, and especially under the chastening influence of affliction, it became developed in his own experience. To the writer he said: "My wife I had recently buried in Italy; my children were dead, my health undermined. My entire earthly prospect was gloomy indeed. God only remained. I lost myself, as it were, in Him; I was hid in Him with Christ. Then I found, while wandering on the banks of the Nile in quest of health, without any process of logic, but by an experimental demonstration, 'the perfect love that casteth out fear.'" The marvellous grace that glorified his greatness with unsurpassed humility in great measure was the effect of this experience on a certain day in Egypt, and the result of the constancy of his faith in this crowning gift of God to believers in this world when they most need it. From the hour of that memorable spiritual transfiguration in the land of the pyramids the doctrine of full redemption through the sanctifying office of the Holy Spirit was very precious to him, and he looked with painful feelings upon anything designed to bring it into disrepute, or lower the standard of piety which it implies. This colossal mind had no difficulty with the question whether consciousness of inner purity is a sufficient proof of entire sanctification. Three years after passing this milestone in his spiritual life, he made this record while too feeble to listen to a sermon: "I never before experienced such rest in Christ— such calm, unshaken faith, such ready, unreserved consent of the heart to the divine will, such an utter surrender of my own will to God's. I cannot find, after much prayerful examination, that I have any disposition to do or to love anything that is not well-pleasing in His sight. I write this with great self-distrust, but as the result of self-examination. Such a state of affections in a Christian so little advanced, and so specially undeserving as I feel myself to be, appears incredible to me, and I am constantly looking for the development of a still unsanctified nature." This implies that such a development had not occurred. A similar testimony was given by President Mahan forty years after his personal experience that "the blood of Jesus Christ cleanseth from all sin," although he was naturally of a temper so quick and violent that his father predicted that in his ungovernable anger he would kill some one and expiate his crime on the scaffold.

Note G

"The moment you submit to God's will and in your heart intelligently believe in the Lord Jesus Christ and accept Him as your Saviour, that moment God who justifieth at the instance of your Mediator will say, 'Your sins are forgiven you for His name's sake;' and God the Holy Ghost will fulfil in your heart the righteousness of the law, certify by the stamp of His royal seal upon your heart that the death penalty of the law against you is cancelled, your sins forgiven, and the love of God, the essential principle of obedience, shed abroad in your heart by the Holy Ghost thus given unto you, and all attested by the Spirit's direct witness, corrobated by the testimony of your own spirit, based on the conscious work and fruit of God's Holy Spirit in your experience" (I John iii.24, Eph. i.13). (Bishop William Taylor.)

Says Rev. Joseph Parker of London:
"Is it not a great honor to be decorated with God's own seal, entitling us to be recognized everywhere in the universe as His adopted sons? What are the decorations which princes bestow as tokens of merit, compared with this sign of the divine approval? That great humorist, Sydney Smith, tells with what pride a little

visitor of his allowed a large red wafer to be stuck in the middle of his forehead every night, signifying that he had behaved well during the day. Once only did the little fellow forfeit the wafer, and then went sobbing and broken-hearted to bed. With less reason have men striven for many a badge of distinction. We all know what deeds have been done for the sake of the French Cross of the Legion of Honor. It is related that a medical student, who had risked his life in a case of contagious disease, smiled sadly when that famous decoration was laid upon his bed, saying, 'It has cost me my life!' If such value be put upon earthly honors, what is that worth which God alone can confer? No earthly coronet or crown approaches the glory of the seal of the Holy Spirit, the sign of adoption into the divine family."

"The present enjoyment of the Spirit is but an *earnest*, a gift beforehand, a pledge of the coming fulness. St. Paul speaks (Rom. viii.23) of those which have the first fruits of the Spirit, and in his other epistles he uses equivalent expressions. What can be meant by such words but that the spiritual life is a continued progression, receiving with its widening capacities richer gifts of the wisdom and holiness of God. The Church is in its infancy as to valuation of spiritual blessing. It is, too, so much engaged in controversy that it can hardly be preparing itself for the completion of the holy promise. By mistaking the part for the whole, it is in danger of setting itself into premature satisfaction, as if it had exhausted the possibilities of prayer. The Church is too much engaged in that worst and most cankering of all worldliness, the elevation of one sect above another, and the angry defence of the transient conveniences of forms. What is delaying the outpouring of the fulness of the Spirit? There is indeed a still sterner inquiry which cannot be put without emotion, yet it may not be honestly suppressed: *Is not the presence of the Holy Ghost in the Church less distinct to-day than in the apostolic age*? Certainly there is not much appearance of Pentecostal inspiration and enthusiasm in contemporary Christianity. Christianity is nothing if not *spiritual*. Why has not a Church eighteen hundred years old a fuller realization of the witness of the Holy Ghost than had the Church of the first century? Has the Church accomplished all the purpose of God and passed forever the zenith of her light and beauty?" ("The Paraclete," pages 373—375)

Note H

"Many a time nothing is wanting but to speak as to a soul already hungry and thirsty, or, if not consciously so, ready to hunger and thirst as soon as the bread and water of life are presented. If the problem is to get souls under sin inspired again, which it certainly is, then it is required that the preacher shall drop lecturing on religion and preach it, testify it, prophesy it, speak to faith as being in faith, bring inspiration as being inspired, and so become the vehicle, in his own person, of the power he will communicate; that he may truly beget in the gospel such as will be saved by it. No man is a preacher because he has something like or about a gospel in his head. He really preaches only when his person is the living embodiment, the inspired organ of the gospel; in that manner no mere human power, but the demonstration of a Christly and divine power. Such preaching has had, in former times, effects so remarkable. At present we are almost all under the power, more or less, of the age in which we live. Infected with naturalism ourselves and having hearers that are so, we can hardly find what account to make of our barrenness." (Dr. Bushnell's "Nature and the Supernatural," page 516.)

"How insignificant all such labored disquisitions compared with the demonstration of the Spirit attending the preaching of one who has received an anointing from the Holy One! Alas! we do not quite know in these days whether any such action is to be expected. We are not quite certain but that the measure of the power of the Spirit received at conversion is all that can be looked for. O that the many would-be prophets who have enjoyed the highest educational advantages of the age, and are yet equal only to the very best 'sounding brass,' may come to believe that for God to be in their hearts and with their mouths is better than all the rest, and that until such an unction is poured upon them from on high, they are not the ministry of the Church which its Lord ascended to bestow." (Rev. C. E. Smith's "Baptism in Fire.")

"The Holy Spirit is able," said Mr. Spurgeon, "to make the Word as successful now as in the days of the apostles. He can bring in by hundreds and thousands as easily as by ones and twos. The reason why we are not more prosperous is that we have not the Holy Spirit with us in might and power as in early times. If we had the Spirit sealing our ministry with power, it would signify very little about our talent. It is extraordinary grace, not talent, that wins the day. It is extraordinary spiritual power, not extraordinary mental power, that we need. Mental power may fill a chapel, but spiritual power fills the Church. Mental power may gather a congregation; spiritual power will save souls. We want spiritual power. O Spirit of the living God! we want *Thee*. Thou art the life, soul of Thy people's success. Without Thee they can do nothing; with Thee they can do everything."

That anointed woman, the Deborah of the nineteenth century, Mrs. Booth, thus preaches: "It is the real, unadulterated Christianity we want, the Holy Ghost reign of Jesus Christ, and then you can have culture or do without it. I say it is a great delusion, and an insult to Jesus Christ, to make out that His reign needs modern culture to help it. A great deal of modern culture has done more to render us effete and powerless than all that ruffianism or heathenism ever did in the world's history! Kingdoms are subdued through *faith*, not through intellect, not through learning, not through modern culture."

Note I

How rarely do we think of the wonderful humility of the Holy Spirit! This is the dispensation of His humiliation thus far, and probably for generations to come. In the Old Testament God the Father was revealed and disobeyed and slighted. Then the Son was manifested, and in His public ministry passed a year in obscurity, a year of public favor, and a year of malicious opposition ending in ignominy. Now is the time when the Holy Spirit is humiliated. He is entirely ignored by the world which denies His existence. He is neglected by many who profess to be His friends. Few, indeed, so earnestly desire Him as to enthrone Him over their hearts. Many believers have vague, crude and unworthy conceptions of His glory and divinity. Instead of self-assertion, He keeps Himself in the background, desiring to give prominence to Christ and not to Himself. "This is the practical lesson: If we are not patient under opposition, ill at ease when unappreciated, and despondent when favor turns into hostility to our efforts to promote the holiness of Christians, it is evident that the Holy Spirit has not yet taken full possession of our hearts, and that we are dishonoring Him. You have not other gifts, because He does not see fit to give them to you. They would spoil some other gift which you have. Now, if this is the true view of Providence— of the whole ordering of the world according to the purposes of *God*,— it does not matter what are our outward circumstances.

Anna was preserved to old age to give thanks for the *Lord's* coming; Simeon was kept alive to see the salvation of the *Lord* and sing the 'Nunc Dimittis;' and Elisabeth was kept barren for a long period of her life in order to bear her witness for the *Lord* in a different way from either. Each string in the great orchestra is under the finger of *God* the *Holy Ghost,* who touches the chord and brings out the tone that is wanted at the right time. How wonderful and tender the patience of the *Holy Spirit* striving with men even before the flood! Think of His patience with us! He might bring out such harmonies from us, and we compel Him to hear such discords!

"This thought will help *you* to be patient, though all seem in disorder. Do not try to set the world right in five minutes. You cannot do it; *God* did not intend you to do it. You have a great ideal of what it ought to be, what it might be; but you have to be patient under this discipline, even as *God* is patient. Be *content*. Your neighbor may have what you have not, and you may have what he has not because 'all these worketh that one and the selfsame *Spirit,* dividing to every man severally as he will'" ("The Presence and Office of the Holy Spirit," Bishop Webb.)

John Fletcher charitably suggests the following lame excuse— the best, however, that can be made— for the dishonor of the Holy Spirit by the silence of the pulpit on this vital theme:

"Some preach the cross of Christ; but they proclaim not the spiritual coming of the risen Saviour. If they even entertain a just opinion of the doctrine for which we plead, yet they are restrained from speaking frequently and freely upon the subject, because as many false Christians have rendered the dispensation of the Son contemptible to the eyes of deists; so, many vainly inspired zealots have caused the dispensation of the Spirit to appear ridiculous before sober-minded Christians. But, notwithstanding the reproach which many fanatics of various sects have brought upon this sublime part of the gospel, by mingling with it the reveries of a heated imagination, yet it will constantly be regarded by every well-instructed Christian as the quintessence of our holy religion."

Spiritual laymen that hold meetings are stigmatized as schismatics. "If, in a parish that is unhappy enough to have a worldly minister, a few persons are happily converted to God and united together in Christ; if, having one heart and one soul, they frequently join together in prayer and in praise, mutually exhorting and provoking one another to love and good works, the unsympathetic pastor, instantly alarmed, imagines that these persons, for the purpose of forming a new sect, are destroying the unity of the church, when, on the contrary, they are but just about to experience the communion of saints. If zealous, he will labor to make it appear that these Christians who are beginning to love as brethren are forming conventicles to disturb the order of the church. Such a minister will give encouragement to companies of jugglers, dancers and drunkards, rather than tolerate a society which has Christian love for its object and basis." ("The Portrait of St. Paul," by J. Fletcher.)

Note K

"It imports us to know that through Jesus only can men entertain the hope of obtaining the gift of the Holy Ghost. Our prayer is a nullity without His prayer.

"He ascended that He might give a greater gift — greater by all that height to which He ascended. He stopped not at any of the grades set forth by the expressions 'principalities, powers, might, dominion.' Not from any such elevation could He give a sufficient gift unto men. Legions of angels would have helped us little. He ascended up far above the highest of heaven's hierarchy. In fact, it was to give Himself to us that He ascended on high, having previously descended to give Himself for us.

"Without the Holy Ghost we have no Christ. Christ, with all His infinite resources, with all His love, all His glory, is brought nigh to the individual believer and made a part of His being by the gift of the indwelling Spirit." (George Bowen.)

This is what Jesus means when He says, "It is expedient for you that I go away; for if I go not away the Comforter will not come unto you." "When I say it will be for your advantage, I do not mean that the Holy Spirit is greater than I am, or a truer friend to you, but that the Spirit will bring you and myself into a more intimate and blessed union than has been yet revealed in your consciousness. Though you have been with me these years, yet there is a moral chasm between us. You must painfully realize the very feeble amount of transforming influence that has been exerted upon you by one who is manifestly God in the likeness of men.

"The desire for sanctification exists in you, but your new and elevated conception of holiness only makes you the more sensible of your great moral deficiencies. If miracles could have given you the victory over sin you would now be the noblest of men. Yet are you still sadly aware that pride, ambition and worldliness have power over you.

"It is one thing that the image of God should have been placed before you; it is a very different thing that you should be changed into that image. You feel the need of some unknown power by which the minds of men may be rendered obedient to the truth, something beyond miracles, something beyond the power of a holy example. Is there not some power in God which can subdue that hostility by which we are hindered from being transfigured through the testimony of a holy life? There is. I ascend on high that the Comforter may come into your utmost selves, and that rivers of living water may flow forth from you, making the desert rejoice and blossom as the rose." (George Bowen.)

"The baptism of the Spirit appears to have been such a blessing that those who received it were fully conscious of possessing it. Not that they all doubted of their own piety before, and that this blessing assured them of their acceptance. It seems plain that Peter and others were sure that they loved the Saviour before the events of the Pentecost occurred. The lips of Christ had told His disciples that they were clean while as yet the Paraclete was not in them; and an angel had assured Cornelius of his acceptance before Peter preached to him the gospel and the Holy Ghost fell on them that heard the word. If they were conscious of acceptance before this, how much more when the Spirit of adoption in their hearts cried Abba, Father! 'I think,' says Calvin, 'that the apostle used this participle (crying) to express greater confidence; for doubt does not suffer us to speak boldly, but holds the jaws as it were compressed, so that the half-broken words hardly come forth from a faltering tongue. On the other hand, crying is a mark of security and of confidence, not at all of vacillating.'" (Dr. J. Morgan.)

"In no age, possibly, have Christian churches been so well equipped for effective service for Christ as they are now. Like marvellous structures of ingenious machinery, our churches stand forth, endowed with wealth, enriched with education, culture and social influence, possessing splendid church edifices, elaborate music and rituals, sound in creeds, confessions and covenants. And yet, alas! these numerous and admirable channels carry but drivelling streams of that divine energy that made the early churches such centres of evangelizing power, where they were composed of disciples whose faith stood not in 'the words which man's wisdom teacheth, but which the Holy Spirit teacheth.' The crying need of the age is not more of such churches or more or better appliances, but a universal baptism of the Holy Spirit. Were this given, the Church could, with her present resources, give the gospel to the world within the next decade." (F. M. Mills, D. D.)

"I believe the Church, with all her external prosperity, is to-day in greater peril than in any of the eighteen centuries of her history. Her very prosperity is her peril. She reminds me of a church in Canada which brought in a report after this fashion: 'We have had a prosperous year. All our pews and sittings are taken. We have a surplus of £50 in the treasury. We have had no conversions, but it has been a very prosperous year.' The world has come into the Church in such a fashion that the Church has become composed of one half wholly worldly people, and the other half of worldly holy people, so that if you do not have a chance to consult the church roll, you cannot tell who belongs and who not. How many people in our modern churches practically know whether there is a Holy Ghost or not? How many of them have ever risen to the conception that their bodies are temples of the Holy Ghost? How many churches have a genuine Holy Ghost prayer meeting? It is either a lecture by the pastor or a social meeting."* The remedy is both divine and human. The Spirit must be poured out, and godly men be ordained to the ministry, converted people do the singing, regenerate men and women be the officiary, and a discipline enforced excluding from the Lord's table all who bring reproach on Christ by wicked conduct.

"If we believe He is a person in the Trinity, let us treat with Him as a person, apply ourselves to Him as a person, glorify Him in our hearts as a person, dart forth

---

*Dr. A. T. Pierson

beams of special and peculiar love to and converse with Him as a person. Let us fear to grieve Him, and also believe on Him as a person." (Goodwin.)

"As Adam's life is reproduced in every child born into the world, so the new, spiritual life of the second Adam is reproduced in every one born of the Spirit. Our life is the reproduction of Christ's spiritual life in His people. The new birth connects us with the second Man, who, by the Holy Spirit, gathers His people under Him by a self-communicating act." (Smeaton.)

"It is one thing to have the Holy Spirit; it is another to have Him completely possessing us. No one can be regenerated without having Him; but there is the other side of it when He fills our entire being and has His way with us." (Kelly.)

"'Spirit,' in the requirement to worship in spirit and in truth, denotes that deepest element of the human soul by which it can hold communion with the divine world. It is the seat of self-collectedness, the sanctuary wherein the true worship is celebrated. Rom. i.9: 'The God whom I serve in my spirit.'" (Godet.)

Chronologically a believer may be living in the dispensation of the Spirit, and yet experimentally he may be living before the day of Pentecost. Objectively he may be in the Spirit because He has been poured out, yet subjectively he may be living in the letter because he has no personal acquaintance with the Spirit.

Note L

"This fountain of the Spirit is not limited to the apostles; it is not surrounded by an iron fence with a narrow gate to which only the priestly class has the key. Jesus precluded any such monopoly when He said: 'He that believeth on me,' learned or ignorant, rich or poor, bond or free.

"'It is a gift which all may share,
From prince to peasant rude;
It glows not more in palace halls
Than in dark solitude.'"
                    (Bishop W. Pinkney.)

"Christ, in the person of the Holy Spirit, is in His Church in all her pilgrimage through this world unto the end. When historic episcopates and ecclesiastical establishments have withered and ceased to bear fruit, this indwelling Christ can bud with new ministries and bring forth in new missionary enterprises. There is a true apostolic succession through which the Holy Spirit is communicated from generation to generation. This succession has rarely been found confining itself to the historical and sacerdotal channels, but it may be traced rather in what Harnack calls 'certain undercurrents of tradition' which have flowed out of sight from age to age. It is usually only a little company who are called into the upper room to receive the baptism of the Holy Ghost and fire; but they receive it for the whole Church, and by a kind of spiritual laying on of hands it is communicated from one to another till multitudes share the blessing.

"In the doctrine of tactual succession there is not only a kind of cheapness and pettiness, but especially a foreshortening of the Spirit's arm, as though the consecrating touch depended on the intervention of some visible ecclesiastic. On the contrary, the hands of the Paraclete have often stretched across a century or generation and set apart a ministry by foreordination long before any bishop or presbytery has moved to set him apart by ordination." ("The Holy Spirit in Missions," by Dr. A. J. Gordon.)

"Some well-intentioned people, but feeble in grace, drink down to the level of forgiveness, but not down to glory and the receiving of the Spirit; they do not realize that 'he that drinketh of the water that I shall give him shall never thirst;' they do not overcome the world; one has almost to make a fresh text for them. This is the defeat wherewith they are worsted, even their little faith."

"We may, indeed, get dying grace, and hold a consecration meeting upon our dying beds, but it is not death that consecrates, nor the grave that sanctifies and cleanses from all sin. We shall begin the next life pretty much where we left off in this." (J. Rendel Harris.)

Note M

The irremissible sin, it is thought by some writers, can be committed only by the backslider from the spiritual life. He may not be an avowed apostate from Christ, but may maintain a profession of Christian faith. Says Rev. W. W. Andrews: "The redemption of the world is as real an act of God as its creation, and the movements of the Holy Ghost are never absent where the Father and the Son are working. And it is step by step against these threefold mercies that the sin of man is suffered to show itself. Beginning with the transgression of His ordinances as the creator and lawgiver, it reaches a higher stage in 'denying the Lord that bought them,' and attains its consummation and climax in that sin against the Holy Ghost for which there is no forgiveness. This triple form of sin shows the wonderful power of man in setting itself against all motives and influences, and in effecting his destruction, although created in God's image and redeemed by the blood of His Son and made partaker of the heavenly life by the renewing of the Holy Ghost. The heathen dishonored God as revealed to them in the ordinances of nature; the Jews rejected

Him as manifested in the crucified Jesus, who gave His life a ransom for their sins; but the greater guilt of the Christian Church will lie in driving the Spirit from His dwelling-place by her pollutions, and turning like 'the sow that was washed to her wallowing in the mire.'"

Members of Schmul's Wesleyan Book Club buy these outstanding books at 40% off the retail price.

Join Schmul's Wesleyan Book Club by calling toll-free:
800-S$_7$P$_7$B$_2$O$_6$O$_6$K$_5$S$_7$
Put a discount Christian bookstore in your own mailbox.

Visit us on the Internet at www.wesleyanbooks.com

You may also order direct from the publisher by writing:
Schmul Publishing Company
PO Box 776
Nicholasville, KY 40340

www.ingramcontent.com/pod-product-compliance
Lightning Source LLC
Chambersburg PA
CBHW071734150426
43191CB00010B/1576